ON FREUD'S
"NEGATION"

**CONTEMPORARY FREUD
Turning Points and Critical Issues**

Series Editor: Leticia Glocer Fiorini

IPA Publications Committee
Leticia Glocer Fiorini (Buenos Aires), Chair; Samuel Arbiser (Buenos Aires); Paulo Cesar Sandler (São Paulo); Christian Seulin (Lyon); Gennaro Saragnano (Rome); Mary Kay O'Neil (Montreal); Gail S. Reed (New York)

On Freud's "Analysis Terminable and Interminable"
    edited by Joseph Sandler

Freud's "On Narcissism: An Introduction"
    edited by Joseph Sandler, Ethel Spector Person, Peter Fonagy

On Freud's "Observations on Transference-Love"
    edited by Ethel Spector Person, Aiban Hagelin, Peter Fonagy

On Freud's "Creative Writers and Day-Dreaming"
    edited by Ethel Spector Person, Peter Fonagy, Sérvulo Augusto Figueira

On Freud's "A Child Is Being Beaten"
    edited by Ethel Spector Person

On Freud's "Group Psychology and the Analysis of the Ego"
    edited by Ethel Spector Person

On Freud's "Mourning and Melancholia"
    edited by Leticia Glocer Fiorini, Thierry Bokanowski, Sergio Lewkowicz

On Freud's "The Future of an Illusion"
    edited by Mary Kay O'Neil & Salman Akhtar

On Freud's "Splitting of the Ego in the Process of Defence"
    edited by Thierry Bokanowski & Sergio Lewkowicz

On Freud's "Femininity"
    edited by Leticia Glocer Fiorini & Graciela Abelin-Sas Rose

On Freud's "Constructions in Analysis"
    edited by Sergio Lewkowicz & Thierry Bokanowski, with Georges Pragier

On Freud's "Beyond the Pleasure Principle"
    edited by Salman Akhtar & Mary Kay O'Neil

ON FREUD'S "NEGATION"

Edited by
Mary Kay O'Neil & Salman Akhtar

CONTEMPORARY FREUD
Turning Points and Critical Issues

KARNAC

Chapter 4, André Green, "The Work of the Negative and Hallucinatory Activity (Negative Hallucination)", reproduced by permission from *The Work of the Negative* (London: Free Association Books, 1999).

First published in 2011 by
Karnac Books
118 Finchley Road
London NW3 5HT

Copyright © 2011 by The International Psychoanalytical Association

All contributors retain the copyright to their own chapters.

The rights of the editors and contributors to be identified as the authors of this work have been asserted in accordance with §§ 77 and 78 of the Copyright Design and Patents Act 1988.

All rights reserved. No part of this publication may be reproduced, stored in a retrieval system, or transmitted, in any form or by any means, electronic, mechanical, photocopying, recording, or otherwise, without the prior written permission of the publisher.

British Library Cataloguing in Publication Data

A C.I.P. for this book is available from the British Library

ISBN: 978–1–78049–025–0

Edited, designed, and produced by Communication Crafts

Printed in Great Britain

www.karnacbooks.com

CONTENTS

CONTEMPORARY FREUD
    IPA Publications Committee   vii
ACKNOWLEDGEMENTS   ix
EDITORS AND CONTRIBUTORS   xi

Introduction
    Salman Akhtar   1

PART I
"Negation" (1925h)
    Sigmund Freud   13

PART II
Discussion of "Negation"

1   Rejection, refusal, denial:
    developing capacities for negation
    Bonnie E. Litowitz   21

2	On "Negation": some reflections following in Freud's wake *Jorge Canestri*	39
3	The negative therapeutic reaction: review, update, and clinical illustration *Brian M. Robertson*	52
4	The work of the negative and hallucinatory activity (negative hallucination) *André Green*	75
5	The Oedipus of the id: the unrepresentable negative and the transformational processes of analysis *César Botella & Sara Botella*	145
6	The negative in dreams *Joachim F. Danckwardt*	165
7	The effects of negation on the analyst–analysand relationship: the paradoxes of narcissism *Jorge Luis Maldonado*	180
8	From psychic holes to psychic representations *Ilany Kogan*	196
9	Negation, negative capability, and the work of creativity *Antonino Ferro*	222

Epilogue
    Mary Kay O'Neil   237

REFERENCES   251
INDEX   271

CONTEMPORARY FREUD

IPA Publications Committee

This significant series was founded by Robert Wallerstein and first edited by Joseph Sandler, Ethel Spector Person, and Peter Fonagy, and its important contributions have greatly interested psychoanalysts of different latitudes.

The objective of this series is to approach Freud's work from a present and contemporary point of view. On the one hand, this means highlighting the fundamental contributions of his work that constitute the axes of psychoanalytic theory and practice. On the other, it implies the possibility of getting to know and spreading the ideas of present psychoanalysts about Freud's *oeuvre*, both where they coincide and where they differ.

This series considers at least two lines of development: a contemporary reading of Freud that reclaims his contributions and a clarification of the logical and epistemic perspectives from which he is read today.

Freud's theory has branched out, and this has led to a theoretical, technical, and clinical pluralism that has to be worked through. It has therefore become necessary to avoid a snug and uncritical coexistence of concepts in order to consider systems of increasing complexities that take into account both the convergences and the divergences of the categories at play.

Consequently, this project has involved an additional task—that is, gathering psychoanalysts from different geographical regions representing, in addition, different theoretical stances, in order to be able to show their polyphony. This also means an extra effort for the reader that has to do with distinguishing and discriminating, establishing relations or contradictions that each reader will have to eventually work through.

Being able to listen to other theoretical viewpoints is also a way of exercising our listening capacities in the clinical field. This means that the listening should support a space of freedom that would allow us to hear what is new and original.

In this spirit we have brought together authors deeply rooted in the Freudian tradition and others who have developed theories that had not been explicitly taken into account in Freud's work.

In "Negation", Freud stated that negation is the way of reaching consciousness of what is repressed without removing the repressive process. In a very synthetic way, he puts at stake the origin of intellectual judgement, its relation to the pleasure principle, the concept of negative judgement as a mark of repression, as well as decisions related to the recognition of the internal and external world, subjective and objective categories, and the role of perceptions and reality-testing in this frame.

The editors, Mary Kay O'Neil and Salman Akhtar, together with the contributors to this volume, accepted the challenge to consider Freudian ideas and update them.

Special thanks are due to Charles Hanly, the President of the IPA, for his support, to the editors, and to the contributors to this volume, which enriches the Contemporary Freud's series.

Leticia Glocer Fiorini
Series Editor
Chair of the Publications Committee of
the International Psychoanalytical Association

ACKNOWLEDGEMENTS

We are deeply grateful to the distinguished colleagues who contributed to this volume. We appreciate their efforts, their sacrifice of time, and their patience with our requirements, reminders, and requests for revisions. With sincerity and affection, we acknowledge the guidance of the members of the IPA Publications Committee, especially its Chair, Leticia Glocer Fiorini. We are also thankful to Jan Wright for her skilful help in preparing parts of the manuscript and to Rhoda Bawdekar for keeping track of all sorts of matters during the book's actual production. Finally, we wish to express our gratitude to Oliver Rathbone of Karnac Books who shepherded this project to its completion and to Klara King for her meticulous copy-editing.

Mary Kay O'Neil & Salman Akhtar

EDITORS AND CONTRIBUTORS

Salman Akhtar is Professor of Psychiatry at Jefferson Medical College and a training and supervising analyst at the Psychoanalytic Center of Philadelphia. His more than 300 publications include 11 books— *Broken Structures* (1992), *Quest for Answers* (1995), *Inner Torment* (1999), *Immigration and Identity* (1999), *New Clinical Realms* (2003), *Objects of Our Desire* (2005), *Regarding Others* (2007), *Turning Points in Dynamic Psychotherapy* (2009), *Comprehensive Dictionary of Psychoanalysis* (2009), *Immigration and Acculturation* (2011), and *Matters of Life and Death* (2011)— as well as 30 edited or co-edited volumes in psychiatry and psychoanalysis, and 7 collections of poetry. He is also a Scholar-in-Residence at the Inter-Act Theatre Company in Philadelphia.

César Botella and Sára Botella are child and adult psychoanalysts in private practice. They are training analysts at the Paris Psychoanalytical Society (SPP). They have also treated psychosomatic patients according to the Paris Psychosomatic School (IPSO). Part of their time is devoted to the teaching and transmission of psychoanalysis as well as to research. International speakers, they have published numerous articles and books, the most recent being *The Work of Psychic Figurability*. They were awarded the Maurice Bouvet Prize in Psychoanalysis.

Jorge Canestri is a psychiatrist, psychoanalyst, and training and supervising analyst for the Italian Psychoanalytical Association and for the Argentine Psychoanalytic Association. He is a full member of the International Psychoanalytical Association and recipient of the Mary S. Sigourney Award in 2004. He is Chair of the Working Party of Theoretical Issues of the EPF, member of the IPA Conceptual and Empirical Committee, and Professor of Psychology of Health at the Roma 3 University. In addition, he is Editor of the Educational Section and a member of the Editorial Board of the *International Journal of Psychoanalysis*, IPA Global Representative (2005–2007), Representative to Europe for the Executive Committee (2007–2009), and President of the Italian Psychoanalytical Association. He has published numerous psychoanalytic papers in books and is the co-author (along with Jacqueline Amati-Mehler & Simona Argentieri) of *The Babel of the Unconscious: Mother Tongue and Foreign Languages in the Psychoanalytic Dimension*. He has edited many books, including *Pluralism and Unity? Methods of Research in Psychoanalysis* (with Marianne Leuzinger-Bohleber & Anna Ursula Dreher), *Psychoanalysis: From Practice to Theory*, and *Language, Symbolisation and Psychosis* (with Giovanna Ambrosio & Simona Argentieri). He is also the Director of the webpage *Psychoanalysis and Logical Mathematical Thought*.

Joachim F. Danckwardt is a training and supervising analyst and a former member of the Executive Board and President of the German Psychoanalytical Association. He has published over 100 papers on various topics in psychoanalytic journals, including the *International Journal of Psychoanalysis* and *Psychoanalysis in Europe, Bulletin of the European Psychoanalytical Federation*. His books include (with Ekkehard Gattig), *The Indication for High-Frequency Analytic Psychotherapy in the Contractual Medical Health Service*, which has been translated into English, Spanish, and Russian. In 2010, he received the Wolfgang Loch-Award 2010 for *On the Gradual Production of New Theories in Psychoanalytic Processes: Sigmund Freud's Third Trauma Theory, the Discovery of Resistance, and Freud's Synthesis Theory for Setting and Interpretation*.

Antonino Ferro is a training and supervising analyst for the Italian Psychoanalytic Society and a member of the IPA and the American Psychoanalytic Association. He has published many articles in the *International Journal of Psychoanalysis*, and several of his books have been translated into many languages. Among these are *Seeds of Illness*,

Seeds of Recovery, with the most recent being *Mind Works: Technique and Creativity in Psychoanalysis*, and *Avoiding Emotions, Living Emotions*, published by Routledge. In 2007 he was selected to be a recipient of the Mary S. Sigourney Award.

André Green is a psychoanalyst who lives and works in Paris, France. He is Past President of the Paris Psychoanalytical Society. He also served as Director of the Paris Psychoanalytic Institute and as Vice-President of the IPA. In addition, he has been co-editor of the *International Journal of Psychoanalysis*, the *International Review of Psychoanalysis*, and *Nouvelle Review de Psychanalyse*. He has written several books, including: *On Private Madness* (1966), *The Work of the Negative* (1993), *The Fabric of Affect in the Psychoanalytical Discourse* (1999), *Life Narcissism, Death Narcissism* (2001), *The Chains of Eros* (2002), *Diachrony in Psychoanalysis* (2003), *Key Ideas for a Contemporary Psychoanalysis* (2005), and *The Resonance of Suffering* (2010). His work has been profoundly influential, and the Award for Extraordinarily Meritorious Service to Psychoanalysis was bestowed upon him at the 45th IPA Congress, held in July 2007 in Berlin, Germany.

Ilany Kogan is a training analyst at the Israel Psychoanalytic Society; a Member of the Scientific Advisory Board of the Fritz Bauer Institute for Holocaust studies, Frankfurt, Germany; Clinical Supervisor at the Department of Children and Adolescents, Eppendorf University Hospital, Hamburg, Germany, and of MAP candidates, Munich, Germany; Supervisor of the Psychotherapy Centre for the Child and Adolescent, Bucharest, Romania; and a teacher and supervisor at the IPA psychoanalytic group, Istanbul, Turkey. For many years she worked extensively with Holocaust survivors' offspring and published and presented many papers on the topic. She is author of *The Cry of Mute Children, Escape from Selfhood*, and *Struggle Towards Mourning*: She was awarded the Elise M. Hayman Award for the Study of the Holocaust and Genocide at the IPA Congress, Rio de Janeiro, for her work in the realm of the second generation of Holocaust survivors.

Bonnie E. Litowitz is on the Faculty of the Chicago Institute for Psychoanalysis, an Associate Professor of Psychiatry at Rush Medical School, and Associate Editor of the *Journal of the American Psychoanalytic Association*. She has been Associate Professor at Northwestern University with joint appointments in the Departments of Linguistics and Communication Sciences and Disorders, and Dean at Erikson Institute, Graduate School in Child Development. Her paper, "Sexuality and Textuality", was awarded the 2001 Chicago Psychoanalytic Society Prize and the 2002 *Journal of the American Psychoanalytic Association* Prize. In 2003 she was presented with the Heinz Hartmann Award for Outstanding Contributions to Psychoanalysis by a Recent Graduate by the New York Psychoanalytic Society. She was selected to deliver the inaugural Ernst and Gertrude Ticho Memorial Lecture at the American Psychoanalytic Association meeting in 2006. She has published over 55 articles on psychoanalysis, psycholinguistics, semantics, and semiotics and has co-authored (with M. Evens, J. Markowitz, R. Smith, & O. Werner) the book, *Lexical–Semantic Relations: A Comparative Survey* (1980). She is the co-editor (along with Philip Epstein) of *Semiotic Perspectives on Clinical Theory and Practice: Medicine, Neuropsychiatry, and Psychoanalysis* (1991) and (along with Glen Gabbard & Paul Williams) of the second edition of the *Textbook of Psychoanalysis* (2011). She is a frequent presenter, panellist, and discussant at meetings and conferences. She has taught undergraduate and graduate students at Northwestern University, where she has served on over 30 dissertation committees.

Jorge Luis Maldonado is a member, training analyst, and professor of the Buenos Aires Psychoanalytic Association. He was also Professor of Psychopathology at Salvador University and was a member of the Latin American Editorial Board for the *International Journal of Psychoanalysis*. He is the author of the book, *Narcissism and the Work of the Analyst: Paradoxes, Obstacles and Transformation*. He has published articles in many journals and has co-authored three books: *Clinical Writings on Perversions and Addictions*, *Aging: the Psyche, Power and Time*, and *New Reflections with Willy and Madeleine Baranger*. He also contributed to *Listening to Hanna Segal: Her Contribution to Psychoanalysis*, by J. M. Quinodoz. He was presented with the FEPAL award by the Latin American Psychoanalytic Federation for his paper, "On Positive and Negative Therapeutic Reactions".

Mary Kay O'Neil is a supervising and training analyst of the Canadian Institute of Psychoanalysis and is in private practice in Montreal, Quebec. Currently, she is Director of the Canadian Institute of Psychoanalysis (Quebec English) and Secretary–Treasurer of the Canadian Institute of Psychoanalysis. She is author of *The Unsung*

Psychoanalysis: The Quiet Influence of Ruth Easser, and co-editor of *Confidentiality: Ethical Perspectives and Clinical Dilemmas, On Freud's: The Future of an Illusion,* and *On Freud's: Beyond the Pleasure Principle.* Her research and publications include depression and young adult development, emotional needs of sole-support mothers, post-analytic contact, and psychoanalytic ethics. She has served on IPA committees, on local, national, and international ethics committees and on the Editorial Board of the *International Journal of Psychoanalysis.*

Brian M. Robertson is a training and supervising analyst of the Canadian Institute of Psychoanalysis, an Associate Professor in the Department of Psychiatry, McGill University, and in practice in Montreal. He is a former Editor of the *Canadian Journal of Psychoanalysis,* a past Director of the Canadian Psychoanalytic Institute, and a past President of the Canadian Psychoanalytic Society. He has presented and published in the areas of long analyses, psychoanalytic research, siblings and the internal world, and teaching and supervising psychoanalysis. In 1992 he was awarded the Miguel Pardos prize for his paper on the supervisory process, and in 2002 he received the Canadian Psychoanalytic Society's Citation of Merit.

ON FREUD'S
"NEGATION"

Introduction

Salman Akhtar

Unlikely though it may seem, an apt starting point for our consideration of Freud's (1925h) concept of negation is in statements made by three eminent political leaders of the last century. Just take a look at the following quotes and you will get the point I am trying to make.

» *Never give in. Never give in. Never, never, never, never—in nothing, great or small, large or petty—never give in, except to convictions of honour and good sense. Never yield to force. Never yield to the apparently overwhelming might of the enemy.* (Winston Churchill, addressing the students at Harrow School, England, 29 October 1941)

» *There were no such thing as Palestinians. When was there an independent Palestinian people with a Palestinian state? It was either southern Syria before the First World War, and then it was a Palestine including Jordan. It was not as though there was a Palestinian people in Palestine considering itself as a Palestinian people and we came and threw them out and took their country away from them. They did not exist.* (Golda Meir, in a statement to the *Sunday Times*, London, 15 June 1969)

» *People have got to know whether or not their President is a crook. Well, I'm not a crook.* (Richard Nixon, at a press conference held in Orlando, Florida, 17 November 1973)

The notion of negation

Winston Churchill's [1874–1965] resolute defiance of failure appeared in the setting of Harrow, a boy's school he had attended as a child. He had ended up there after having had difficult times at two previous schools, though his performance at Harrow proved no different from that at the others. Churchill's tough exterior might also have drawn tributaries from other traumatic experiences of his childhood; it is well known (Gilbert, 1992; Jenkins, 2002) that his cold and stern mother would often return unopened the letters he wrote to her from boarding school, instructing him to correct a misspelled word in the postal address before she would open it. Little Winston would comply; to act otherwise would be to "give up" on the much-needed tie with his mother and "give in" to the anguish of unbelonging. And yet it is not far-fetched to assume that the thoughts of giving up (out of anger) and giving in (due to libidinal fatigue) occurred to him. His forceful incantation to the contrary thus appears an attempt to bury the impulse to accept a severely painful reality and, of course, its later derivatives. Faced with utter helplessness, Churchill was "reduced to being omnipotent" (Bion, cited in Grotstein, 2007, p. 33).

Golda Meir [1898–1978], in declaring that there are no Palestinian people, gave voice to the conflict in upholding the creation of Israel at the cost of displacing some native dwellers of that land. To say that there are no Palestinian people was in effect saying that "I repudiate my knowledge that such people exist because recognizing their existence would cause me conflict and distress". Finally, we have Richard Nixon [1913–1994], who secretly taped all conversations in the Oval Office and instigated the burglary at the Democratic National Committee's office at the Watergate building in Washington, DC, and its subsequent cover-up. He was compelled to call himself "not a crook" only because of his deeper awareness to the contrary.

What these public statements have in common is precisely what

Freud called negation. According to him, negation denotes the appearance in consciousness of something one has desperately attempted to ward off; however, it becomes conscious in an inverted form. "I *never* thought that my brother would steal from me", one declares. "I'm *not* being competitive with you", another pronounces. Such statements, Freud asserts, betray the contrary. The former individual *does* suspect his brother and the latter *is* being competitive, but neither can fully accept this aspect of their psychic reality. Negation offers them a psychological mid-point between an affectively meaningful dissolution of repression and the total banishing of disconcerting mental contents by repression. In Freud's own words, negation is "a lifting of the repression, though not, of course, an acceptance of what is repressed" (p. 236). An individual employing negation becomes aware of the reverse of what he has tried not to know. And that is what he reports: the inverted truth.

This brings up the difference between negation and lying. Negation involves *unconscious* sequestering of the emotional validity of the psychic truth; even the intellectual awareness of that truth is limited to its inverted form. Lying, in contrast, involves *conscious* sequestering of what is known and felt to be true. When an individual using negation says "I never thought of such and such", he is speaking the truth; indeed, he has never consciously thought of such and such. However, when a liar says "I never thought of such and such", he is not speaking the truth; he has thought of it and he knows that he has. Negation involves deceiving oneself. Lying involves deceiving others.

Some concepts related to negation

The mechanism Freud described appears distinct and clear on the surface. However, careful scrutiny reveals conceptual and dynamic overlaps between negation and some other defensive operations of the ego. These include: (1) repudiation, (2) denial, (3) disavowal, (4) isolation of affect, and (5) undoing. Let us take a closer look at them, one by one.

» *Repudiation*: Also called "foreclosure" by Freud (1894a), repudiation refers to the end-point of repression and the elimination of an idea from consciousness and of the fact that this has occurred. According to Freud, "the ego rejects the incompatible idea together with its affect and behaves as if the idea had never occurred to the ego at all" (p. 58). Viewed as such, repudiation and negation seem to lie on the opposite ends of the "repression spectrum". The former erases repression itself, and the latter creates a partial opening in the repressive barrier of affect. Both repudiation and negation follow repression and alter what it has achieved.

» *Denial*: This unconsciously operative ego defence works by obliterating the awareness of a painful external reality (Freud, 1926d [1925]). Anna Freud (1936) elaborated further on this concept, but she never departed from Freud's view that denial involves the erasure of a piece of perception. In contrast, Klein (1935, 1946) used the term denial to denote the obliteration of internal reality, especially the importance of the objects on which one depends. In her view, denial is an aspect of "manic defence" (Klein, 1935) and helps dispose of disagreeable qualities of a needed object, leading to its idealization. But how does denial relate to negation? The answer depends upon whether one is using the Freudian or Kleinian definition of denial. Freudian denial obliterates perception before it can become a part of psychic reality, whereas negation addresses a repressed content of psychic reality; the two mechanisms are quite different. Kleinian denial, however, comes close to negation, since both deal with aspects of psychic reality. The difference between them is that such denial is violent towards the internal word, whereas negation involves a certain reconciliation with the repressed mental contents.

» *Disavowal*: Freud used this term at first (1924d) for the little girl's refusal to acknowledge her lack of a penis and later (1927e) to explain the fetishist's maintaining two contradictory attitudes by which he simultaneously acknowledges and repudiates the absence of a penis in women. Unlike denial, disavowal leads to splitting of the ego. This also makes disavowal distinct from negation, since there is no cleavage of ego in the latter. Moreover, while disavowal is characterized by contradictory attitudes in two consciously experienced, though separated, ego segments, negation holds one attitude consciously and the other unconsciously.

» *Isolation of affect*: In his paper, "Negation", Freud states that "we can see how in this [negation] the intellectual function is separated from the affective process. With the help of negation only one consequence of the process of repression is undone—the fact, namely, of the ideational content of what is repressed not reaching consciousness. The outcome of this is a kind of intellectual acceptance of the repressed, while at the same time what is essential to the repression persists" (p. 236). Curiously, it is precisely the lack of intellectual acceptance (I *never* thought of my mother in this connection) that Freud held to be the hallmark of negation. How, then, to account for the contradiction? It is hard to say, but my sense is that Freud actually stumbled on a new concept here, a concept that would be elucidated two decades later by Anna Freud (1936) under the designation "isolation of affect".[1]

» In negation, repression is partially undone by allowing the repressed into consciousness in its *negative* form. In isolation of affect, repression is partially undone by allowing the repressed into consciousness in its *positive* form. An individual using negation exclaims, "I *never* thought that my husband should die", as opposed to the one using isolation of affect, who declares, "I *have* thought of my husband dying, but I have no idea why, since I've no feeling of anger or hostility towards him". The two mechanisms are thus different. However, there is some similarity, too, between negation and isolation of affect. This resides in the fact that neither permits the emotional counterpart of the de-repressed idea into conscious awareness.

» **Undoing:** This is a defence mechanism first described by Freud in 1909 (1909d) and further elaborated by him in 1926 (1926d [1925]). It involves the ego's warding off anxiety by committing an act opposite to an instinctual deed that has been actually committed or is imagined to have been committed. In Fenichel's (1945) words, in undoing "something is done which, actually or magically, is the opposite of something which, again actually or in the imagination, was done before" (p. 153). The act often follows a drive intensification as a consequence of external or internal events. For instance, someone stopping over at a friend's apartment might say "please do not offer me a drink" in a rather transparent effort to reverse the morally conflicted and shy desire to ask for a drink. Something is becoming conscious here and is reversed by stating its opposite. And, herein lies the similarity between undoing and negation. Both express the opposite of what is meant: undoing, in the form of inverse action, and negation, in the form of inverse thought. But since the boundary between thought and action can get blurred, it is possible to conceive of undoing as "negation via action" and of negation as "undoing via thought". However, such parallelism overlooks the fact that undoing diminishes one's contact with internal reality, while negation prepares the ground for increased knowledge of it.

Having clarified—or at least, having made an attempt to clarify—the phenomenological and dynamic reach of Freud's concept of negation, we can move on his linking negation with the function of judgement.

Freud's digression into the function of judgement

It seems a bit "unfair" to call Freud's comments on the function of judgement in this paper a "digression": after all, they extend over more than half of this five-page paper. And yet, the sense one gets upon encountering this portion of the paper is of being distracted from the main point. Nonetheless, perseverance yields much that is of significance—for instance:

» The function of judgement is made of two mental activities: (a) assessing whether something possesses a particular attribute or not, and (b) whether that object is merely a figment of imagination or exists in actuality.
» The "pleasure-ego" accepts or rejects an object, whereas the "reality-ego" determines whether the object can be found in external reality.
» Since all mental presentations originate from perception, the function of reality-testing is not to find the object but to re-find it.
» A precondition for reality-testing is that "objects shall have been lost which once brought real satisfaction" (1925h, p. 238).

» Judgement is an intellectual accomplishment that sets the ground for motor action.

Freud's ideas about the function of judgement make sense, and their refinement in Rangell's (1969) discussion of the "decision-making function of the ego" lends them further credence. However, when Freud (1925h) links his ideas about the function of judgement with negation, matters begin to take a different turn. He states that:

> The polarity of judgement appears to correspond to the opposition of the two groups of instincts which we have supposed to exist. Affirmation—as a substitute for uniting—belongs to Eros; negation—the successor to expulsion—belongs to the instinct of destruction. The general wish to negate, the negativism which is displayed by some psychotics, is probably to be regarded as a sign of a defusion of instincts that has taken place through a withdrawal of the libidinal components. [p. 239]

This passage seems to overextend the concept of negation. An ardent ally of the ego turns into an undercover agent of the id. Rather than facilitating psychic growth (by de-repressing some material), negation now appears to be destructive to the mind (by erasing the representable altogether). One begins to note that Freud's definition of negation is Janus-faced and might even contain two separate concepts: "benign negation", which enlarges mental contents, and "malignant negation", which diminishes them. The former yields epistemic benefits and thus seems to be motivated by what Freud (1923b) termed "ego instincts"; the latter creates psychic holes and thus appears to be mobilized by self-directed aggression.

Such conceptualization clears up some things but leaves some other things ambiguous. For instance, it remains unclear whether all that seems not psychically representable comes under the purview of negation. And can this non-representable ever be represented? How are little girls' genitals, which are often unnamed or mislabelled (Lerner, 1976), psychically represented, for instance? Does the dread of castration arise only from the sight of the female genital, or can "penis-lessness" be imagined otherwise as well? And what about an only child imagining that he has siblings, an orphan "creating" parents for himself, an amputee experiencing phantom limb phenomena? The conscious representation of what is present as being absent lies at the heart of negation, but does the representation of what is absent as present also fall under its rubric? Clearly, more thought is needed here.

Nonetheless, it is undeniable that Freud's delineation of the instinctual underpinnings of intellect laid the groundwork for what Bion (1957, 1970) later described as "attacks on linking" and "black holes", as well as for Green's (1993) "negative hallucination" and "negative hallucination of thought". Thus, Freud's digression might actually have anticipated matters of considerable theoretical and technical importance. While the elucidation of all such issues is beyond the scope of this introductory essay, Freud's own ideas about the technical handling of negation certainly warrant attention here.

Technical handling of negation

Two statements in Freud's paper stand out when it comes to the consideration of psychoanalytic technique *vis-à-vis* negation. The first is to be found in the paper's opening paragraph, and the second constitutes its last sentence. Let us take the two in order. The sentence in the opening paragraph reads as follows: "In our interpretation, we take the liberty of disregarding the negation and picking out the subject matter alone of the association" (1925h, p. 23). This seems to make sense. But upon further thought, something appears to be unclear here. Does Freud's use of the word "interpretation" refer to how the analyst *understands* the patient, or does it refer to how the analyst *speaks* to the patient? The first "translation" of the word "interpretation" poses no problems; the patient's use of negation is instinctively deciphered by the analyst, but he is in no hurry, under no compulsion, to unmask the repudiated aspect to the patient. The second translation of the word "interpretation" has, however, the potential of causing difficulty. It condones—in fact, encourages—a brusque and authoritarian manner of relating to patients. To "disregard" the patient's defensive posture and point directly to what is difficult to admit into consciousness can foreclose the understanding of the anxiety that is motivating the defence. Worse, a penetrating intervention of this sort (e.g., "you *are* being competitive", "it *is* your mother that you hold responsible for your childhood pet getting lost") can traumatize the patient and adversely affect the therapeutic alliance. Yet another problematic outcome might be that the patient is "impressed" by the cleverness of the analyst and, thus mesmerized, submits to his pronouncement. In effect, the interpretation is met by compliance and not by further reflection and deepening of association. Keeping all this in mind, it seems preferable to see Freud's use of the word "interpretation" in the sentence quoted above as applying only to the analyst's *understanding* and not to the analyst's *speaking*. Doing so is congenial to the unhurried and step-wise nature of the psychoanalytic process.

Freud's other statement regarding the technical handling of negation appears as the last sentence of his paper: "There is no stronger evidence that we have been successful in our effort to uncover the unconscious than when the patient reacts to it with the words 'I didn't think that' or 'I didn't (ever) think of that'" (1925h, p. 239). This statement leaves two questions unanswered. Whom is Freud calling "we" here? And, what does "it" stand for when he talks of the patient's reacting to "it"? If Freud's "we" stands for "we analysts", then the picture of analytic technique that emerges is authoritarian and one-sided. If, however, the "we" stands for the analyst–analysand duo, then a more egalitarian give-and-take comes to the fore. Similarly, if the "it" refers to "our *effort* to uncover the unconscious", then the patient's exclamation that he didn't think this or that might actually be correct rather than an evidence of negation; after all, it is the analyst who has "uncovered" the unconscious, and the analyst may be wrong. However, if the word "it" refers to the unconscious content, then Freud's statement makes perfect sense. In a sense, it is the patient—not the analyst—who has brought up the unconscious content, only to recoil from it through the use of negation. To put it bluntly, to qualify as negation, the use of "I did not think of . . ." must be spontaneous on the part of the patient. To refute something in response to the analyst's suggestion is not negation. It is important to keep this in mind, since without such proviso any and all disagreement on the analysand's part can be regarded as a resistance. The spectre of false confession and "gaslighting" (Barton & Whitehead, 1969) is then not far away. To reiterate, disagreement with the analyst's intervention is not the same as negation.

Conclusion

Freud's concept of negation, elucidated in just five pages, turns out to be highly textured and full of nuances. Its phenomenological borders touch upon many other concepts and yet somehow remain distinct. His two technical recommendations for dealing with negation boil down to an interesting paradox. Both statements hint at an oracle-like, declarative stance on the analyst's (in this case, Freud's) part. At the same time, however, both statements can be read in a way that makes it possible to imagine a less authoritarian psychoanalytic technique. In his paper on negation, Freud comes across as a stern arbiter of the "truth" about the unconscious, but the text's "layering of significance" (Kristeva, 1987, p. 6) is a testimony to his genius as a thinker and writer. And it is this richness of conceptualization that our book seeks to celebrate. It brings together contributions on the topic of negation from distinguished colleagues from diverse analytic cultures. They address the phenomenological (Canestri), developmental (Litowitz), instinctual and metapsychological (the Botellas, Green), oneiric (Danckwardt), and technical (Ferro, Kogan, Maldonado, Robertson) ramifications of Freud's 1925 proposals. Actually, assigning such topical designations to these multifaceted essays is unfair, as each of them contains varying features and sheds light on both theoretical and technical facets of the topic under consideration. Deploying the mechanism of negation right here, I conclude by *not* claiming our book to be outstanding.

Note

1. Freud's (1926d [1925]) own use of the term "isolation" was in a different context. He described "isolation" as a defence that, after a painful event has taken place, "interpolates an interval during which nothing further must happen ... the experience is not forgotten but instead is deprived of its affect, and its associative connections are suppressed or interrupted so that it remains as though isolated" (p. 120). Freud also used the expression "isolation" for the capacity to keep irrelevant materials away from the mind while concentrating on a task.

PART I

"Negation"
(1925h)

Sigmund Freud

NEGATION

THE manner in which our patients bring forward their associations during the work of analysis gives us an opportunity for making some interesting observations. 'Now you'll think I mean to say something insulting, but really I've no such intention.' We realize that this is a rejection, by projection, of an idea that has just come up. Or: 'You ask who this person in the dream can be. It's *not* my mother.' We emend this to: 'So it *is* his mother.' In our interpretation, we take the liberty of disregarding the negation and of picking out the subject-matter alone of the association. It is as though the patient had said: 'It's true that my mother came into my mind as I thought of this person, but I don't feel inclined to let the association count.'[1]

There is a very convenient method by which we can sometimes obtain a piece of information we want about unconscious repressed material. 'What', we ask, 'would you consider the most unlikely imaginable thing in that situation? What do you think was furthest from your mind at that time?' If the patient falls into the trap and says what he thinks is most incredible, he almost always makes the right admission. A neat counterpart to this experiment is often met with in an obsessional neurotic who has already been initiated into the meaning of his symptoms. 'I've got a new obsessive idea,' he says, 'and it occurred to me at once that it might mean so and so. But no; that can't be true, or it couldn't have occurred to me.' What he is repudiating, on grounds picked up from his treatment, is, of course, the correct meaning of the obsessive idea.

Thus the content of a repressed image or idea can make its way into consciousness, on condition that it is *negated*.[2] Negation is a way of taking cognizance of what is repressed; indeed it is

---

[1] [Freud had drawn attention to this in (among other places) the 'Rat Man' analysis (1909*d*), *Standard Ed.*, **10**, 183 *n*.]

[2] [The German '*verneinen*' is here translated by 'to negate' instead of by the more usual 'to deny', in order to avoid confusion with the German '*verleugnen*', which has also in the past been rendered by 'to deny'. In this edition 'to disavow' has in general been used for the latter German word. See the footnote on this point in 'The Infantile Genital Organization' (1923*e*), p. 143 above.]

235

already a lifting of the repression, though not, of course, an acceptance of what is repressed. We can see how in this the intellectual function is separated from the affective process. With the help of negation only one consequence of the process of repression is undone—the fact, namely, of the ideational content of what is repressed not reaching consciousness. The outcome of this is a kind of intellectual acceptance of the repressed, while at the same time what is essential to the repression persists.[1] In the course of analytic work we often produce a further, very important and somewhat strange variant of this situation. We succeed in conquering the negation as well, and in bringing about a full intellectual acceptance of the repressed; but the repressive process itself is not yet removed by this.

Since to affirm or negate the content of thoughts is the task of the function of intellectual judgement, what we have just been saying has led us to the psychological origin of that function. To negate something in a judgement is, at bottom, to say: 'This is something which I should prefer to repress.' A negative judgement is the intellectual substitute for repression;[2] its 'no' is the hall-mark of repression, a certificate of origin—like, let us say, 'Made in Germany'.[3] With the help of the symbol of negation, thinking frees itself from the restrictions of repression and enriches itself with material that is indispensable for its proper functioning.

The function of judgement is concerned in the main with two sorts of decisions. It affirms or disaffirms the possession by a thing of a particular attribute; and it asserts or disputes that a presentation has an existence in reality.[4] The attribute to be

---

[1] The same process is at the root of the familiar superstition that boasting is dangerous. 'How nice not to have had one of my headaches for so long.' But this is in fact the first announcement of an attack, of whose approach the subject is already sensible, although he is as yet unwilling to believe it. [Freud's attention had first been drawn to this explanation by one of his earliest patients, Frau Cäcilie M. Cf. the long footnote on the subject in the first of Freud's case histories in *Studies on Hysteria* (1895d), *Standard Ed.*, 2, 76.]

[2] [Freud's earliest statement of this idea seems to have been in his book on jokes (1905c), *Standard Ed.*, 8, 175. It re-appears in the paper on 'The Two Principles of Mental Functioning' (1911b), ibid., 12, 221, and in the metapsychological paper on 'The Unconscious' (1915e), ibid., 14, 186.]

[3] [In English in the original.]   [4] [This is explained below, p. 237.]

decided about may originally have been good or bad, useful or harmful. Expressed in the language of the oldest—the oral—instinctual impulses, the judgement is: 'I should like to eat this', or 'I should like to spit it out'; and, put more generally: 'I should like to take this into myself and to keep that out.' That is to say: 'It shall be inside me' or 'it shall be outside me'. As I have shown elsewhere, the original pleasure-ego wants to intrjoect into itself everything that is good and to eject from itself everything that is bad. What is bad, what is alien to the ego and what is external are, to begin with, identical.[1]

The other sort of decision made by the function of judgement —as to the real existence of something of which there is a presentation (reality-testing)—is a concern of the definitive reality-ego, which develops out of the initial pleasure-ego. It is now no longer a question of whether what has been perceived (a thing) shall be taken into the ego or not, but of whether something which is in the ego as a presentation can be rediscovered in perception (reality) as well. It is, we see, once more a question of *external* and *internal*. What is unreal, merely a presentation and subjective, is only internal; what is real is also there *outside*. In this stage of development regard for the pleasure principle has been set aside. Experience has shown the subject that it is not only important whether a thing (an object of satisfaction for him) possesses the 'good' attribute and so deserves to be taken into his ego, but also whether it is there in the external world, so that he can get hold of it whenever he needs it. In order to understand this step forward we must recollect that all presentations originate from perceptions and are repetitions of them. Thus originally the mere existence of a presentation was a guarantee of the reality of what was presented. The antithesis between subjective and objective does not exist from the first. It only comes into being from the fact that thinking possesses the capacity to bring before the mind once more something that has once been perceived, by reproducing it as a presentation without the external object having still to be there. The first and immediate aim, therefore, of reality-testing is, not to *find* an object in real perception which corresponds to the one presented, but to *refind* such an object, to

---

[1] See the discussion in 'Instincts and their Vicissitudes' (1915*c*) [*Standard Ed.*, **14**, 136.—Freud took up this question again in the first chapter of *Civilization and its Discontents* (1930*a*).]

238   NEGATION

convince oneself that it is still there.¹ Another capacity of the power of thinking offers a further contribution to the differentiation between what is subjective and what is objective. The reproduction of a perception as a presentation is not always a faithful one; it may be modified by omissions, or changed by the merging of various elements. In that case, reality-testing has to ascertain how far such distortions go. But it is evident that a precondition for the setting up of reality-testing is that objects shall have been lost which once brought real satisfaction.

Judging is the intellectual action which decides the choice of motor action, which puts an end to the postponement due to thought and which leads over from thinking to acting. This postponement due to thought has also been discussed by me elsewhere.² It is to be regarded as an experimental action, a motor palpating, with small expenditure of discharge. Let us consider where the ego has used a similar kind of palpating before, at what place it learnt the technique which it now applies in its processes of thought. It happened at the sensory end of the mental apparatus, in connection with sense perceptions. For, on our hypothesis, perception is not a purely passive process. The ego periodically sends out small amounts of cathexis into the perceptual system, by means of which it samples the external stimuli, and then after every such tentative advance it draws back again.³

The study of judgement affords us, perhaps for the first time,

---

¹ [Much of this is foreshadowed in *The Interpretation of Dreams* (1900)*a*, *Standard Ed.*, **5**, 565–7, and, more particularly, in the 1895 'Project' (Freud, 1950*a*; Section 16 of Part I). Here the 'object' to be refound is the mother's breast. Cf., too, a sentence which occurs in a similar connection in Section 5 of the *Three Essays* (1905*d*), *Standard Ed.*, **7**, 222: 'The finding of an object is in fact a refinding of it.']

² [See *The Ego and the Id* (1923*b*), p. 55 above. But Freud made the point repeatedly, beginning with the 'Project' of 1895 (at the end of Section 17 of Part I). A list of references will be found in Lecture XXXII of the *New Introductory Lectures* (1933*a*). Incidentally, the whole topic of judgement is discussed at great length and on much the same lines as the present ones, in Sections 16, 17 and 18 of Part I of the 'Project'.]

³ [See *Beyond the Pleasure Principle* (1920*g*), *Standard Ed.*, **18**, 28, and 'A Note upon the "Mystic Writing-Pad" ' (1925*a*), p. 231 above. It may be remarked that in this last passage Freud suggests not that the ego but that the *unconscious* 'stretches out feelers, through the medium of the system *Pcpt.-Cs.*, towards the external world'.]

an insight into the origin of an intellectual function from the interplay of the primary instinctual impulses. Judging is a continuation, along lines of expediency, of the original process by which the ego took things into itself or expelled them from itself, according to the pleasure principle. The polarity of judgement appears to correspond to the opposition of the two groups of instincts which we have supposed to exist. Affirmation—as a substitute for uniting—belongs to Eros; negation—the successor to expulsion—belongs to the instinct of destruction. The general wish to negate, the negativism which is displayed by some psychotics, is probably to be regarded as a sign of a defusion of instincts that has taken place through a withdrawal of the libidinal components.[1] But the performance of the function of judgement is not made possible until the creation of the symbol of negation has endowed thinking with a first measure of freedom from the consequences of repression and, with it, from the compulsion of the pleasure principle.

This view of negation fits in very well with the fact that in analysis we never discover a 'no' in the unconscious and that recognition of the unconscious on the part of the ego is expressed in a negative formula. There is no stronger evidence that we have been successful in our effort to uncover the unconscious than when the patient reacts to it with the words 'I didn't think that', or 'I didn't (ever) think of that'.[2]

[1] [Cf. a remark in Chapter VI of the book on Jokes (1905c), *Standard Ed.*, **8**, 175, footnote 2.]

[2] [Freud had made this point in almost the same words in a footnote added in 1923 to the 'Dora' analysis (1905e), *Standard Ed.*, **7**, 57. He once more returned to it in his very late paper on 'Constructions in Analysis' (1937d).]

PART II

Discussion of "Negation"

1

Rejection, refusal, denial: developing capacities for negation

Bonnie E. Litowitz

In 1925 Freud published a brief paper on negation. This paper has endured as a classic, not because Freud could produce the definitive explanation of this concept in such a few pages, but because he brought to public awareness a fundamental and pervasive aspect of how the mind works. Since its publication, psychoanalytic writers, as well as those from other disciplines, have returned again and again to the paper as a point of departure for their own explorations of its insights.

Coming to psychoanalysis with a background in formal linguistics and developmental psycholinguistics, I was aware of the importance of negation in logic (and therefore in all scientific inquiry). But I was also aware that children are not born with the capacity to negate as Freud described it. A capacity for negation has its own course of development, during which it takes different forms. In a paper published in 1998 (Litowitz, 1998) I explored further logical and developmental implications of Freud's original insights, a review of which I present below.

Much has changed in me and in psychoanalysis since my first exploration. I still endorse what I wrote about the importance of negation in logic and the description of a developmental sequence. The latter is—I believe—even more relevant today as psychoanalytic theorists widely incorporate academic developmental data in their focus on the pre-oedipal period. However, returning to these topics now, I am more impressed than ever with the relevance of negation for the whole variety of mental functioning we encounter in clinical practice. And, consequently, I feel even more strongly about the contribution to our work to be gained from an awareness of the different developmental manifestations of negation as these appear in therapeutic interactions.

In 1925 Freud was continuing to delineate what would become identified as "Freudian theory" by expanding on the revision he had already made to the concept of defence, adding denial as another form of the defensive structure of repression. Today, we practice at a time of multiple psychoanalytic perspectives that have evolved out of Freud's original models. Although each perspective or school elaborates and focuses on a particular defensive structure, no perspective—not even one that questions the concept of a dynamic unconscious (Stern, 2004)—can claim to be psychoanalytic without some concept of defence. Brenner best articulates why this is so: "To discuss defense in terms of *defense mechanisms* is wrong . . . [implying] that there are special mechanisms of defense. . . . This is not the case. . . . Anything that comes under the heading of normal mental functioning or development can be used defensively. Modes of defense are as diverse as psychic life itself" (2006, pp. 117–118). Brenner then goes through each familiar "mechanism", demonstrating that in each case something is negated or denied. He concludes: "every defense denies something. . . . [Denial] is merely a synonym for defense" (p. 120). Thus, Brenner reworks Freud's sequence (defence and repression are one and the same, extended in 1925 to make denial and repression types of defence) into the proposition that all subsequent elaborations of defences are the same—that is, some form of saying "no" or "not". Furthermore, if all defences are just "normal mental functioning or development" used to negate/deny something (e.g., anxiety), then we have found: the deeper insight of Freud's paper on how the mind works; a reason for its enduring fascination to theorists; and the rationale for understanding how this normal mental capacity develops.

Freud on negation

Freud begins the 1925 paper with clinical examples of statements made by patients, such as the following: "Now you'll think I mean to say something insulting, but really I've no such intention"; "You ask who this person in the dream can be. It's not my mother"; "I've got a new obsessive idea... but no, that can't be true". All the examples in the paper are linguistic, verbal statements that contain an explicit sign of negation: "not" or "no". These statements, Freud says, are judgements, and judgements involve "two sorts of decisions: affirm[ing] or disaffirm[ing] the possession by a thing of a particular attribute; and assert[ing] or disput[ing] that a presentation has an existence in reality" (1925h, p. 236). Thus, Freud described his examples in philosophical terms, often referred to as prediction (attribution) and reference (existence).

Philosophers view statements, such as Freud's examples, as embodying propositions and expressing truth (i.e., a positive statement) or falsehood (i.e., a negative statement) about those propositions. A proposition can be represented in logical shorthand as P, which can be recast in expressions of the propositional calculus (i.e., symbolic logic) as either P, which is true, or –P, which is false. Further, since P is itself a shorthand expression for a predicate (f) and its argument (x), P or –P can be recast in the predicate calculus as: $f(x)$ or $-f(x)$. An example involving existence could be: "it's mother" $[f(x)]$ or "it's not mother" $[-f(x)]$; of attribution: "mother is good" or "mother is not good". But propositions can also be as complex as: "I intend to say something insulting."

In symbolic notation, the underlying proposition is always positive, since negation is one of the small set of (Boolean) operators that affect propositions but are not part of the propositions themselves.[1] Consequently, it is not really the case that a negative statement means its opposite; rather, more correctly, the former entails the latter. A negative statement always entails its positive proposition (but not vice versa) because a negative statement is a statement of a proposition (by definition positive) plus a negative operator: "A judgment of nonexistence has necessarily the formal status of a judgment of existence... thus negation is first acceptance" (Benveniste, 1971, p. 73). Therefore, what Freud says is true of the examples he offers, and in logic it is called denial. In fact, the noun in the original German title of Freud's 1925 paper—*Die Verneinung*—is more usually translated as "denial" in just this logical sense (Ricoeur, 1970, p. 314).

Questions of lexical choice and translation pervade discussions of this topic, as I discuss below. Suffice it to say at this point that Freud is using the formal properties of propositions in order to explain why it is that statements containing a negative sign actually affirm the existence of what they seem to deny. However, Freud did not explore here the full implications of the negative operator in logic and their role in manifestations of denial. The fact that the negative operator has scope over the whole proposition (rather than being part of the proposition itself) means that negation can be transposed within the proposition. For example, if one takes the underlying proposition. "the swan is black" [black (swan)] and adds a negative operator, one can generate "the swan is not black" [−black (swan)]. But transposing negation within the proposition can also generate "it is not the swan that is black" [black (−swan)]; or "it is not (the case) that the swan is black" [−(black (swan))]; and so forth. As negation spreads across the whole of language, it can be expressed indirectly and in complex ways beyond syntax—for example, through morphology as prefixes to words (a−, un−, dis−, ir−) and even through prosody (Lyons, 1977, p. 775). Thus one can see how multifarious the expressions of propositional negation can be and, therefore, the many opportunities for denial that language affords. In this respect, propositional negation contrasts sharply with the constraints of performative negation, as is discussed below.

Having presented examples of the statements he wants to explain and a description of their logical structure, Freud builds an explanation based on his theories of libidinal investment in bodily zones and on the ego's developing capacities. Early developmental phases are dominated by the pleasure principle: what is taken in is good and internal, while what is spit out is bad and external. However, as the reality principle becomes dominant, the child must determine whether what he takes in and is good is "there in the external world, so that he can get hold of it whenever he needs it" (p. 237). As a consequence, the ego is forced to develop a capacity to distinguish between subjective and objective realities, an "antithesis [that] does not exist from the first" (p. 237). Thus, Freud constructs a careful explanation of the clinical examples in terms of a developmental continuum, each stage sublated into the next: the dialectics of the body (in–out) become the attributions of good–bad; and these, in turn, become, at the object level, the dialectics of subjective–objective.[2] Once language becomes available, its multiple forms of negation afford another level—that of saying (knowing) and denying (not knowing), which introduces the dialectics of conscious–unconscious.

In choosing an appropriate translation for the various German terms for negation, the editors of the *Standard Edition* had already used "to deny" for *verleugnen* and therefore chose to translate *verneinen* as "to negate" for the 1925 paper. However, Laplanche and Pontalis note ambiguities within German among these terms themselves:

> In German, "*Verneinung*" denotes *negation* in the logical and grammatical sense (there is no verb "*neinen*" or "*beneinen*"), but it also means *denial* in the psychological sense of rejection of a statement which I have made or has been imputed to me, e.g. "No, I did not say that" or "I did not think that". In this second sense, "*verneinen*" comes close to "*verleugnen*" (or "*leugnen*"), to disown, deny, disavow, refute. [Laplanche & Pontalis, 1973, p. 262]

In such examples, the negative operator has moved outside the propositional statement (–P), to a higher, epistemic statement about the whole proposition: "I did not know that (P)." Freud concludes his paper on negation with just such examples: "There is no stronger evidence that we have been successful in our effort to uncover the unconscious than when the patient reacts to it with the words, 'I didn't think that' or 'I didn't (ever) think of that'" (p. 239; see also Freud, 1905e [1901], p. 57; 1937c, p. 263). In other words, while a negative statement of denial unconsciously circumvents repression by both saying and not saying what is both known and not known, in this strongest evidence of successful analysis the patient consciously acknowledges the process of repression, which hides what is known by one part of the mind (id) from another part (ego).

In a series of papers that Freud wrote distinguishing denial from disavowal, he sought to tie verbal denials to repression and interagency conflicts (i.e., as a horizontal split in the psyche), and to oppose these intrapsychic defences to the perceptual defence of disavowal as a response to external danger. Freud first introduced disavowal in describing "Fetishism" (1927e), but he later extended it to encompass a boy's efforts to allay his anxiety about his own castration by denying [*verleugnen*] his perception that a woman lacks a penis (1940a [1938], 1940e [1938]). Finally, Freud further "normalized" disavowal as a general defence of childhood:

> Let us return to our thesis that the childish ego, under the domination of the real world, gets rid of undesirable instinctual demands by what are called repressions. We will now supplement this by further asserting that, during the same period of life, the ego often enough finds itself in the position of fending off some demand from the external world which it feels distressing and that is effected by means of disavowal of the perceptions which bring to knowledge this demand from reality. Disavowals of this kind occur very often and not only with fetishists. [They are always half-measures, incomplete because] the disavowal is supplemented by an acknowledgement. [Freud, 1940a (1938), p. 203]

In their close reading of Freudian texts, Laplanche and Pontalis (1973) claim "a justification for distinguishing between '*verneinen*' and '*verleugnen*'. Towards the end of his work, Freud tends to reserve the latter verb [*verleugnen*, translated by the editors of the *Standard Edition* as "disavowal"] for the refusal to perceive a fact which is imposed by the external world" (p. 262). Unfortunately, the distinction does not remain clear even for Freud, who also used disavowal to describe the disjunction of idea from affect, where the affect is repressed [*Verdrängung*], but the idea is disavowed [*Verleugnung*] (1927e, p. 153). Inversely, other writers have used it to describe an affect/idea split in which affect is disavowed. Complicating matters further, *verleugnen* can also denote "to disown", as when one perceives external reality and may experience the affect as well, but feels it is not one's own (i.e., belongs to another, as in projection).[3]

Basch (1981) discusses the difficulties in translating ordinary German verbs [*leugnen, verneinen*] that appear in Freudian texts as substantives [*Verleugnung, Verneinung*] in a specialized vocabulary. For example, Basch notes that, although Anna Freud (1936) delineates types of denial (by fantasy, word, or act), she actually uses *Verleugnung* in the original German. Later writers (e.g., Dorpat,

1984; Stewart, 1970) often collapse disavowal and denial under the latter term and, as did Jacobson, contrast it with repression: "in each [denial of reality and repression] we find two contradictory ideas or attitudes. [In the former] both remain in the go, thus causing a split in the ego; [in the latter] one exists in the ego and the opposing one in the id" (1957, p. 77). In his review of these concepts and terms Basch concludes that it is not perception *per se* but only its meaning that is repudiated in disavowal, thereby following Freud's ultimate position: disavowal is a ubiquitous early defence, necessarily prior to repression, which must await the resolution of the Oedipus complex.[4] In his review Basch was making a distinction that would become further elaborated by self psychologists for whom a vertical split within the self (versus a horizontal split between systems or agencies of the psyche) takes on major theoretical importance (Goldberg, 1999). Denial (= repression) continues to be used by many writers as the foil against which to define the particular defence that is key to their theoretical perspective (e.g., dissociation; Stern, 2010).

Developmental psycholinguistics

Putting aside terminological ambiguities, I return now to Freud's original examples of verbal or logical denial in order to examine the precursors of the ability to express this form of denial. It is remarkable that the explanation Freud offers in 1925 parallels the development of capacities to express negation as described by developmental psycholinguistics. Researchers in this field share with Freud an appreciation of the decisions underlying judgement as the most mature form of negation—namely, logical denial. However, what they add to Freud's account are studies of how the capacity to express logical denial develops, demonstrating that each precursor stage has its own form of negative expression.

Denial has been an important focus of psycholinguistic study, and a brief review of the modern era in linguistics may be helpful in explaining why. The revolution in linguistics ushered in by Chomsky's *Syntactic Structures* (1957) pried grammatical descriptions loose from anthropology and descriptions of specific languages and, in a search for universal structures, connected linguistics to the mathematical formulae of symbolic logic and analytic philosophy. Developmental psycholinguistics emerged as a discipline when researchers sought to demonstrate how competence in these universal structures is "acquired" (versus "learned", as behaviourists had claimed) in particular languages by children innately endowed with capacities to do so. Certain capacities are considered uniquely human because they are possible only with language; and denial is one of these. Therefore, from its beginnings as a discipline in the 1960s, developmental psycholinguistics sought data to demonstrate the acquisition of the uniquely human capacity to deny.

As a consequence, negation has been studied extensively from grammatical, semantic, and pragmatic points of view in children acquiring many different languages.[5] The results of these studies can be summarized in three basic findings. The first of these was well known to Freud: namely, that the core of negation is to deny a corresponding—implicit or explicit—affirmative statement (Volterra & Antinucci, 1979, p. 283). Negation entails an affirmative statement—but not vice versa. Second, examining language evidence from children in a wide range of circumstances, it became clear that there are several types of negation expressed by children in a stepwise series of stages towards mastery of the mature syntactic form. Third, researchers found that the syntactic form itself undergoes a systematic but uniform change across languages: from negative marker before the sentence—"No cookie"; "No want cookie"; "No Sally want cookie"—to negation marked within the sentence—"Sally no/not want cookie"; "Sally doesn't want a cookie" (i.e., the transposition of negation within the proposition as described above).

What types of negation did researchers identify, and in what developmental sequence do they appear? Several types were posited in early studies (Brown, 1973; Pea, 1980, reviewed in Tomasello, 2003) based on their communicative function: to express rejection; to express refusal; to express nonexistence, disappearance, or unfulfilled expectations; and to express denial. Nonexistence, disappearance, and unfulfilled expectations were important types for psycholinguists because of their implication in truth-functional negation or denial, which "express[es] judgments on the use of language by others to predicate properties and existence of things" (Pea, 1980, p. 182). In other words, these researchers' goals were similar to Freud's—finding the precursors to logical or propositional denial.

The two remaining functions—to reject and to refuse—were viewed as the earliest forms of negative expression, roughly mastered by the end of the first year of life. By contrast, expressions of the other functions are mastered in the second year; while denial is mastered only at the end of that year (Pea, 1980).[6] Denial is last acquired because it is uniquely dependent on verbal capacities; that is, denial can be expressed only verbally. By contrast, earlier types of negation can be expressed both verbally and through gestures.[7]

Rejection and refusal are less discussed in both research and clinical contexts, which have been dominated by explorations of the precursors to logical negation. To clarify the relationship of these earliest expressions of negation—rejection and refusal—I turn to Spitz's (1957) early exploration of how negation develops in normal infancy. Spitz observed that the same movement that the infant uses to find the breast (i.e., rooting) later becomes a means to avoid or turn away from food: "The motor pattern exists; this pattern has a function—first to achieve food, later to avoid it" (Spitz, 1965, p. 193). A third stage, the "semantic no", occurs at 15 months, when the child turns away from another person. In other words, "the very same movement, when it reappears in the second year of life as the 'No' gesture, is endowed with the meaning of the avoidance behaviour (namely refusal)" (Spitz, 1957, p. 94). However, the earlier refusal (i.e., rejection) of food is "objectless and still only the manifestation of the psychophysical state of the child" (Spitz, 1965, p. 193). Only in the third stage is it indicative of "elementary reciprocal object relations", but "each of the first two phases contributes to the third" (Spitz, 1957, p. 94).[8]

Rejection—literally pushing or throwing back—may be connected to "dismell", which Tomkins (1962–63) lists as a primary innate affect based on its evolutionary role in protecting organisms against bad food. To be able to avoid what is perceived as bad, therefore, must be evolutionarily very basic, appearing early in the infant's repertoire of responses to its environment (but subsequent to nutrient-seeking). By contrast, refusal proper, I agree with Spitz, involves another person: specifically, the command of another person (Volterra & Antinucci, 1979, p. 288). In this later response to the environment one is not just rejecting food or the breast but setting oneself up in opposition to another's wishes. Therefore, refusal must appear later than rejection, although perhaps not as late as Spitz's "semantic no" (i.e., at fifteen months). It is important to note that, even though refusal involves the command of another person, it does not yet involve the statement of a proposition in a dialogue with another person, a condition necessary for denial.

The proposed emergence of a sequence for the expression of negation corresponds to a long tradition of hypothesized developmental sequences in the psychoanalytic literature (Palombo, Bendicsen, & Koch, 2009). The key question for such structural and epigenetic models is the fate of earlier stages: does each subsequent stage integrate and replace the previous stages at a new level of organization and regulation (Gedo & Goldberg, 1973, p. 12), or do earlier stages "persist, both in their original 'primitive' forms and in the various progressively more 'mature' forms they may attain" (p. 156)? Do old forms persist but take on new functions (Hartmann, 1939; Spitz, 1957; Slobin, 1973)? I am suggesting here that the earliest forms of negation—rejection and refusal—remain viable and appear in our clinical interactions with patients, indicative of defensive uses of negation that first appear developmentally to solve problems the child faced within the first year of life. At the same time, the later language-dependent form of denial may also appear; but the mere presence of "not" or "no" does not automatically indicate the particular type of negation, nor does it make clear, psychologically, its developmental function.

Clinical examples

Rizzuto (1988) describes patients with bulimarexia as suffering from defects in early communicative uses of language who rely on "patterns of early mentation related to oral incorporation and ejection" (p. 385). Many such patients have suffered deprivation and abuse in their early years, and they tend to spend sessions spewing forth a litany of complaints and slights suffered at the hands of others, including the therapist. One is reminded of Melanie Klein's suggestion that the ego's first mode of defence is not repression but expulsion (Stein, 1994). For patients with severely pathological interactions with caretakers early in life, the use of another person to establish subject–object relations, as in refusal, may have been problematic. For such patients, the emergence of refusing behaviours in treatment may signal progress (versus a regression).

Novick (1990), for example, describes a severely abused and exploited patient

> who spent the first year and a half of her analysis in constant berating of me and the process, hurling accusations about my criticizing and judging her, or bitterly cataloguing her resignation and reproach that I was of no use to her. . . . After a one-week break in the treatment due to her vacation, [the patient] started an argument about the treatment setting and provoked me to note, as I had in the past, how she complained about my making the rules, but she retained de facto control, for instance, by her refusal to use the couch" [Novick, 1990, pp. 345–346]

In response, the patient threw herself angrily onto the couch and "after some initial speeches about how impossible it was to talk to anyone in that position, she subsided into a silence fraught with an extraordinary degree of tension" (p. 346).

Novick explains this behaviour in terms of attachment and separation issues: she and the patient "seemed suspended in a transference actualization of the developmental moment when the toddler is struggling to define himself as separate from mother but cannot feel comfortable or whole consistently by himself" (p. 346). Alternatively, in terms of forms of negative expression, one might view the litany of abusive complaints as the patient's use of the analytic setting to serve as the container for her *rejected*, spewed-forth malignant maternal introjects; then one might judge this girl's *refusal* to use the couch as a developmental step forward, made possible by prior analytic work. One wonders if the price of hanging on to the needed analyst is compliance, prematurely giving up a needed step in the use of negation to establish oneself in a meaningful dialogue where, ultimately, *denial* might be possible.

However, even for those who have attained the possibility of denial in therapeutic dialogue, earlier forms of negation may emerge in the treatment. For example, Shapiro (1979) describes a patient in analysis who presented a dream and "raced through his associations, obviously shifting to a content which bore little discoverable relationship to the manifest content of the dream. When he was asked for further associations to the dream, he balked". Shapiro interpreted the patient's resistance as

> a parallel to his feelings in marriage that the longer he stayed with his wife, the more he felt trapped by what others expected of him. He denied this with little affect and proceeded on another track. Later, he slapped his head and noted that he had said 'No', as he had so frequently done with his wife and mother, because he could only feel free and autonomous when he opposed others. He felt that what they or the analyst said were challenges and were therefore to be denied. [Shapiro, 1979, p. 115–116]

In other words, although the patient appeared to be denying the propositional content of the interpretation, he acknowledges that he was actually refusing to comply with the performative requirements of the analytic dialogue. He has to defend against the intrusion of the other person—mother, wife, analyst—in order to protect his own subjectivity by refusing to enter into a dialogue at all.

Performative negation

In order to understand the difference between propositional negation, expressed through verbal forms of denial, and earlier forms, expressed performatively, it is useful to begin with a closer look at the infant's experiences. The infant's subjective experiences are analogical—that is, continuous along dimensions of greater or lesser intensity. The earliest forms of negation are similarly analogical. For example, gestures such as shaking one's head to reject an object are continuous and permit varying degrees of intensity. In contrast to the infant's analogical experiences, language systems are digital, introducing discrete categories and distinctions.[9]

One author who has examined Freud's concept of negation in terms of an analogical–digital distinction is Anthony Wilden. According to Wilden (1972), "not" introduces the digital into analogical systems and is "a necessary (but perhaps not a sufficient) condition for natural language" (p. 188). So, for example, other species can reject food or refuse a mate but cannot deny or negate.

In the same way, human babies, who are first attuned to and master the analogical aspects of their language system (i.e., prosodic speech patterns), can reject food and refuse mother with or without digitalized language forms, but they cannot deny their own or others' thoughts without "not" (or its equivalents). However, as new language forms are mastered, they first serve old functions (Slobin, 1973, p. 184); for example, "no" often accompanies gestures of rejection and refusal. Increasingly, the child's environment demands that he use words to express himself, and ultimately all forms of negation can be expressed verbally.

Language is acquired in contexts of caretaker–child interactions where "utterances not only serve to express propositions, but also perform actions" (Levinson, 1983, p. 243). Since the early 1960s, philosophers of language have examined how speaking is always also enacting—that is, doing something with words (Austin, 1962; Searle, 1969). A theory of speech acts posits that messages (i.e., propositional content) are always embedded in particular pragmatic enactments, on which interpretation of the proposition depends. Each type of speech act has a different "illocutionary force" that affects its truth-value. Thus, for example, the proposition used in examples above—"the swan is black"—will have different meanings if embedded in a command ("I insist that the swan is black"), a request ("I ask you if the swan is black") or an assertion ("I claim that the swan is black"). Only the last of these makes a claim about the truth-value of the statement, but, since the performative verb (insisting, requesting, asserting) is rarely explicitly stated, ambiguities arise about how to interpret propositional messages. Instead, one must rely on the relationship of the speaker ("I") and addressee ("you") to determine how the message should be interpreted (Litowitz, 2005, 2011).[10]

As described already, a statement can be negated in many ways, as the negative operator may move from outside to inside the underlying proposition. However, as Lyons explains, the predicate calculus cannot accommodate negation at the illocutionary or performative level of speech acts (1977, p. 773). Performative negation would negate not the proposition but, rather, the performative action in which the proposition is embedded: "I do not claim [P]"; "I do not ask you [P]". With performative negation (also called "neustic" negation), Lyons states that we express our refusal or inability to perform the illocutionary act of asserting, promising, or whatever it might be. But to do this is in itself to perform an illocutionary act: an act of non-commitment [i.e., non-compliance]. Acts of non-commitment are to be distinguished, on the one hand, from saying nothing and, on the other, from making descriptive statements. [Lyons, 1977, p. 770]

However, clinically we often find that negation *is* expressed by saying nothing, as in responses of silence or empty chatter, which we label "resistance".

Understanding the differences among negative expressions and when they first arise in development is an effort to push clinical listening beyond "resistance" to ask: resistance to what or to whom? My contention is that acts of non-commitment are performed as refusals (i.e., acts of non-engagement or non-compliance) towards the end of the first year of life. When refusals appear later in life or in treatment, the same form is being used to express the same defensive function: to establish or safeguard one's subjectivity against the impingement of another.

Developmental psycholinguistic research supports the sequencing of caretaker–child communication in pragmatic contexts prior to the ability of the child to generate even the earliest forms of propositional negation. Young children correctly interpret the speech act before they have full mastery of the embedded propositions; in this way they move from communicational to grammatical competence (Bates, 1976; Bruner, 1975a, 1975b, 1983). As a result, children master capacities of negation at the illocutionary level before they master the intricacies of propositional negation.[11] In other words, after rejection (which is still based in their own psychophysical experiences) children master the ability to refuse to engage with another subjectivity, and only later, when engaged as an "I" to a "you", do they make judgements about the truth or falsity of propositions (e.g., "It's not my mother").[12]

In his major philosophical study on the function of negativity in the constitution of the subject, Ver Eecke (1984) comes to a similar conclusion: Freud's classic paper reveals more than one type of negation, with developmental implications. Using Lacan's (1957, pp. 374–408) and Hyppolite's (1956) distinction between *denegation* and *negation*, Ver Eecke calls one type the "no" [*non*] or "denial", and the other, "not" [*ne pas*] or "negation". The distinction Ver Eecke is articulating (albeit with confusing terminology, from our perspective) is directly parallel to the differences I have described between earlier types of negation (rejection and refusal) and logical or truth-functional denial. In the former types of negation

> the speaking person is a prisoner of the expression he used. He cannot vary his negative judgement; he also cannot give a positive content which he wants to clarify or want to defend by his negative proposition. Finally, he gets irritated when he is contradicted. He cannot confront his point of view with that of others. The other is ... not a partner but an outsider. [Ver Eecke, 1984, p. 152]

By contrast, the latter type of negation is "founded upon a confrontation with the other, whereby the speaker tries to defend intersubjectively a personal vision of reality", a truth (p. 153).

Ver Eecke's single first stage seems to incorporate aspects of both rejection and refusal (1984, pp. 144, 186). However, I believe that distinguishing between these two earliest types can be clinically useful by providing a contrast between the spewing-forth and demanding containment of malignant affects/introjects (Bion, 1967), on the one hand, and conflicts around intersubjective engagements, on the other, as in the following clinical example. A borderline patient of mine, although much improved over a long and often stormy treatment, still can experience difficulty in her closest relationships. At those times she will spend the better part of sessions spouting expletives and decrying: "I'm done!" "I've had it!" "I'm so over X!" Emptied of rage and venom she will become calmer but refuses my interpretations with "No, it's not that [my P]"; "It's just that [her P]". I see this change in responses as a movement from ejecting (rejecting) to refusing, even almost denying. Indeed, she is often capable now of engaging with me in an intersubjective dialogue where we can negotiate her truth and my truth. However, other defensive forms of negation resurface when she is in states of narcissistic injury or experiencing particular conflicts. Identifying the form of negation helps me to articulate those states and conflicts for her, thereby making them available as joint referents in our dialogues.

Conclusion

During the first years of life, every child is faced with making challenging distinctions, which he will need throughout his life: desirable versus dangerous, internal versus external, self versus other, his thoughts versus others' thoughts. At the same time, language acquisition is proceeding *pari passu*, and its resources become available to the ego (self) as forms of protection while meeting these challenges. In noting at the start of this essay that any aspect of normal development can be used defensively (Brenner, 2006), one is reminded of Freud's emphasis on the ego's use of defences for protection, especially during its early growth period.

> The mechanisms of defence serve the purpose of keeping off dangers. It cannot be disputed that they are successful in this; and it is doubtful whether the ego could do without them altogether during its development.... Moreover these mechanisms are not relinquished after they have assisted the ego during the difficult years of development. [1937c, p. 237).

For Freud, specific defences "become fixated in [the] ego. They become regular modes of reaction of [one's] character" (p. 237).

The developmental sequence of forms of negation proposed here is not meant to suggest the predictability of such "regular modes" or "fixations". Quite the contrary: I am suggesting that all modes remain available, and one or the other may predominate, disappear, or reappear during the course of a treatment. While all forms of negation can be seen as resistances, awareness of differences in types may help clinicians to determine what the patient is defending against and at what level of development his current internal struggle is being waged. The types of negation provide sources of information regarding the nature of the relationship to the analyst/therapist that the patient is evoking for defensive reasons; whether one views the defence as against wishes, anxiety, fragmentation, loss of boundaries, or whatever. While for Freud the patient's struggle is intrapsychic—forces pushing for expression or held in check, mental agencies split or in opposition (Jacobson, 1957)—the developmental view presented here adds an interpsychic or intersubjective perspective consistent with post-Freudian theoretical approaches (e.g., object relational, interpersonal, self psychological). If, in the end, "everyone's defensive repertory is as broad as his or her range of mental functioning" (Brenner, 2006, p. 121), then examining when and why these resources emerge should help us to better understand the varied and shifting defensive positions encountered in our clinical interactions.

Notes

1. Other operators are: conjunction; disjunction; material implication; and biconditional implication. However, Peirce determined that all five can be derived from just two primitives: conjunction and negation (Sowa, 1984, p. 386).
2. "Sublated" is used here as the usual translation of *Aufhebung* in Hegelian dialectics, defined in *Webster's Third New International Dictionary* as, "to cancel but also preserve and elevate (an element in a dialectic process) as a partial element in a synthesis".
3. As the Kris Study Group monograph illustrates, little agreement exists on definitions and distinctions concerning denial and disavowal (Fine, Joseph, & Waldhorn, 1969).
4. For a succinct critical review of major works in psychoanalysis and philosophy that relate to Freud's 1925 paper, see also Ver Eecke (1984, pp. 2–11).
5. English, Italian, French, German, Japanese, Hebrew, Finnish, Samoan, Luo, Korean, Tamil, English as a second language, American Sign Language (Bloom, 1970; Bowerman, 1973; Brown, 1973; Ferguson & Slobin, 1973; Hoffmeister & Wilbur, 1980; Keller-Cohen, Chalmer, & Remler, 1979; McNeill & McNeill, 1968; Tomasello, 2003; Volterra & Antinucci, 1979).
6. An additional type—"self-prohibition"—is evident from around the age of eighteen months in response to negative responses from the environment and interpreted by Spitz (1957, 1965) as identification with the aggressor, leading to superego development. However, Lichtenstein (1971) differentiates between prohibitions that promote ego growth ("coaching no") and other sanctions ("malignant no") that derail ego development, generating heightened aggression and sexuality.
7. Gestural expressions may substitute for or accompany verbal expression but are no less symbolic. Darwin (1872) observed over a century ago that even the negative headshake is less universal than would be expected and gestures of affirmation are more variable still.
8. Cf. "sublation", described above.
9. Matte-Blanco's "bi-logic" (1975) offers an alternative perspective.
10. Watzlawick, Beavin, & Jackson (1967) distinguish between the "report" (i.e., propositional statement) and the "command" (i.e., relationship

of speaker and hearer) into which statements are embedded. Ambiguities and contractions can arise between digital report and analogical command, and some may lead to pathological patterns of communication.

11. The first forms of propositional negation use the performative negative "no"—i.e., new functions first use old forms (Slobin, 1973).

12. Writers have observed an inability to master the performative "I-the-speaker address you-the-hearer" and negative signs in autism and psychosis (Litowitz & Litowitz, 1983; Shapiro, 1979; Shapiro & Kapit, 1978; Ver Eecke, 1984).

2

On "Negation": some reflections following in Freud's wake

Jorge Canestri

I should like to begin by saying that I shall be speaking about negation as a psychoanalytic notion—in other words, as a specific defensive mechanism—leaving aside any consideration about the importance of the concept in other fields, as well as any discussion of an etymological or philological nature.

Concepts, especially in our field, are not univocal; but in some particular cases, such as the one we are dealing with, they seem to be pervaded by a disordered polyvalence and changeability. By this I do not mean to say that concepts should not evolve, change, and expand; on the contrary, these processes are part of the elaboration of a concept and are normal and desirable. Could it therefore be argued that the concept of negation as a defence mechanism has undergone this type of elaboration as a result of the progress made during the history of psychoanalysis, and that the original intent of the concept has been changed? A statement such as this is only partially valid when it concerns negation. There are many works that examine this defence mechanism and its consequences, the two most pertinent ones being Ferenczi's (1913) paper: "Stages in the Development of the Sense of Reality" and Laforgue's (1926) discussion on scotomization entitled "Verdrängung und Skotomisation".

Owing to the repercussions that her work has had in the analytic field, I consider that Melanie Klein played an important role in extending—perhaps beyond measure—the concept of negation, to the point of including in it mechanisms that should, instead, be carefully distinguished from it. In her research project on very early childhood, Klein (1928, 1935) suggests that negation is a very premature mechanism, prior to repression and active without distinction in all pathologies. Thus, affects, drives, psychic reality, external reality, anxiety, and so forth can all fall under negation. Initially differentiated from Laforgue's scotomization (criticized and rejected by Freud), it ends up by taking possession of it and including it.

I do not want to burden you by repeating the whole history of the concept in question, but I should like to take another look at the actual idea of negation or *Verneinung* as enunciated by Freud in 1925.

Freud's notion

In the bare and desolate landscape of so-called "literature for children", the Italian writer Gianni Rodari has cultivated a little wood that is strong and playful. In his book: *Twice upon a Time There Was a Baron Called Lamberto* (1978), I found the idea of quite an unusual way of rejuvenating. He said that his character, Lamberto, returned to the days of his youth thanks to those people who were commissioned to repeatedly say his name. Who knows whether concepts are invigorated if they are re-examined? And so to *Die Verneinung*: a short text—two pages in German—and yet incredibly dense with meaning. At first sight it could appear to be about analytic technique, and that it certainly is, but it is also much more. It is a "knot" or intersection where the various problems of the theory that Freud was developing converge. I will briefly mention some of them in a list that is not exhaustive, but only attempts to summarize the complexity of a thought that in this text is perhaps condensed to the maximum.

The backbone of the article is made up of the theory, not explicitly stated, of the constitution of the subject of the unconscious. Manifestly, on the contrary, Freud develops the theme of the inscription of the experience and the creation of the concept of reality operated by the judgement of existence, analyses the meaning of the object in psychoanalytic theory, hypothesizes the genesis of thought in the insurgence of the explicit symbol of negation, distinguishes negation from psychotic negativism, and so forth: the list could be continued. However, in this occasion, I have chosen the problem of the definition of the Freudian concept of negation [*Verneinung*], in view of the laxity with which it is frequently considered and used. I shall try to find within the text those arguments that authorize us to highlight the differences that exist between the defensive mechanisms that Freud put forward in the neuroses [*Verdrängung, Verneinung*]. Subsequently, I shall refer to clinical practice in an attempt to discover the source of the questions that I am going to propose.

I shall now move on to a short comment on the text, emphasizing points that are relevant to the theme. Freud begins the article with examples from which he draws a very clear conclusion. I quote the passage: "Thus the content of a repressed image or idea can make its way into consciousness, on condition that it is *negated*. Negation is a way of taking cognizance of what is repressed; indeed it is already a lifting of the repression, though not, of course, an acceptance of what is repressed" (pp. 235–236). In this passage we have to remember the footnote where Strachey justifies the translation of the German "*verneinen*" by "to negate" instead of "to deny".

From this statement and the following one in which Freud describes the details of the operation carried out in the subject every time he/she tries to grasp something that has been repressed, it appears that:

» negation is subsequent to repression;

» it is a mechanism that enriches thought with contents that are otherwise inaccessible, and this occurs through the use of the symbol of negation;

» repression remains; it is not eliminated, it is only revoked, abrogated [*Aufhebung*]. I will not discuss the many problems that still continue to divide analysts concerning the nature of the revocation, or of the splitting between intellectual function and affective process, or whether affective process indicates primordial symbolization or something else.

It is an established fact that repression must exist in order to be able to speak of negation, and this is sufficient for me to explain the theme I am dealing with, inasmuch as negation is a way of accessing the repressed contents and is characteristic of the essential non-acknowledgement (in the constitutive sense) that the subject suffers in regard to what determines it.

If Freud had ended the text after this statement, the imprint would have been substantially technical. But he immediately proposes a consideration of the psychological origin of the function of negation. Here begins what I will call the speculative part of his treatment. Others speak of mythical exposition. I have nothing against this if the idea of myth is interpreted according to the meaning given to it by Levi-Strauss (1958), as a sort of logical instrument that establishes a bridge between an initial problem and one flowing from it.

I could speak of speculative treatment in the sense that Freud suggested when he said that certain ideas follow each other, repeatedly combining material deriving from experience with that which is purely speculative, accepting the fact that in this way the degree of uncertainty increases and that it is just as possible to make a positive discovery as it is to make a shameful mistake.

Taking up again the classic distinction between attributive judgement and judgement of existence, Freud claims that the function of judgement consists in conceding or refusing a quality to a thing (attribution) or admitting or contesting the existence in reality of a representation (existence). Attributive judgement can be expressed in the oral drive impulses—incorporate–expel—and trace a primeval groove between what I introduce into myself and what coincides with the original pleasure-ego [*Lust-Ich*], and what is foreign to me and is rejected by me on the basis of the quality of being unpleasant. Freud calls it a question pertaining to the outside and to the inside. The "inside" is representation, trace, inscription, sign. All these are names that were used alternatively in Freud's works and serve to describe the subjective, which appears when the second decision of judgement tries to find the representation in the perception (reality). The thing (*das Ding*, the object of satisfaction) must exist in the reality.

I shall quote an excerpt that concludes this second part: "The first and immediate aim, therefore, of reality-testing is, not to *find* an object in real perception which corresponds to the one presented, but to *refind* such an object, to convince oneself that it is still there" (pp. 237–238). And shortly afterwards: "But it is evident that a precondition for the setting up of reality-testing is that objects shall have been lost which once brought real satisfaction" (p. 238).

Recapitulating the model—for indeed it is a model—it must be noted that:

» A primary/primeval groove is delimited by the work of affirmation (*"Die Bejahung, als Ersatz der Vereinung, gehört dem Eros an"*: "Affirmation—as a substitute for unification—belongs to Eros) and of expulsion (whose consequence—*Nachfolge*—a posteriori will be negation).

» Affirmation [*Bejahung*] implies the inscription of a representation; the expulsion, on the contrary, implies its absence and its belonging to what has been expelled to reality.

» The object of satisfaction, which intervened in the corresponding experience, is lost.

» This is the necessary condition for the installation of reality-testing, whose final aim is to retrieve the object.

Going on with his considerations, Freud makes this model tally with the drive model, attributing to affirmation, as I have already said, the quality of *Ersatz* of unification, thus belonging to Eros, and to negation the character of *Nachfolge*, the consequence of expulsion—that is, the possession of the *Destruktionstrieb*, the destructive drive. Freud wonders whether psychotic negativism should not be interpreted in the sense of an already-happened defusion of drives [*Triebentmischung*], a return to a pure state, a decantation of the drives?

Negation, therefore, allows thought a first level of independence from the effects of repression, and it is the type of relation that the neurotic and normal subject has with the unconscious. Will the mechanism that acts in the psychoses and in the perversions not have other characteristics that could perhaps be deduced from the previous model? Instead of confusedly extending the negation mechanism, as Klein had done, Freudian research sought for alternative pathways. That Freud worked hard to find a specific mechanism, different from negation, that would serve to confront the problems regarding the psychotic and perverse pathology is too well known to require proof. Just as well known are the texts that bear witness to this: "The Loss of Reality in Neurosis and Psychosis" (1924e), "Psycho-Analytic Notes on an Autobiographical Account of a Case of Paranoia (1911c [1910]), and so forth.

The object in this context

I do not want to explore the possibilities of expanding the hypothetical model without first saying a word about the object—essential for the task in hand. What can be deduced from the schema postulated in relation to the object in psychoanalysis? I emphasize that the object of satisfaction is that thing [*Ding*] that, having been lost, has left a sign of itself—a representation—that, in its absence, acts as the driving force and cause of a pursuit. Reality-testing is connected with the possibility of retrieving the object. In my search for an analogy that would express this relationship between presence (of the representation) and absence (of the object) and their reciprocal interaction, the *Tao Te Ching* (c. AD 300; Duyvendak, 1954) came to mind. The following lines from it describe, with the skill and delicacy of a Chinese paintbrush, an alternative simile:

> Though thirty spokes may be joined in one hub, the utility of the carriage lies in what is not there.
> Though clay may be moulded into a vase, the utility of the vase lies in what is not there.
> Though doors and windows may be cut to make a house, the utility of the house lies in what is not there.
> Therefore, taking advantage of what is, we recognize the utility of what is not.

This analogy describes a query that the model solves: how what is not there—the object—is used by taking advantage of what is there—the representation. This is how we establish a relationship with reality, says Freud. But suppose that what should be there is not there? At this point we could start hypothesizing about the model.

I take as a starting point the primeval groove that is the *conditio sine qua non* of what follows. In fact, if Freud states that the affirmation, as *Ersatz* of unification, is installed "inside" a primary representation [*Vorstellung*], and that the negation, afterwards, will be a consequence [*Nachfolge*] of the decision to expel, in its turn belonging to the *Destruktionstrieb*, then this *Vorstellung* must exist in order to be able to afterwards confront it with the object that is retrieved in reality. If this representation is not there, then reality, corresponding to this absence of representation, is not re-discovered.

In an example that Freud gave in his work "The Neuro-Psychoses of Defence" (1894a), he reasoned about the hallucinatory psychosis of a mother who cradled a piece of wood in her arms during the mental illness that followed her son's death. Freud presumes, in these cases (Meynert's amentia), the existence of an extremely strong and successful form of defence: expulsion, the rejection of the incompatible idea (intolerable: *unverträglich*, cf. note by J. Strachey)—in this case the death of her son—together with its own affect. The subject subsequently behaves as though this idea had never existed, entering into psychosis because, moreover, part of the reality is connected to the idea, a reality from which she obviously detaches herself. This is the premise for the hallucination.

Returning to the example, when one thinks of a piece of wood in the place of a dead child, usually one neglects the fact that there is no relation of substitution but, rather, a relation of absolute identity—a characteristic of psychosis. The relation of substitution implies that there is an element in the place of another, taking its place, in so far as a replacement is possible, that is of a symbolic nature.

A represents and therefore substitutes for *B* (it could be illustrated with the symbolic equation of the feminine Oedipus: a child instead of a penis). In the mother's hallucinatory madness the wood is the child: *A* does not represent *B*, it *is B*. And it is the child because there is no representation of the death of the child. The reality that corresponds to this absence is a presence about which it is difficult to reflect.

If the hallucination, and therefore the reality in question, is defined only in relation to the nonexistence of the sensitive material that promotes the corresponding intentionality in the perception, and this, in its turn, according to Taine (1870), is considered a real hallucination, then it is difficult not to find oneself at a dead end—unless, like Freud, one raises the question of the subject who splits in the act of expelling an incompatible representation, whose absence operates on another level—the level of reality that is not a retrieval, but a hallucination—a return from reality of the excluded idea whose effectiveness is, paradoxically, increased.

From what has been said above, a definition can be suggested of the relationship of the subject with a reality that is far from the roughness that analytic post-Freudian conceptualization has sometimes revealed. However, it must be said that a model of this kind is propaedeutical and leaves the main question unanswered. An isolated mechanism cannot explain a psychotic structure. It is inevitable to feel the need to theorize the constitutive modalities of the subject, a path followed by Freud in both theory and clinical work. As an example, I mention his work on President Wilson that usually goes unnoted (Freud & Bullitt, 1939/1966).

Clinical illustrations

First clinical vignette

I would now like to present a particular "moment" of an analysis that may lead to certain reflections on the matter we are dealing with. In the "moment" I have selected, I feel one can catch a glimpse of an effect of the action of a defensive mechanism that is detached from negation in the Freudian sense and draws near to the concept of a more radical mechanism (*Verleugnung*/denial/disavowal—*Verwerfung*/repudiation or foreclosure) of *Verneinung*, as I have tried to understand it. The analysis I am speaking about was carried out in two languages, English and Spanish. This was necessary because, owing to her childhood bilingualism, the analysand associated spontaneously in both languages.

I will call the patient S.

At the beginning of one of her weekly sessions, S rebukes the analyst for not paying enough attention to the "culor" of her pretty blouse. The slip of the tongue consists of substituting the letter "o" ("colour" in Spanish) with the letter "u", and also a change in the pronunciation of the second "o", which becomes phonetically like the English "er". In correcting the lapsus, the analysand recognizes a precise composition in the new word. It is a mixture of "*color*", "colour" and ____, a word that she flatly refuses to pronounce, saying that it is coarse and vulgar. Afterwards, she admits that it is "*culo*" [arse, ass]—a word that she says is not in her vocabulary; instead, she uses the word "*cola*", tail. "*Cola*" is a word that in Spanish describes the caudal appendix of an animal (tail) and also glue—the mixture used to stick two things together. But, in the ambiguous language that adults sometimes use with children when speaking of sex and the body, and which children then use themselves, it also means both genitals and buttocks.

It must be pointed out, however, that her associations in English denote a good knowledge of the names for the sexual parts of the body, such as "buttocks", "bottom", "bosom", and so on, with some particular expressions taken from Scottish (her maternal grandmother). Leaving aside this "knowledge", she only uses the word "tits" from the "Old English" to speak of breast, and the above-mentioned "*cola*" to make a vague reference to an imprecise area between the waist and thighs. "*Cola*" had an equivalent in English—"tail"—which she describes as "something that hangs". But these two words are not interchangeable; the words "tits" and "*cola*" from her childhood vocabulary that have remained alive and active are sufficient for her to speak—or, rather, not to speak—about the body and sex. The associations shift from the blouse to the buttocks, apparently following the patient's wish to make the analyst look at her. But what should this glance have noticed, and to what should it bear witness afterwards, when closing the circuit of the sought-after recognition? Surely not the beauty or harmony of her figure—whether upper or lower—because, in her unconscious knowledge about the etymology of the word "colour", the erotic invitation conceals a very different desire. In fact, I find out immediately that the analysand's theory is a stubborn defence of the lack of differentiation between the sexes when men and women are dressed alike or when they are naked but seen from behind.

At this point in the session the patient remembers a dream of the night before that is partly distressing and partly happy. In the first half S dreamed that a metallic object broke away from her mouth and scattered into space. I will not analyse this aspect of the dream, nor will I talk about the related associations. In the second half, she enacts a rearrangement of the first half: she sees herself with a tin of "Plasticola" in her hand, and she says to herself that with it she would repair the damage done before. "Plasticola" is the brand name of a synthetic plastic glue, as the word indicates. Literally, it is *"cola plastica"* [synthetic glue], but if the words are inverted, it can also mean artificial, false, supplement, an orthopaedic element, or plastic surgery of the *"cola"* [tail, buttocks].

In the passage I have quoted, it is not difficult to recognize an expression of the tenacity with which S kept up a childhood belief that she had purposely used in order to refuse the idea of castration, but there was also an indication of the crisis in the above-mentioned belief. Either there was no difference between the sexes, or the situation could be remedied. The seduction revealed in the slip of the tongue and in the care taken in dressing and putting on make-up to come to the session—then explicitly admitted by the patient—cannot succeed in diverting attention. Here seducing means obtaining the consensus and complicity of the other: "Isn't it true that a glance from behind cannot differentiate; isn't it true that if there is a difference, in one way or another it can be remedied?" In this case, can one speak of a negation of sexual differentiation, a negation of castration?

The process in S's case appears to go well beyond the limits that Freud describes in the *Verneinung* [Negation] in order to acquire the characteristics of a real shattering, a splintering. S knows and doesn't know; there was a moment when—as Freud said about the Wolf Man—she didn't want to know anything about castration. The defence appears to be more radical in an approach to processes of a psychotic nature.

A shorter vignette

Another analysand began his analysis by proposing a riddle that he thought was of great interest and attraction. This did not derive from the content or the structure of the riddle, which was a familiar combination of antitheses, but from the way in which it presented an essential problem he himself had. Inasmuch as my speech must be straightforward without the complication of riddles, as promised by Aeschylus in Prometheus, I will repeat the riddle in its longer and more explicative version, that of Aristotle, even though the analysand was fascinated by one sentence only. Aristotle says:

> Homer consulted the god to know who were his parents and which was his homeland, and the god replied thus: the island of Io is the homeland of your mother, and it will receive you when you are dead; but beware of the riddle of young men. ... He reached Io. Here, seated on a rock, he saw some fishermen drawing near to the shore and he asked them if they had anything. Because they had not caught anything and had no fish, but were picking fleas off themselves, they answered him: "What we caught we threw away; what we didn't catch we carry with us", referring with a riddle to the fact that the fleas they had caught, they had killed and thrown away, and those they had not caught, they carried in their clothes. Homer, unable to solve the riddle, died of dejection. [Aristotle, *De Poet*, Fr. 7 (A11), in Colli, 1977, p. 32]

The sentence that attracted the analysand was the fishermen's reply—that is, the riddle itself. Turning it over and over in his mind, he thought he could see a ray of hope for his problems. And he was not wrong. He carried around with him, like uncaught fleas, something that he had not taken (admitted): in his particular case, an unregistered death that re-presented itself with the agonizing force of a hallucination. Like Homer, who died from dejection, and Calchas, who was overcome by the sleep of death for not being able to solve a riddle, the psychotic has to deal with something that he cannot grasp, and this extreme defence creates a laceration that obscures and that must not be confused with negation.

Concluding thoughts

These brief reflections are an attempt to review the Freudian concept of negation. Sandler has often emphasized (e.g., 1983) that the frontiers of psychoanalytic concepts are fairly elastic, and that this characteristic must not necessarily be considered negative. However, these pages state that the Freudian concept of negation would benefit from greater precision if it is not to be confused with concepts that are certainly close to or related to it. Post-Freudian psychoanalysis—for example, André Green's important construction on "the negative"—has definitely widened the area that the concept could cover.

Melanie Klein (1932, 1935) was perhaps the first to attribute to negation the character of a very early mechanism that preceded repression. Without questioning the validity of her clinical observations and the utility of her conception from the viewpoint of defence mechanisms, I think that it would not be appropriate to superimpose this concept on the Freudian one. I consider just as debatable the interpretation provided by Lacan (1957, pp. 374–408), who, in his comment to Hyppolite (1956), talks about denial, thus fostering, as mentioned above, a certain conceptual confusion. This work suggests a reading of the Freudian text in which it is stated that negation is subsequent to repression, that it is needed in order to enrich thought with contents that would otherwise remain inaccessible, that this is possible thanks to the use of the symbol of negation, and that repression is revoked, abrogated, but not eliminated.

All this makes negation a characterizing element of the essential non-acknowledgement of the subject with regard to his main determinations. The proposed interpretation subsequently analyses the speculative model created by Freud in order to explain the psychological origin of the function of negation, pointing out the importance that is attributed in it both to the representation—trace of the initial statement—as well as to the loss of the object of satisfaction. On these two elements depends the installation of reality-testing and the "retrieval" of the object.

Probably the considerations that Freud gives to the object in his model are those that allow a glimpse of the problems resulting from non-neurotic pathologies. With the metaphoric assistance of the *Tao Te Ching* and of an Aristotelian enigma, a central query of these pathologies is revealed—that is, the possible absence, not of the object, but of the representation, and the consequences deriving from it.

Through two small clinical examples I have tried to place negation among those defence mechanisms of Freudian theory that include "*Verleugnung*" [denial, disavowal] and "*Verwerfung*" [repudiation, foreclosure]. The first example refers to *Verleugnung* and the second to *Verwerfung*. Both mechanisms, in the wake of the Freudian project, allow us to draw closer to the non-neurotic pathologies, which claim the attention of contemporary psychoanalysis to a greater extent. As the greatest scholars have always said, all of Freud's writings can be the subject of many and new interpretations. "Negation", in particular, offers itself for continuing reflection, as if what it can give to the attentive analyst could never be exhausted.

3

The negative therapeutic reaction: review, update, and clinical illustration

Brian M. Robertson

In "Negation" (1925h), Freud understands the concept of the negative as a defence against what is repressed. At the same time, the presence of such a defence is acknowledgement of the repressed. As a consequence, "negation" when recognized can represent an intellectual acceptance but not an emotional acceptance or rejection: "the intellectual function is separated from the affective process" (p. 236). Intellectual and emotional acceptance or rejection provides the underpinnings for the concept of the negative therapeutic reaction (NTR). This chapter proposes to trace the Freudian concept, the subsequent development, and the contemporary understanding of NTR.

The negative therapeutic reaction is a clinical concept that Freud first described in *The Ego and the Id* (Freud, 1923b). He used the appearance of the phenomenon in the analyses of certain patients to illuminate the existence of an unconscious guilt in such patients. Further, he used the concept to demonstrate the existence of the superego, as one of the mental agencies making up his new structural theory of the mind. This intimate involvement with the birth of the superego, and the structural theory itself, has lead to the widespread use of the concept in the psychoanalytic literature. However, it has not been the subject of intensive investigation in the literature in spite of its frequent usage in clinical discussions and in papers dealing with other clinical and theoretical topics. This relative absence following Freud's original contribution was noted by Sandler in 1970 (Sandler, Holder, & Dare, 1970). A recent search on PEP utilizing negative therapeutic reaction in the title revealed some 34 articles and commentaries specific to the concept.

Negative therapeutic reaction: Freud's concept

Freud's most complete description of the negative therapeutic reaction appears in *The Ego and the Id* (1923b). He sets the stage by stating that the, "superego is always close to the id and can act as its representative *vis-à-vis* the ego. It reaches deep down into the id and for that reason is farther from consciousness than the ego is" (p. 49). Freud then turns to clinical facts and states as follows, in a well-known passage,

> There are certain people who behave in a peculiar fashion during the work of analysis. When one speaks hopefully to them or expresses satisfaction with the progress of the treatment, they show signs of discontent and their condition invariably becomes worse. One begins by regarding this as defiance and as an attempt to prove their superiority to the physician, but later one comes to take a deeper and juster view. One becomes convinced, not only that such people cannot endure any praise or appreciation, but that they react inversely to the progress of the treatment. Every partial solution that ought to result, and in other people does result, in an improvement or a temporary suspension of symptoms produces in them for the time being an exacerbation of their illness; they get worse during the treatment instead of getting better. They exhibit what is known as "the negative therapeutic reaction". [Freud, 1923b, p. 49]

In such patients Freud concludes that the need for illness is more powerful than the wish to recover. Further, he notes that this resistance to cure is the "most powerful of all obstacles to recovery" and more formidable than the "familiar ones of narcissistic inaccessibility, a negative attitude towards the physician and clinging to the gain from illness" (p. 49). The analyst is faced with "a moral factor, as sense of guilt, which is finding its satisfaction in the illness and refused to give up punishment or suffering" (p. 49). The patient does not perceive this guilt consciously but, rather, experiences himself as ill. As Freud notes, the analyst faces a very difficult task to convince the patient of his guilt—the motivation underlying his continuing conviction that he is ill.

In an otherwise pessimistic view of the possibility of resolving this most tenacious of resistances to analysis, Freud (1923b, p. 50) noted, in a long footnote, a particular kind of negative therapeutic reaction, one with a more favourable prognosis. This is based on "borrowed guilt": this form of unconscious guilt is the product of the analysand's identification with another person who was, once, "the object of an erotic cathexis".

Freud foreshadowed this downturn during treatment in a number of his earlier writings. In the technical papers he discusses an intensification of the conflicts and the symptoms that may occur as repression lifts, occasioned by a more understanding attitude towards the neurosis, or by the patient's wish to prove to the analyst the dangers of therapy (Freud, 1914g, p. 152). In his case study, "From the History of an Infantile Neurosis", Freud describes the Wolf Man as exhibiting "transitory 'negative reactions'; every time something had been conclusively cleared up, he attempted to contradict the effect for a short while by an aggravation of symptom which had been cleared up" (Freud, 1918b [1914], p. 69). However, it is only in *The Ego and the Id* (1923b) that Freud describes the negative therapeutic reaction as a specific concept differing from the more typical resistances encountered in analytic work. In this sense the analyst has to deal with a patient who at every stage of the analysis prefers suffering to cure.

Freud reconsiders the negative therapeutic reaction in "The Economic Problem of Masochism" (Freud, 1924c). As part of his discussion of moral masochism, he returns to his idea that an unconscious sense of guilt is the motivation underpinning the appearance of this particularly entrenched resistance in an analytic process. He underscores the strength of this resistance, stating, "I pointed out the sign by which such people can be recognized (a 'negative therapeutic reaction') and I did not conceal the fact that the strength of such an impulse constitutes one of the most serious resistances and the greatest danger to the success of our medical or educative aims" (p. 166). Freud stresses that the patient's suffering is key to moral masochism and to its manifestation in the negative therapeutic reaction during analysis. He meets the objections of patients tormented by harsh consciences who find it difficult to accept that they suffer similar unconscious guilt feelings without being aware of them by emphasizing their "need for punishment". He also notes that a neurosis that has frustrated strenuous therapeutic efforts may disappear if reality, in the form of personal, material, or professional disaster, intervenes in the life of the patient. What is required by the individual is that a "certain amount of suffering" is maintained.

In 1937 Freud turned his attention to constructions and discussed their place in analytic technique. While it is the patient's task to remember what he has repressed, the analyst's is to construct what has been forgotten from the fragments that remain in the clinical material. In discussing the problem of confirming or disconfirming the analyst's constructions, Freud raises some of the issues that he had previously pursued in his "Negation" paper. He discerns that both a "yes" and a "no" in the patient's response must be confirmed in subsequent material; paradoxically, both are ambiguous in that "yes" may disguise a negative and "no" may conceal a confirmation. Of particular note here is that Freud refers directly to the NTR, and he refers again to his belief that it is a specific and serious form of resistance. He states,

> If an analysis is dominated by powerful factors that impose a negative therapeutic reaction such as a sense of guilt, a masochistic need for suffering or repugnance to receiving help from the analyst, the patient's behaviour after he has been offered a construction often makes it very easy for us to arrive at the decision that we are in search of. If the construction is wrong, there is no change in the patient; but if it is right or gives an approximation to the truth, he reacts to it with an unmistakable aggravation of his symptoms and of his general condition. [Freud, 1937d, p. 265]

Not withstanding his emphasis on the superego and masochism to explain the negative therapeutic reaction, Freud, in his last discussion of the concept, introduces a direct linkage between the negative therapeutic reaction and the death instinct, beyond the superego and masochism. In "Analysis Terminable and Interminable", Freud states,

> No stronger impression arises from the resistances during the work of analysis than of their being a force which is defending itself by every possible means against recovery and which is absolutely resolved to hold onto illness and suffering. One portion of this force had been recognized by us, undoubtedly with justice, as the sense of guilt and need for punishment, and has been localized by us in the ego's relation to the superego. But this is only the portion of it which is, as it were, psychically bound by the super-ego and thus becomes recognizable; other quotas of the same force, whether bound or free, may be at work in other, unspecified places. If we take into consideration the total picture made up of the phenomena of masochism immanent in so many people, the negative therapeutic reaction and the sense of guilt found in so many neurotics, we shall no longer be able to adhere to the belief that mental events are exclusively governed by the desire for pleasure. These phenomena are unmistakable indications of the presence of a power in mental life which we call the instinct of aggression or of destruction according to its aims, and which we trace back to the original death instinct of living matter. [Freud, 1937c, pp. 242–243]

It appears that for Freud the negative therapeutic reaction signalled the presence of a very specific clinical phenomenon in the analytic situation where the resistance to recovery cannot be explained by recourse to the usual modes of understanding resistances. This concept goes beyond the usual causes of therapeutic failure such as faulty technique, countertransference interference, or inappropriate interpretations. Its essence lies in its paradoxical nature: the patient gets worse following improvement or encouragement by the analyst. This paradoxical reaction cannot be understood by the operation of the pleasure principle alone; accordingly, it goes beyond the usual structural resistances to analytic progress. Both Sandler (Sandler, Holder, Dare, 1970) and Laplanche and Pontalis (1973) note correctly that the concept has been extended beyond Freud's specific definition by some authors in the literature to encompass a characterologically based negativism or contrariness on the part of the patient in analysis. It is thus employed to designate any particularly deep-rooted resistance encountered during analysis.

Negative therapeutic reaction: later contributions

A few years before Freud described the negative therapeutic reaction, Abraham (1919) had published a paper that foreshadowed the writings of later analysts. He made certain observations about a small group of patients who demonstrated chronic resistances to analysis. He noted the following characteristics: an eagerness to be analysed, together with subtle resistances against free association; sensitivity to loss of self-esteem, coupled with a readiness to experience humiliation; defences against the transference involving identification with the analyst; concerns about the "superiority" of the analyst; the unmistakable appearance of envy in the transference; problems in object relations with fathers; disordered narcissism; the presence of anal sadistic traits.

With reference to envy, Abraham states, "Neurotics of the type under consideration grudge the physician any remark that refers to the external progress of their analysis or its data. In their opinion he ought not to have supplied any contribution to the treatment; they want to do everything all by themselves" (p. 307). Not surprisingly, he concludes that the analysis of such patients is difficult because, "analysis is an attack on the patient's narcissism, that is, on that instinctual force upon which our therapeutic endeavours are most easily wrecked" (p. 310).

While Abraham does not identify the negative therapeutic reaction in his paper, there is a consensus among later authors that he was describing similar patients to those later identified by Freud in 1923 (Olinick, 1964; Riviere, 1936; Rosenfeld, 1987; Spillius, 2007).

Just before Freud's final discussion of the negative therapeutic reaction (1937d), two well-known analysts published papers on the concept from different theoretical viewpoints. Horney (1936) begins her paper with an affirmation of Freud's original definition of the concept. She makes the important point that the concept should not be applied to every deterioration of an analysand's condition. It should be confined to a situation in which the analysand shows an increase in symptoms, becomes discouraged, or threatens to leave analysis, immediately following either encouragement by the analyst or interpretative work that would reasonably be expected to bring relief. Initially, the patient experiences relief: this is followed by symptomatic increase and discouragement, often associated with disparagement and hostility of the analyst in overt or disguised forms.

Horney then describes several possible reactions to a successful interpretation by the analyst that she found to characterize patients who exhibit negative therapeutic reactions. The analyst's intervention may provoke competitiveness with the analyst, or a feeling of painful, humiliating exposure of the patient's weakness or inadequacy. In addition, there may be fears of recovery in those phobic of success. Also, the analyst's words may be experienced as an unjust accusation by the unconsciously guilty, or as rejection by those hungry for the analyst's love. In their turn, patients may strike back at the analyst with rage, devaluation, accusations, and regressions, in the form of a return of symptoms or acting out.

Horney concludes her paper with some technical recommendations for dealing with negative therapeutic reactions. She advocates a close attention to the analysand's reactions to interpretations, followed by the typical sequence of relief followed by regression. She also endorses a here-and-now approach to interpreting in such cases rather than the use of constructions of childhood events, attitudes, and experiences.

Riviere's (1936) classic paper makes use of Klein's formulation of the depressive position in approaching analysands who exhibit negative therapeutic reactions. She argues that Freud in *The Ego and the Id* (1923b) was not as pessimistic about the analysability of such patients as generally supposed. For Riviere, negative therapeutic reactions are more likely to occur in narcissistic patients. The impulses to attack the analyst's interventions are part of a manic defence against a catastrophic underlying depression. She believes that in these refractory cases there are other factors involved in their resistances than the severity of their superegos. She states,

> My contribution to the understanding of especially refractory cases of a narcissistic type will therefore consist in the two proposals (*a*) that we should pay more attention to the analysis of the patient's inner world of object-relations, which is an integral part of his narcissism, and (*b*) that we should not be deceived by the positive aspects of his narcissism but should look deeper, for the depression that will be found to underlie it. [Riviere, 1936, p. 306]

The negative therapeutic reaction

The dreaded depression in such patients is defended against by omnipotent control of inner psychic reality—the manic defence—which, in turn, leads to a distorted sense of outer reality. The denial inherent in this attitude relates especially to the ego's dependence on its objects. For the patient, "The psychic truth behind his omnipotent denials is that the worst disasters have actually taken place; it is this truth that he will allow the analysis to make real, will not allow to be 'realized' by him or us" (p. 312).

Although Riviere states that such patients can be analysed, she does not minimize the difficulties. A central issue is that these patients do not feel worthy of help until they have repaired and resurrected the dead and damaged internal objects. Analysis is aimed at helping the patient to surmount his difficulties. This is experienced by him as a temptation to give up the crucial task of repairing his damaged internal objects and is thus resisted fiercely. There remains some hope that the analyst may manage to reach the patient emotionally through the transference and so help him to tolerate the pain involved in cure and the depressive position.

Klein did not write specifically about the negative therapeutic reaction. However, she discusses it in "Envy and Gratitude" (1957). Envy is central to her understanding of the concept. Envy, constitutionally based, is present from birth, and the first object of envy is the feeding breast. In the analytic situation this envy is rekindled—as Klein states,

> We find this primitive envy revived in the transference situation. For instance: the analyst has just given an interpretation which brought the patient relief and produced a change in mood from despair to hope and trust. With some patients, or with the same patient at other times, this helpful interpretation may soon become the object of destructive criticism. [Klein, 1957, p. 185]

As with Horney, Klein observes that some analysands envy the analyst's success and competitively devalue his efforts. Klein discusses the defences against such envy and the attacks on the analyst and the analysis that it motivates. She believes that the envy is often deeply unconscious, heavily defended against, and split off from the rest of the psyche. The analyst must proceed cautiously in fostering awareness of this envious, split-off aspect of the self lest the patient be overwhelmed with his own destructiveness. Gradually, the integration of the destructive aspect takes place and the patient is able to cope with his own destructiveness directed at loved objects by employing less primitive defences. Progressively, as this process unfolds, the analysand's projections onto the analyst diminish, and he consequently becomes a less dangerous figure: the analyst also, no longer the target of envious attacks, finds it easier to help his patient with further integration. As Klein states, "the negative therapeutic reaction is losing in strength" (p. 225).

Olinick (1964, 1970) reopened the topic of the negative therapeutic reaction in the literature with two publications that approached the concept from a predominantly ego-psychological viewpoint. He also emphasizes that the term should be reserved for a relapse in a patient's condition following an accurate interpretation or some hope for improvement in an analysis. It is a transference resistance of variable severity, emanating from the superego, occurring in a sadomasochistic individual prone to depression. Olinick highlights the presence of negativism in the character structure of such analysands, employed defensively to preserve the self from the encroachments of a preoedipal, depressed maternal object. In his cases there is also a background of an absent father, unavailable as a figure of identification for the analysand.

Olinick, and other American authors of this era, with the exception of Loewald, eschew Freud's idea that the death instinct is involved in these severe cases. However, Olinick does acknowledge the presence of the primitive destructiveness that underpins many of the manifestations of the negative therapeutic reaction with these words: "they attempt to mold the analyst into a subjectively accurate rendition of a lost introject; and they persistently annihilate the object by means of projection of the threatening introject. They destroy lest they be destroyed" (p. 568). He also stresses the importance of countertransference issues in such cases, a point taken up again by Orgel (2007) in his recently published discussion of Horney's 1936 paper.

Asch (1976) begins by dispensing with Freud's final formulation of the negative therapeutic reaction as linked to the unbound aspects of the death instinct. He regards this as having a biological basis and "more as a part of his philosophy than as clinically derived" (p. 385). He then enumerates and discusses three additional etiological factors to Freud's unconscious sense of guilt.

1. The masochistic ego: a developmental distortion linked to psychopathology of the ego ideal.
2. Unconscious guilt expanded to encompass a variety of preoedipal fantasies of harm to primary objects.
3. A characterological defence against regression to fusion with an ambivalently regarded preoedipal object.

Asch also points to the importance of countertransference issues in the handling of analysands who have negative therapeutic reactions.

Of note, as exemplified by Olinick and Asch, is the tendency of American ego psychologists of this era to speak more optimistically of the analytic outcome with such patients. Another example is Brenner, cited by Olinick (1970), who concluded his contribution to the panel by stating that analysts should treat the negative therapeutic reaction as they do any other transference resistance. In contradistinction to this tendency are the contributions of Laplanche and Pontalis (1973) and that of Loewald (1972).

Laplanche and Pontalis (1973), in their discussion of the negative therapeutic reaction, raise the issue of whether Freud considered this resistance to emanate from the superego. They answer in the affirmative with reference to Freud's idea of borrowed guilt, which he describes in a footnote to his discussion of the negative therapeutic reaction in *The Ego and the Id*. Here the patient's sense of guilt is "a 'borrowed' one—when it is the product of an identification with some other person who was once the object of an erotic cathexis" (Freud, 1923b, p. 50). They also note that in "Inhibitions, Symptoms and Anxiety" Freud, while detailing the source of various resistances, mentions those emanating from the superego and refers indirectly to the negative therapeutic reaction. This resistance "seems to originate from the sense of guilt or the need for punishment; and it opposes every move towards success, including, therefore, the patient's recovery through analysis" (Freud, 1926d [1925], p. 160).

However, they also point out that Freud had initially left room for features of the negative therapeutic reaction that cannot be fully understood in terms of the superego or secondary masochism. In "Analysis Terminable and Interminable" Freud linked the NTR with the death instinct. When the NTR proves an irreducible obstacle to therapeutic progress, the cause is intimately intertwined with the death instinct, which "becomes recognisable; other quotas of the same force, whether bound or free, may be at work in other, unspecified places" (Freud, 1937c, p. 242). Laplanche and Pontalis hold that by his use of the term NTR, Freud intended to designate a very specific clinical phenomenon, where resistance to cure is not linked to the usual explanations.

Loewald (1972) delineates the difficulties for analysts in reaching a consensus about the concept of the negative therapeutic reaction. Freud's definition is problematic for many analysts, involving, as it does, complex problems of guilt, masochism, and the life and death instincts. To go beyond Freud's understanding is to widen the field and include any deep-seated transference resistance or entrenched negativism on the part of the analysand.

Loewald supports and adds to Freud's understanding. He underlines the need for punishment in such patients and their intense struggle against diminishment of suffering and the amelioration of their condition. As such, he suggests that the actions of the patient are directed not necessarily against the interventions of the analyst but against any possibility of change. If they are directed against the interventions of the analyst, they may be analysable. However, as Loewald states,

> ... in severe cases such an imbalance is rooted in problems of early psychic development, in the precursors of morality, conscience, and guilt which antedate the Oedipus complex and the formation of the superego—where destructive forces got out of hand ... and affected the very fiber of the person *before* they could be bound, as Freud says, by the superego and in the tension between ego and superego. [Loewald, 1972, p. 240]

He places this early development as the result of tensions in the early mother–child matrix of interaction. For Loewald, instinctual drives are codetermined by the mother–child interactional environment. Accordingly, some objections to the death instinct are muted. He states,

> The intensity of destructive tendencies and of their narcissistic entrenchment in the negative therapeutic reaction would depend, predominantly, on early interactions which favour a distorted organization of both destructive and libidinal, destructive and creative, drives, and favour a lack of balanced coordination of them. [Loewald, 1972, p. 242]

Loewald's ideas find support in the writings of three other analysts, each from a different psychoanalytic culture. Pontalis (1981), in a paper regrettably only published in French, entitled "No, Twice No",[1] discusses the negative therapeutic reaction in a unique yet profound fashion. After reviewing some of the relevant literature, he considers the word "reaction" and expands on it. He suggests that the negative therapeutic reaction involves a particular form of intensely ambivalent object relation with the preoedipal maternal object that traps the individual forever in the grip of a deadly struggle of action and reaction. Thus, Pontalis writes of his patient Fabienne,

> Thinking of Fabienne, and others, I will not talk here of identification: the word which suggests a minimum of divergence, of play, between two subjects would be too weak. But of *possession*: possession by an internal foreign body which continuously and violently intrudes, and exercises its mastery from within, as if the mother was taking the place of the drive; whence, in return, a passionate effort to 'possess' it, this foreign body, to control it, equally without let up or respite, in projecting it to the outside. [Pontalis, 1981, p. 64][2]

The transference–countertransference is invaded in its turn by this endless struggle of opposing forces wherein the analyst's interventions are treated as violently intruding forces to be repelled at all costs.

Rosenfeld (1987) places an analysand's narcissistic object relations as central to an understanding of the negative therapeutic reaction and illustrates his ideas with two detailed case reports. Earlier, Rosenfeld (1971) had previously formulated the concept of destructive narcissism, linked to Freud's ideas of the death instinct and applicable to the negative therapeutic reaction. For him,

> destructive omnipotent parts of the self can be idealized but remain disguised or silent and split off so that their existence is obscured ... one is only aware of an apparent lack of

relationship to the outside world . . . modes of relating of this kind have a very powerful effect in preventing dependent object relations and keeping external objects permanently devalued, with serious consequences for psychoanalytic therapy. [Rosenfeld, 1987, p. 87]

A patient with predominantly narcissistic object relations who has experienced relief in some form as a result of the analyst's work in a session is thus particularly prone to developing a negative therapeutic reaction. The analyst's words are viewed as a threat by the omnipotent, narcissistic, and split-off aspects of the self, particularly if they have helped the patient to face the reality of his dependent needs. The danger is that the patient will become aware of how much he is in the clutches of his own omnipotence; anything that exposes this domination will be silently denigrated and destroyed.

More recently, in a paper devoted to a consideration of the death instinct, Kernberg (2009) also discusses the negative therapeutic reaction. He considers the negative therapeutic reaction as one of the phenomena that led Freud to develop the hypothesis of the death drive, rather than the idea of an aggressive drive. Kernberg describes three forms of the negative therapeutic reaction, of increasing severity, and of increasingly gloomy prognosis in terms of a successful outcome to psychoanalytic treatment. For him, the presence of unconscious guilt underpinning the reaction is the mildest form, followed by unconscious envy of the therapist, most prevalent in narcissistic patients. The severest form of negative therapeutic reaction is that appearing as highly motivated self-destructiveness. The self-destructiveness is linked, according to Kernberg, to an unconscious identification with a sadistic object whose mastery of the individual is such that they believe they can only be in a relationship with someone who will destroy them.

Before turning to current clinical material of my own, I will briefly discuss a clinical paper that illustrates a particular kind of NTR referred to by Freud (1923b) in a well-known footnote. He noted that in some patients their NTR is based upon what he referred to as "borrowed guilt". The borrowed guilt, leading to manifestations of this resistance, "is the product of an identification with some other person who was once the object of an erotic cathexis. A sense of guilt that has been adopted in this way is often the sole remaining trace of the abandoned love-relation and not at all easy to recognize as such" (Freud, 1923b, p. 50). If this former object cathexis can be "unmasked", then the therapeutic success can be "brilliant". Levy (1982) describes such an outcome in documenting in some detail the long, difficult, but ultimately successful analysis of a young depressed woman whose depressive, masochistic character was linked to an unconscious identification with a controlling and masochistic maternal object. When the unconscious, murderous rage against this maternal object surfaced, the young woman's negative therapeutic reaction came close to fatally disrupting her analytic gains.

I will now discuss some clinical material of my own, which exemplifies some of the features of the negative therapeutic reaction in a current psychoanalytic therapy.

Case vignette

I was referred H by his analyst, who was about to retire. At the initial interview H informed me that he had had two previous analyses but continued to be troubled by chronic anxiety and bouts of depression. These symptoms had worsened over the last four years. A large, imposing man of 65 years, H spoke articulately in a loud voice that was confident if not dominant in tone. I had an early impression of a considerable disjunction between his manner of speech and its content. He gave the overall impression of a man who had achieved much in his life, but his narrative was of someone who had managed to make his successes largely through the efforts of others. In his account of his working life he admitted that he was the director of his company, a family business begun by his late father. He had entered the business after he had dropped out of professional school in his first year due to increasing anxiety. Speaking of his work as director, he avowed that he owed his successes, which he reluctantly admitted, largely to his wife, who worked closely with him.

As time went on, I learnt more of his tendency to underplay his role in his personal and work achievements. His motto in life was "leave no fingerprints": in other words, he took great pains to avoid any claim that he had been a central agent or even instrumental in events that took place in his family or in his business life—especially if they in any way enhanced his personal prestige or could be counted a success by outside observers.

Over time, I learnt more about him that was in striking contrast to his frequent statements of inadequacy. He had been married for some 40 years; he had five children, all successful professionals; between them, they had given him ten grandchildren. . . . On careful questioning by me, H revealed himself to be a loving and devoted father and grandfather. This was in marked contrast to his own authoritarian and punitive father. His father believed in excessive physical punishment and seems to have singled out H in particular. He recalled many such beatings. In addition, his father did not hesitate to verbally abuse H. Comments such as "You're the cause of all the trouble around here" were common. This abuse continued into adult life. When H suggested a new approach in the business, his father shouted that "this is a house of cards, and you with your crazy ideas will knock it down!"

When he and his wife were not engaged in their work, which required frequent travel, they visited their various offspring and seemed to be accorded a warm welcome in each home. Of his business life there seemed little doubt that he had taken the marginal family business and turned it into a profitable enterprise. Contrary to his statement that his wife was responsible for this success, it emerged that he had only recruited her into the business in the last five years. It was also clear that this recruitment had been the latest in a number of successful business moves H had made through the years, after his father and older brother had died.

H had entered analysis soon after his failure at professional school. Although he had been able to complete life tasks with notable success, he continued to suffer from anxiety, which at times was debilitating, and occasional bouts of mild to moderate depression. His suffering was considerable and appeared to worsen as he aged and as his life unfolded successfully. His second analyst prescribed anxiolytics and antidepressants with some relief, but he was never without high levels of anxiety.

The events I describe unfolded over some 10 days. They illustrate just one example of his negative therapeutic reaction and his terror of success, at least as this might be represented intrapsychically. As it became apparent to me overtime, H could take appropriate action in his working, social, and personal life that assured successes in these spheres provided he did not represent these successes in his mental life. H's mood had been progressively worsening, and his wife insisted that she would take a weekend vacation in another city, whether or not he would accompany her. Reluctantly, he agreed. In spite of his habitual pessimism, he enjoyed the weekend. His anxiety was in abeyance, and his spirits lifted as he and his wife experienced the varied attractions of the city.

However, as their flight approached home, his anxiety returned and increased the next day.

H opened his Tuesday session with the statement that he had rarely felt as bad as he did at the moment. He described intense anxiety, dread of the future, and a disturbed night of sleep with early-morning awakening. Familiar ruminations had returned, including one that involved his younger sister, whom he and his deceased older brother had bought out of the family business after his father's death. He spent much time worrying that his sister, who had been left some of the real estate associated with the business in the deal, would claim that she deserved a greater share of the business linked to her real estate holdings. Despite reassuring consultations with his legal advisors and his own investigations, which suggested his concerns had little merit, he continued to evoke this financial spectre when he was anxious and depressed.

In the Tuesday session we dealt with a number of issues that we had identified as tending to lead to periods of anxiety and depression, particularly after some lifting of his symptoms. The theme of his guilt about his success in business, compared with his father, older brother, and his sister surfaced. We were also able to identify a possible dynamic underpinning his return of symptoms following the enjoyable sojourn with his wife in another city.

Relations between his father and his wife had never been close. His father suspected his wife of being after the family money, and his wife reciprocated these suspicions with a lively dislike of her own. H had admitted previously that he would never have asked his wife to join the business if his father had been alive. I had observed that when H talked of his father's abusive attitude towards himself, he rarely expressed anger. In fact, he had previously talked about his idealization of his father, which was in full force at least from his early latency until mid-adolescence. This idealization defended him against rage at his father and may well have been the conscious counterpart of his growing persecutory anxiety. Gradually, I had come to the conclusion that because of his intense ambivalence towards his father he had never mourned him, thus dealing neither with his love nor his hate for his father. In effect, his father lived on and was effectively in H's fantasy still running the business and, in effect his life.

The enjoyable trip out of town with wife, now an integral part of the business, would have been a direct affront to his father. In the session I brought this issue to H's attention and coupled it with further comments about how he had not mourned his father, a topic we had touched on previously. He seemed to accept this as linked to his depressed and anxious mood. He also told me for the first time that after his father died, his brother had put up a photo of his father in the office. When his brother died, H took the photo down: it rests under a stack of old files on a shelf in his office. He also described for the first time in this session an incident between him and his father on the morning after his wedding day. He and his wife had spent the wedding night at a local hotel. When they returned to their new apartment, his father had called and informed him that the hotel had called him to complain about a coverlet missing from the honeymoon suite. His father had then asked whether or not his wife had "inadvertently" taken the coverlet. Of note was his lack of reaction to this egregious act, which was not the first time his father had openly impugned his wife's motives.

H seemed to accept my tentative formulation of his relapse after the weekend. As the session wound down, he seemed more relaxed and stated that he felt somewhat better. It appeared as though our work had led to a diminution of his anxiety and to a lessening of his depressive affect. His next session was in two days, and I reflected hopefully on the possibility that we had made some progress.

My optimism was premature. He returned to his next session accompanied by his wife, who had insisted on coming to his session to talk to me. He gave the following account of events. For sometime after the session he had felt much better. However, by that evening his anxiety had increased and had continued unabated. His depressed mood had returned in force, now complemented by some abdominal pains. H presented a picture of silent suffering as his wife angrily detailed her concerns and her doubts that the therapy was helping. Of note was that once his wife had expressed her anger and concerns, she described her own assessment of her husband's dynamics. She confirmed his abusive childhood, especially at his father's hands, and also her husband's positive features, his business acumen and his successes as husband and father. In the joint session she pleaded with him to forget his past and relish his abilities.

H's paradoxical negative reaction to the apparently successful work of the preceding session brought the issue of his transference to the fore. For most of the therapy this had been positive, and he had expressed gratitude at times for the work we did together. Generally, I had become aware of an overly respectful attitude to me, with little manifest aggression or its derivatives in humour, for example. However, hints of negative feelings appeared from time to time. He became very concerned about his behaviour in my office. Once he expressed concern about some of my mail that lay on the entrance floor as he turned to go into the waiting room prior to a session. He might read the address of the sender and thus be accused by me of prying into my affairs. He ruminated over an incident in my washroom where he became convinced that he had "accidentally dripped" on the washroom carpet as he was urinating. This incident induced a recurrent fear that I might retaliate against him verbally or, worse, "kick me out of therapy".

Although there are many issues involved in H's psychodynamics, I will focus on a few to highlight his negative therapeutic reaction. First, his telling comment that he tried "to leave no fingerprints". This strongly suggested that he was guilty of some unspecified crime, or crimes, and was carefully concealing his tracks from the authorities and the police. The crime was patricide—in his unconscious fantasy linked to his rage against his persecutory and abusive father. Associated in his mind was the linkage between his father's oft-repeated comment about how he would bring down "the house of cards", the family business, and his father. H had previously told me that his father was a rather fearful businessman who distrusted innovation and change. In feeling much better after the vacation trip and then subsequently after the session, he had unconsciously reinforced his sense of guilt, not just about father, but also potentially about his hidden rage in the transference. The fact that he brought his wife to the session strongly suggests, among other issues, a further attempt to emphasize his weakness and inadequacy in the face of the dangerous analyst–father.

Conclusion and discussion

The negative therapeutic reaction remains a psychoanalytic concept in good standing, provided that it is clearly defined. Freud's definition has been reconfirmed and elaborated over time. It has also been extended to encompass ideas that overextend the original definition. The descriptive essence of the concept is as follows. During an analytic session the analyst's interpretive work either deepens understanding of the patient's issues or offers encouragement to the patient. Paradoxically, the patient who may initially feel relieved returns to analysis with a worsening of his condition—namely, an increase in symptoms, various negative transference manifestations, or a history of acting out. The concept should not be extended to include any tenacious resistance to an analytic process or to encompass a character-based negativism, which may manifest as a general opposition to the treatment.

The relationship between the clinical concept of the negative therapeutic reaction, Freud's concept of negation (Freud, 1925h), "the work of the negative" (Green, 1993), and the intrapsychic forces of destruction exemplified by Freud's concept of the death instinct is complex and deserves careful theoretical and clinical investigation beyond the present chapter. With respect to the death instinct, the negative therapeutic reaction that Freud encountered clinically was one of the phenomena that lead him to introduce the concept of a destructive drive. Of note here is that Freud's definitive description of the negative therapeutic reaction appeared in *The Ego and the Id* (1923b) with his reformulation of the structural theory. As such, it was closely linked to the appearance of the dual instinct theory in *Beyond the Pleasure Principle* (1920g), his further investigations of masochism in "The Economic Problem of Masochism" (1924c), and the appearance of his paper on negation in 1925. For Freud, negation as a concept is a defence against what is repressed, as in my patient's statement early in our work together that "I have nothing to do with the business, my wife runs it". Freud also underlines negation's dual role as an important element in freeing thinking from repression: he states, "With the help of the symbol of negation, thinking frees itself from the restrictions of repression and enriches itself with material that is indispensable for its proper functioning" (Freud, 1925h, p. 236).

Negation is both a defence against the repressed and a simultaneous acknowledgement of it at the same time. Freud elaborates this idea as follows:

> the intellectual function is separated from the affective process. With the help of negation only one consequence of the process of repression is undone—the fact, namely, of the ideational content of what is repressed not reaching consciousness. The outcome of this is a kind of intellectual acceptance of the repressed, while at the same time what is essential to the repression persists. [Freud, 1925h, p. 236]

Parsons (1999) points out that in the psychoanalytic situation the critical issue is whether negation is being used only defensively or whether it is an agent for the establishment of psychic reality and its engagement with the individual's external world. If used mainly for defensive purposes—that is,

> to establish psychic reality as a defensive structure, efforts to reduce it will indeed be treated as attempts at conquest and resisted as such. The difference lies in whether negation is a fixed state to be held on to, or a mobile and flexible activity, a provisional suspension of ordinary reality to be moved on from when it has served its purpose. [Parsons, 1999, p. 71]

The negative therapeutic reaction can then be understood as a localized clinical example of psychic structure employed as a massive defence against engagement with the analytic situation's potential for enabling structural change. The negation of the analyst's interpretive efforts prevents a more flexible and creative interchange between psychic reality and the world.

Green, in a series of publications (1993, 1998, 2005), has elaborated Freud's concept of negation with his extensive investigation of the "work of the negative" in psychoanalytic theory and clinical experience. This "work" involves some measure of disinvestment of objects, rejection of perception, and ego depletion. Green states:

> I have proposed gathering together all these related mechanisms: repression, splitting or disavowal, foreclosure or rejection and negation, in the concept of the 'work of the negative'. This gathering is justified by the fact that all of these mechanisms are elaborations of the prototype of repression. All of them imply a judgement of acceptance or refusal: a question whose answer has to be given in terms of yes and no. [Green, 1998, p. 660]

He adds a number of his own concepts to this list, including negative hallucination, negative narcissism, and the ego's sense of self-disappearance. Of significance in the negative therapeutic reaction is his concept of negative hallucination. Characteristically, this phenomenon is behind a patient's sudden emptiness of thought—as typically stated: "My mind's just gone blank". Green states that this can occur in a wide variety of psychic constellations to varying degrees of severity, from the normal to the psychotic. He links negative hallucinatory phenomena to a dual action: on the external side an extremely distressing perception leads to a negative hallucination so undesirable as to lead to denying the existence of the perceived objects; on the internal side an unconscious representation of a wish (abolished) presses towards consciousness but is defended against at the preconscious–conscious barrier, and the space occupied by the denied perception is left vacant (Green, 2005).

My patient affords a clinical example of a negative hallucinatory process.

We were discussing his anxieties about travelling, which he did frequently both for his business and for pleasure. I suggested that his oft-quoted explanation—the sense of being isolated and helpless far from his home—might hide the opposite: that it was in fact his competence and ability to cope well with foreign travel that threatened his role of the inadequate, loser son of an abusive father.

In the next session he stated that he had felt at ease while on a business trip that involved a series of flights to another part of the country. He then recalled accurately only a phrase of an interpretation of mine, namely, "It is what you do when away . . .". My patient then reworked my comment into its negative form by recalling that

I had agreed during the previous session that it was his helplessness and inadequacy that was at issue. When I reminded him of what I had actually said, he had no recall of my words, even when I gave him details of what I had actually said. This differs from repression, whereby the patient, once reminded, will usually recall the analyst's comments. H had blanked out my words and their meaning: the threatening perception was abolished.

While there is some agreement concerning the definition of the negative therapeutic reaction, there is less clarity or certainty when it comes to explanations of this clinical phenomenon. It appears that there are a number of possible causes. Certainly, unconscious guilt and the need to suffer should always be considered. However, the motivations behind the analyst's inference of unconscious guilt can vary from preoedipal fantasies of harming the primary object to oedipal fantasies of killing the father, as was assuredly one of the conflicts that lay behind my patient's manifestations of the negative therapeutic reaction. Underlying envy of the analyst, often coupled with defences against dependency, and a subsequent wish to devalue or destroy his interventions, is another element in the manifestations of the negative therapeutic reaction.

The place of identification in explanations of the concept is less straightforward. One of most common suggestions is that of identification involving an intensely ambivalent relationship with a masochistic parent—usually a maternal object. My own sense, both from a survey of the literature and from my own clinical experience, is that, at least in severe cases of negative therapeutic reactions, the individual's experience is one of being possessed, invaded, or mastered by the object. This fatal struggle, in turn, enters the analytic arena and can subvert the transference–countertransference relationship and reduce it to a never-ending struggle between the participants. One such fantasy that I have encountered clinically that relates to this possession by the object is one in which the patient believes that there is only so much good available in the world. If the patient feels better, is relieved, or is hopeful, it means that this has been taken from someone else, at the other's expense. If this fantasy predominates, progress in the analysis may become impossible.

Freud's original conceptualization of the role of the death instinct remains controversial as a factor in the negative therapeutic reaction. However, one can imagine a situation in which the early interaction between self and object is so marked by ambivalence that both intense self-destructive impulses and wishes to destroy the object are let loose. This could certainly create unmovable resistances to a successful analysis as Freud and others have predicted. Clinically, this would be a manifestation of the death instinct. Clearly, not all instances of the negative therapeutic reaction represent impasse and a failed analysis. We do not fully understand why some patients can change and others cannot. It would be helpful if we could study in detail specific instances of analytic interventions with particular patients that led to negative therapeutic reactions.

Notes

1. In French, "Non, deux fois non".
2. My translation.

4

The work of the negative and hallucinatory activity (negative hallucination)

André Green

Any proposal to introduce yet another notion into psychoanalytic vocabulary is usually met with reserve. It is feared that such an addition would simply further encumber a theoretical machinery which one would prefer to lighten if anything. This is especially true when the notion proposed can neither claim to be a novelty nor to meet a lack, but seems rather to emerge from the depths of what one thought had been definitively forgotten—a sanction for its unjustified claim of usefulness.

The notion of negative hallucination which I shall examine in this chapter can be traced back to the heyday of hypnotism, before the birth of psychoanalysis even. Nowadays, perhaps, psychoanalysts are less familiar with it than the public who have come across it in books or films, even though the term itself may not be familiar to them. Its posterity was ensured by Maupassant's *Le Horla* written in 1887, a work whose literary filiation goes back to Hoffmann, Gogol, and Dostoevsky. We also need to take into account the part played in its conception by the demonstrations of Charcot and Bernheim, great masters in hypnotism, which the author witnessed, as did Freud. Barely three years later, in 1890, Freud mentioned negative hallucination for the first time in an article entitled "Psychical (or Mental) Treatment" (1890a). The hypnotist's order was sufficient to suppress the perception of an object which "tried to impose itself" on the hypnotized patient's senses. This was just the first of quite a long series of examples taken from hysterics as well as normal people. Occasionally, Freud cites one of his own experiences, the phenomenon appearing independently of any context of suggestion and in a thoroughly spontaneous manner. What may be surprising is the link established unhesitatingly between hallucination and a phenomenon of negation—since what is involved is the denial of an object's existence. From the first, it was accepted that it was not enough to compare the observation with normal perception as being a simple lack, but that it should be compared with hallucination as its counterpart. In positive hallucination ("perception without an object") there is something in excess [*l'en plus*] which corresponds to what is lacking [*l'en moins*] in negative hallucination ("non-perception of an object"). One must also note in the initial descriptions the common reference to a force which weighs upon the hypnotic subject from without, having the power to make him see what is not there or coercing him into remaining insensible—in the etymological sense of the term—to what is there. Yet, as we have already seen, the phenomenon can appear without the intervention of this external force. This extraneous will may also be replaced by an *internal* force which the subject does not recognize as being part of himself. Nor does he realize that it acts against his own will or without his knowing it, but the motive is always the same: to act against what he seems to want consciously. Breuer, who was less scrupulous than Freud with regard to the terms he used, speaks in this connection of a "negative attitude" (Breuer, in Freud, 1895d, p. 26).[1] When the force acts from inside the subject there are clues which enable one to infer its existence indirectly—for example, hysterical conversion, which shows that it derives from outside the psyche; obsessive representation, whose content does not appear to account for its obsidian tenacity, leading us to look for the displacement which it was subject to; and, finally, hallucination which designates quite clearly the projection of its offshoots recognized in Freud's earliest writings. The discovery of this internal force soon makes it clear what it is that resists its manifestation—that is, repression, which now becomes the focus of attention. These first investigations relied on an active investigative method, whether hypnotic or not.

One can easily imagine how the invention of psychoanalysis would greatly diminish interest in negative hallucination by laying emphasis on the organization of the internal world. However, the paradigmatic value of the symptom remains. And even if it has not given rise to many new developments, we are reminded of it through direct and indirect signs at key moments during the re-examination of central concepts of analytic theory. We will have ample cause to come back to this later.

Thus negative hallucination is a psychic mechanism which relates to two categories: hallucinatory activity and the negative. The former will lead us to study its relations with perception and unconscious representation, and the latter calls for a close analysis of its relation to other more familiar defences (repression, splitting, negation, etc.).

Hallucination: a defence neurosis or psychosis?

However frequent the allusions to the strange phenomenon of negative hallucination in Freud's writings were (see, in this connection, Couvreur, 1992; Duparc, 1992), particularly at the beginning, though less so thereafter, it is clear that the institution of the psychoanalytic setting and the selection of those for whom the method was suitable would favour other notions which needed to be given prior consideration—that is, representation rather than perception, psychic reality rather than external reality, the reaction to absence rather than presence, the reference to memory rather than sensibility to the present, the understanding of fantasy rather than the relation to the observable world. Whereas in his early clinical contributions Freud never tired of comparing hysteria and obsessional neurosis to paranoia and to hallucinatory confusion (Meynert's amentia), little by little, these two latter conditions ceased to be a part of this comparative approach (see in this regard Freud, 1896b, 1950a [1887–1902]. However, they both present hallucinations, either in the clinical picture of chronic delusion in paranoia, or during the oneirism caused by hallucinatory confusion. One would be wrong in thinking, however, that hallucination is a synonym for psychosis—acute or chronic. Quite the opposite. During the period when Freud was almost exclusively interested in hysteria, he included the hallucinations of hysterics among the symptoms he examined. The fact is that at this stage in his thinking all these conditions which I have just mentioned were seen as belonging to the "psycho-neuroses of defence". It was at this point (Freud, 1896b) that the mental process of "defence" or of "repression" entered the picture, one year *after* the publication of the "Project".

A reading of "Further Remarks on the Neuro-Psychoses of Defence" (1896b) is of interest on two accounts. On the one hand, Freud analyses the various symptoms (hysteric, obsessional, paranoiac—hallucination playing, of course, a major role in the last of these) in relation to each other, comparing the psychic mechanisms specific to each category. But, on the other hand, however interesting these psychic constructions may be, he relativizes their distinctive features by tracing them back to the common mechanism which accounts for them: repression and its corollary, the return of the repressed. Hallucinatory activity loses importance in two respects. First, the privilege—which it has sometimes enjoyed in semiology—of being a sign by means of which psychosis can be identified is erased by being included within a neurotic framework. Second, the analysis of its mechanism subordinates it to being simply one of the vicissitudes of the return of the repressed. From then on the problem lies elsewhere. Rather than wearing oneself out searching for the meaning and function of hallucination by means of an active technique of investigation, the priority now is how to gain access to the repressed. Instead of searching for it actively, it turns out to be better to arrange things in such a way that it reveals itself spontaneously: this is the invention of analysis. But that implies sacrificing hallucination, which does not lend itself so easily to the analytic game as the other two neuroses. Negative hallucination and positive hallucination make way for more manageable subjects of study. To put it another way, negativizing the therapeutic situation by the adopting of criteria such as free association, floating attention, and benevolent neutrality is less favourable to the observation of negative symptoms which appear under normal conditions of observation or during hypnosis.

As analytic treatment became increasingly codified, the clinical features of hallucination were no longer taken into account. Does this mean that hallucinatory activity ceased to have a place in Freud's thinking? As we shall soon see, nothing could be further from the truth. On the one hand, we cannot help thinking that he needed little persuasion to turn away from the psychoses, which were considered unsuitable for psychoanalysis; we know that he had no great inclination for tackling them. On the other hand, Freud had the ambition of being much more than a specialist in neuroses; his theories were intended to cover the whole field of psychopathology. And much more than that even, since their range of application extends beyond clinical practice. It might as well be said that he could not neglect the study of psychosis even though its fixations and regressions might have prevented its analysis. Under these circumstances the publication of Schreber's *Memoirs* was a godsend: the richness of the patient's introspection, the quality of the document which he puts at the disposition of his doctors and the precision and insight which he demonstrates, surpass by far the most in-depth psychiatric observations. The possibility we have of studying it carefully compensates largely, under these circumstances, for the lack of immediate data which only an analysis can gather. This is then an unhoped-for opportunity to renew our understanding of psychosis which will make it possible to test the conceptions developed by psychoanalysis over the last dozen years or so.

While we can only admire the way Freud elucidates and interprets the pathology of the *Senatspräsident*, there is also good reason to be surprised in certain respects. Dr Weber's diagnosis, which Freud (1911c [1910]) reports without further discussion, is "hallucinatory insanity" (p. 24). Now Freud's brilliant analysis says almost nothing of Schreber's hallucinations. What I mean is that Freud approaches the case from the angle of delusion and the mechanism of paranoia but shows only very limited interest in hallucination. Admittedly, from time immemorial, the analysis of hallucinatory delusions has laid emphasis alternatively either on the aspect of delusion or on that of hallucination in order to maintain that one was responsible for the genesis of the other. Did Freud simply join ranks with those who opted to give pride of place to delusion? Can the priority which was given to the study of repression, the libido, the ego, and their relations only be explained by the place accorded to delusion? Even if this is so, it scarcely exempts us from examining more closely the hallucinatory phenomenon which remains the sign of a very distinctive mental functioning. Moreover, Freud does not shirk this completely: he defines hallucination briefly with a formulation of great importance when he describes the return, by an external path, that of perception, of what was *abolished* on the inside—and not just suppressed or repressed. This is no doubt the essential point, but stopping there means being content to note the fact in passing, giving the impression that we do not want to dwell on the implications of what we have put forward. Freud (1911c [1910], p. 69) practically acknowledges this himself, deferring further discussion until later.[2] Once again, Freud's approach has two aspects to it. On the one hand, as we have seen, the elucidation of hallucinations in psychosis, qualified nonetheless as hallucinatory, disappears with the analysis of repression—as in neurosis. But on the other, with hindsight and not immediately, Freud pinpoints a difference. He revises his position: what is involved is not suppression affecting the inside (that is, an action connected with repression) but of *abolition*. Is it repression which is involved? Freud does not say and asks us to wait until he is ready to communicate his thoughts on projection, which, however, he never does. We know we are indebted to Lacan for his contribution of foreclosure, but I am not certain that his commentaries exhaust the question either. What is important is to explain how hallucination is related to an *abolition*, considered by Lacan to be a flaw in symbolization. The Phallus and the foreclosure of the Name of the Father are supposed to satisfy our curiosity and fulfil our expectations. Really?

The enigma of Freud's declining interest in the symptom of "hallucination" can be explained by the connection established between this pathological phenomenon and dreams whose normality cannot be contested. We are led to look for their common denominator by constructing a model which accounts for each of them and is worthy of consideration in its own right for its general validity which goes far beyond any theoretical forms resulting from it.

An outline for a model—drifting towards dreams

While Freud's interest in the symptomatology of hallucination waned, he wanted to get to the core of hallucinatory activity. Even before the discovery of repression, which did not play the slightest part in his first theoretical construction, he prepared the ground for his future model in the "Project" of 1895. The advantage of this work—even if Freud disowned it—is that it gives us a very precise idea of the notion he had of the basic elements of psychic life and the essential principles of their functioning. Accordingly, after the definition of neurones and quantities in motion, that is, minimal "atomic" elements—in the etymological sense of the word—and the relations uniting them, comes the first description of the two major experiences of "psychology": satisfaction and pain. The experience of satisfaction brings out the analogy between perception and hallucination (Freud, 1950 [1895], p. 319). The reactivation, under the pressure of states of tension and wishing, *of mnemonic memories of the wished-for object and of the reflex movement* produces a hallucination, he writes. There is no difficulty in recognizing what was later to become hallucinatory wish-fulfilment although it is not named as such at this stage. On the contrary, the experience of pain aims at avoiding the return to the psyche of the memory of painful experiences. The coupling of the two "experiences" will form the basis of the future pleasure–unpleasure principle. Already in this first attempt to organize his theories into a whole, Freud establishes a close connection between hallucination and primary process.[3] In spite of modern interpretations which have attempted to separate the temporal and structural meanings of the term primary, for Freud, the term undoubtedly covers both aspects. Thus primary denotes what is assumed to exist at the beginning of psychic life in the short-circuit "reflex", desired object–presented object as (if it was) real, by constructing theoretically what constitutes its foundations to which the psyche may be obliged to return, flouting many earlier acquisitions when, for example, reality becomes too unbearable because of the deficiencies which have to be endured.

We can therefore understand the paradoxical position in which Freud found himself: as a clinician he appears to give less and less importance to hallucinations; as a theoretician, on the contrary, he gives it a place which it had never been given before. Once the model was "outlined" it gave rise to all sorts of developments and constructions which generation upon generation of psychoanalysts would try and amend in order to improve it.

Alongside these neurobiological fictions, however, Freud's essay contains two parts which are still of great interest today: the analysis of a hysterical symptom (the proton pseudos) and an initial exposition of his ideas on dreams in which this phenomenon is linked with hallucination ("we shut our eyes and hallucinate"), announcing what is to follow, that is, the book on dreams and the case of Dora, subtitled *Dreams and Hysteria*. There was another reason which led Freud to turn his attention to dreams. He has been misled by clinical experience. He had believed in the trauma of seduction. There was a great danger of giving too much credit to what patients say. For, in spite of claims to the contrary, it was not a question of fantasy having replaced seduction. Finding the solution so easily would be too much to hope for. It was much more troublesome to have to admit that the criteria available were insufficient to determine when seduction had occurred and when it had not. By considering the problem in terms of the subject's psychic productions alone, the field of fantasy was circumscribed more adequately. With the phenomenon of dreaming this anticipated "reality-testing" was no longer an issue. Furthermore, in response to the drawback of the subject's eventual fantasizing (conscious? unconscious?), Freud does not make use of the illusory measure of a verification which would rely on the power of consciousness but, on the contrary, turns towards the analysis of a mechanism of fantasy freed from the suspicion of being intentional in origin. The truth of a dream would dispel any doubts as to the narrator's intentionality. Clinical considerations were to be dealt with later. It was an exemplary approach bearing witness to a deep familiarity with the powers of the negative.

This "Project" was to lead to the theoretical development set out in *The Interpretation of Dreams* (1900a). It might be helpful here to recapitulate on a number of well-known findings with the purpose of shedding new light on them. Instead of proceeding in a progressive way, we shall adopt another approach. Let us consider that the conclusions that Freud drew from *The Interpretation of Dreams* were not so much discoveries made in the course of an investigation, whose eventual outcome was unknown, as demonstrations of hypotheses drawn from his earlier trials and errors. They may be summarized as follows:

1. Nothing can be learnt directly from clinical experience. Comparative semiology itself can say nothing about the *raison d'être* and meaning of symptoms. Only recourse to psychic mechanisms seen from a dynamic and comparative standpoint can throw light on the diversity, the structure and function of symptoms which are subject to more general key principles.
2. The distinction between normal and pathological is based on different modes of functioning originating a group of common factors. In other words, normal and neurotic people are inhabited by the same desires and the same fears, but these have got nothing to do with what they admit to each other spontaneously in the course of ordinary exchanges. Pathology is only mysterious and often incomprehensible because it arises from an intensification (involuntary) of the procedures which habitually contribute to the concealment of these preoccupations, an intensification which is proportionate to the increasing fear (often justified) that their activation makes them visible in spite of precautions taken to prevent this. One cannot simply say that what is pathological is mysterious and enigmatic. It would be better to admit that what is mysterious and enigmatic in a normal person is liable to become the source of pathology in a neurotic. This mysterious, enigmatic characteristic—which Laplanche focused on—no doubt comes from the complexity of psychic structure, but before asserting this in too transcendental a manner, we need to find out what men "openly" hide, if I may put it like this, and draw all the necessary conclusions concerning the way this constrains them to function psychically in relation to what they conceal from themselves, without being aware of it. This is all the more true in that Freud was led by experience to make the following observation: although men have secrets, they are incapable of keeping them. Furthermore, it is not so much others whom they betray as themselves. The key to this, then, is to be found in the disclosure of what exists within the normal person, without his being aware of it, but which, unlike the neurotic, he has managed to render

unintelligible. In other words, the pathology corresponds to the visible struggle between the return of the repressed and repression, whereas this same struggle is indiscernible in the normal person because of successful repression. But the fact that there is no apparent struggle should not deflect our attention from what is some distance from it and makes its return at a later time. So, if the common factor is repression, this must be related to what it seeks to repress.

3. The success of repression in the normal person is very relative. Not only are there signs of misfunctioning, but there is a space and time in which the lessening of censorships, even if it does not lift repression, attenuates the act of repression enough for "steam to be let off" and to relieve the internal tension created by it. Dreams are an attempt to prevent the untimely return of the repressed and, more often than not, they enable the normal person to avoid the outcome of the conflict. However, unlike in cases of misfunctioning, it is not possible with dreams to cancel immediately what they have betrayed, by correcting them. They succeed in forming *another* reality. So man has the power to create a second world within the confines of sleep in which he can fulfil desires, making himself believe in the reality of this other world where this fulfilment occurs. This is what hallucinatory wish-fulfilment achieves. The "realization" signifies just as much the achievement of satisfaction as the creation of a reality in which such a satisfaction becomes possible. Finally, hallucination is the mode of functioning which manages to create this other world in which desire, by not succumbing to repression, exists in a form, thanks to which the wish, which is disguised so that it cannot be identified, can take its place in a universe of "realization", indiscernible from reality. Nevertheless, the lowering of censorship in dreams is far from being equivalent to a suppression of repression. It is only through dream work that wish-fulfilment is achieved. It is also important to emphasize that even at the heart of this other reality of dreams, the dreamer is not conscious that the wish has been fulfilled. This can only be inferred from dream analysis. In spite of these special conditions, what takes place—the manifest content—is unavoidably subject to compromise. The hallucinatory fulfilment is complemented by the dream work which widens the gap between the

latent content—which remains unsuspected—and the manifest content which the dreamer beholds in its hallucinated form. But the price to be paid for dreams creating a second reality is the sense of incoherence and absurdity experienced by the dreamer. There are thus two effects of the negative which need to be explored successively in dream work and in secondary elaboration.

4. What is instructive then is not so much the dream itself but what can be inferred from the study of its functioning which results in hallucinatory wish-fulfilment. This is useful as a model. The observation we made earlier about the hallucinatory nature of the primary process can therefore be sustained. It does not follow from this that all wish-fulfilment is accomplished by means of hallucination, just as the primary process does not necessarily take on a hallucinatory form. It is sufficient to admit that the wish can take on these extreme forms in certain cases, convincing us thereby of the power it can occasionally deploy. The advantage of the full model is that it shows us how far we can go. We must still bear in mind, however, that there is a risk involved in functioning beyond the permitted limits of the biological activity of sleep by exceeding the latter's restricted spatio-temporal conditions. On the other hand, confining wish-fulfilment and then primary process to their hallucinatory mode is too restrictive. The example of unconscious fantasy shows that the primary process may fall short of its hallucinatory fulfilment and its conscious form in order to be "dreamed", but it is not, however, a dream. This being so, wish-fulfilment and primary process will be able to monopolize the psychic characteristics of dream functioning, *without however going as far as hallucinatory functioning*, but knowing that it is a possibility. Unconscious representations will take over from hallucinations. Sometimes both can merge, as in dreams. Usually they can be distinguished, as in waking life, where one can designate by a process of deduction an unconscious representation for which, by definition, there is no evidence in consciousness. What conclusions can be drawn then about the relations between unconscious representation and hallucination? Quite simply: the unconscious representation can never be *perceived* either from the inside or from the outside. It can acquire a form which can be represented after

it has first been elaborated by the subject himself or by another person who elaborates the subject's thought for him. But in this case it will only be a conscious representation which is supposed to have some similarity with the unconscious representation which cannot be known. The preconscious representation is perceived from the inside, and only in this way. Hallucination is a representation, essentially unconscious, which is transformed into perception by being transposed outwards, due to the impossibility of its acquiring an acceptable form for the subject even just within himself. It can only be perceived from the outside (unlike the preconscious representation) by passing itself off, if need be, as a perception, that is, as originating from the outside. When we speak of an internal perception, we are not referring to a representation or a psychic event which can be represented or thought about, in other words which can be apprehended as an object [*objet*] of the psyche, but rather which is sensed in the way sensations coming from the outside are, sometimes carrying very little significance. On the other hand, we are bound to conclude that wish-fulfilment and primary process tend towards hallucinatory activity, so much so that the problem arises *a contrario*: how is the spontaneous tendency towards hallucinatory activity to be restrained? Freud was to wrestle with this problem for more than twenty years.[4]

The return of the negative hallucination

In "A Metapsychological Supplement to the Theory of Dreams" (1917d [1915]), a major revision of his papers on metapsychology (1915c, 1915d, 1915e), Freud comes back to the comparison between dreams and hallucination understood in the light of the first topography and with the help of the notion of investment. Three states are seen as being very similar: dreaming, acute hallucinatory confusion, and the hallucinatory phase of schizophrenia (which replaces here what was formerly known as paranoia). The first two can be included under the general title of "wishful hallucinatory psychosis" (Freud, 1917d [1915], p. 230). The third can be accounted for by the return of investments towards objects. Freud then comments that it is not enough to bring unconscious wishes into consciousness for them to be taken as realities. Belief in reality seems to be bound up with perception through the senses or regression to hallucination. But how does hallucination come about? Regression would be an unsatisfactory answer since we can let very clear visual mnemic-images invade consciousness without taking them for real perceptions. In other words, twenty years later, the hallucinations of hysterics were no longer necessarily considered to be hallucinatory. Reliving (regressive) is not hallucination.

What is at stake in this discussion is the relationship to reality. This task falls to perception but, as (wishful) hallucination is so similar to it that it is difficult to tell them apart, it may be assumed that the psyche has equipped itself with a supplementary contrivance: reality-testing. Under normal conditions, perception and wishful hallucination can be differentiated —that is, the subject does not take his wishful hallucinations for realities any more than he takes the shadow of the object for the object, thanks to the contrivance in question. Nonetheless, amentia and dreams can succeed in putting it out of action.

The following solution may be given: the system *Cs.*, otherwise called *P.* (perception), can be invested from within and not, as is normally the case, from without alone. It is in this sense that regression can lead to hallucination. What is involved then is not only vividness or regressive reliving—that is, the aesthesic intensity of the representation— but also the possibility it has of occupying the terrain of consciousness and seeing to it that there is no longer any distinction between internal and external reality. Or, to be more exact, that internal reality succeeds in passing for external reality. The reality principle, postulated for some time and recently theorized in the "Formulations on the Two Principles of Mental Functioning" (1911b), arms itself with a test before being subjected to a "judgement" (of existence). It is now that Freud (1917d [1915]) adds the note which was the starting-point for my elaboration: "I may add by way of supplement that any attempt to explain hallucination would have to start out from *negative* rather than positive hallucination" (p. 232).[5]

With this single notation, Freud gives us a glimpse of an entire psychic constellation at the origin of hallucinatory production. The latter is thought to result from a dual action originating from an interface between:

» its external face: an undesirable, insupportable or intolerable perception leads to a negative hallucination expressing the wish to reject it to the point of denying the existence of the perceived objects;

» its internal face: an unconscious representation of a wish (abolished) which seeks to enter consciousness but which finds itself prevented from doing so by the barrier of the system Cs. (P.). The latter gives way to the pressure put on it and the space occupied by the denied perception is now vacant.

The conjunction of these two aspects gives us reason to suppose that a potentializing of effects may be involved, that is to say, the unbearable perception is "irreconcilable" (to use an old expression of Freud's) with the unconscious representation and, rather than the latter disappearing, it is the perception which is invalidated. The space which has been liberated by the negative hallucination is occupied, through projection, by the unconscious representation in a form which cannot easily be defined. But we could imagine that it takes on the attributes of perception, not in a way which would lead to their being confused, but through the form which denial takes in this case which "whitens" whatever presents itself to the mind, suggesting the intervention of a mechanism which Freud qualifies as "pulling away" from what is perceived. Between external reality which presses against internal reality, and internal reality which refuses to give way, the psychic apparatus has decided in favour of the latter, to the point of giving it the credence accorded to perceptions, as if the latter had done away with censorships. Thus negative hallucination is the process by which the ego can break off or interrupt its relations to reality. It can therefore justifiably be considered as the major process which governs relations between reality and the ego and which can, in extreme cases, extend to the durable process of repressing reality which Freud describes in psychosis. This is carried out thanks to a withdrawal of investment, or in more extreme circumstances by a disinvestment.[6] With respect to this, the voluntary renunciation occurring in dreams can be distinguished from the extensive and obligatory "repression"[7] found in amentia.

Perception and denial–splitting

Freud was to come back to this question at a later date. With the benefit of the hindsight needed for presenting an overview of his ideas and trying to focus on the essential points on the pretext—a fortunate one for us—that he was giving a talk (imaginary) to an audience which was keen to learn of the recent acquisitions of psychoanalysis, Freud (1933a) wrote:

> This system (*Pcpt.–Cs.*) is turned towards the external world, it is the medium for the perceptions arising thence, and during its functioning the phenomenon of consciousness arises in it. It is the sense-organ of the entire apparatus; moreover it is receptive not only to excitations from outside but also to those arising from the interior of the mind. We need scarcely look for a justification of the view that the ego is that portion of the id which was modified by the proximity and influence of the external world, which is adapted for the reception of stimuli, comparable to the cortical layer by which a small piece of living substance is surrounded. In accomplishing this function [representing the external world "to the id"], the ego must observe the external world, must lay down an accurate picture of it in the memory-traces of its perceptions, and by its exercise of the function of "reality-testing" must put aside whatever in this picture of the external world is an addition derived from internal sources of excitation. [Freud, 1933a, p. 75]

He added that thought activity is interposed between a need and an action. Two functions are emphasized here:

» the task of reproducing an accurate picture of the external world with particular insistence on the distinction between the internal or external source of excitations and information;
» the setting up of a limit which functions as an interface adapted both for the reception of stimuli and as a protective shield against them.

It is not difficult to see that these two functions are bound to contradict each other.

Freud's clarification of the relations between hallucination and perception should not lead us to believe that they are the only cases where the question of the relations of reality perception arises. There is a new allusion to it in the short article on "The Loss of Reality in Neurosis and Psychosis" (1924e). The importance of hallucinatory activity corresponds to the need to create a new reality by procuring a constant influx of new perceptions. Alongside this hallucinatory excess, of which psychosis is an example, we should also consider the case where negative hallucination (of which positive hallucination is the corollary) does not occur, although there is indeed a misfunctioning of perception. This is the case with fetishism. Here too the perception is intolerable: the boy refused "to take cognizance of the fact of his having perceived that a woman does not have a penis" (Freud, 1927e, p. 153). What is happening exactly? Freud raises the question: is this scotomization? This would, however, suggest that the perception had been completely erased. He adds: "In the situation we are considering, on the contrary, we see that the perception has persisted, and that a very energetic action has been undertaken to maintain the disavowal" (p. 154). He proposes instead the mechanism of *Verleugnung* or—following Jean Laplanche's translation—disavowal. In other words, in negative hallucination disavowal involves doing away with perception and in *Verleugnung* it involves denial: the subject cannot believe his eyes, but it is precisely because he can see and not because he is blind.

All these situations suggest that it is necessary, where perception is concerned, to separate its object from the judgement which it makes of what it perceives. From now on the idea of a "neutral" perception is seriously challenged. And the difference between perception and wishful representation is not so clear as one might think. However, it is precisely the preservation of perception which interests us as well as the introduction of a split mode of judgement in which the correlate of perception is the creation of a double language which both recognizes and denies castration simultaneously. Furthermore, what results is a clinging to the fetish as a substitute for the penis which perception showed to be lacking. The article "Fetishism" (1927e) not only sheds light on perversions, it is also a remarkable analysis of certain thought processes which are no less instructive than those which can be inferred from the couple representation–hallucination.

Internal perceptions—body and thought

We are naturally inclined to associate perception with the ego's relation to the external world. This restriction of the perceptive field is in fact a convenient oversimplification. In Chapter 2 of *The Ego and the Id*, which is also the title of the work as a whole, Freud sets himself the task of redefining the different ways in which something becomes conscious, for this is our only means of knowing. With this purpose in mind, he divides up perceptions according to their origin. He contrasts those which come from without through the senses with those which come from within: sensations and feelings. To them he adds thought-processes which will become perceptions through the interposition of word-representations.

Two kinds of internal perceptions can thus be contrasted: those arising from the body and those connected with thought. As far as the first are concerned, Freud reneges, in order to state the opposite, on the opinion he had expressed in the "Papers on Metapsychology" with respect to the non-existence of feelings, that is, of unconscious affects. Feelings therefore can indeed be repressed (and not just suppressed).

But that is not all. Classical psychiatry taught us long ago of the existence of Cotard's "delusion of negations" which is observed much less frequently now because the evolution of the affection, during which it appeared, has been stopped, thereby preventing its manifestation. In the course of Cotard's syndrome, after a melancholic phase, the patient often presents a far-reaching negativist attitude. The whole world is dead, the subject no longer has any parents, and so forth. But the most curious thing is the negation of organs: the patient claims he has no organs any more inside his body. This generates as an indirect consequence a delusional megalomania: the absence of organs leads to the idea of immortality, and at the same time the body, losing its limits, feels it is expanding so that it comes to occupy the whole universe (Ey, 1950). Thus the sense of one's own body, on which the most immediate consciousness of one's existence is based, can be disavowed, which destroys the perception of it.

Although nowadays these strange clinical pictures are less frequently observed, other much more discrete forms can be seen to stem from comparable problems. Thus alexithymia, as described by Sifneos, does not only designate an absence of words to name affects but also, in the sense in which I understand it, the inability to experience affective states, that is to say, to become conscious of them. McDougall (1986) has gone more deeply into the analysis of patients presenting manifestations of this kind, postulating that unconscious affect is cut off from the system of word-representations.

In other words, without an appropriate "reading" which would make it possible to think about their meanings, affects can never be dominated. All these cases, which are similar to those studied by P. Marty's Psychosomatic School, lead us to compare psychosis and *psychosomatosis*. This approach raises such complicated and far-reaching problems that they cannot be discussed here. We have confined ourselves to mentioning briefly the possible negativizing of sensations linked to the body itself and to affects. By linking them with negative hallucination, we are making the hypothesis that hypochondria or certain passionate manifestations, which are more or less delusional, occur against a background of negative hallucination in the sphere of the body or that of the emotions. As for the eventual relevance of such a hypothesis, applied to psychosomatic disturbances, we may suppose that the shutting-down of the preconscious barrier mentioned by P. Marty might stem from the same phenomenon whose extension would also be relevant to other topographical barriers.

In the comparative analysis of symptoms which Freud undertakes in the article "Further Remarks on the Neuro-Psychoses of Defence" (1896b) we can read:

> A thing which is quite peculiar to paranoia and on which no further light can be shed by this comparison [with obsessional neurosis], is that repressed self-reproaches return in the form of thoughts spoken aloud. In the course of this process, they are obliged to submit to a two-fold distortion: they are subjected to a censorship, which leads to their being replaced by

other, associated thoughts or to their being concealed by an indefinite mode of expression, and they are referred to recent experiences which are no more than analogous to the old ones. [Freud, 1896b, pp. 184–185]

This hallucinatory activity is amply illustrated in Schreber's Memoirs, even if it is not given particular attention. However, in his later works, Freud proposes an original and new conception of language. He attributes it with the function, thanks to verbal mnemic residues, of making thought-processes perceptible. In short, language allows thought to be "externalized". Nevertheless, it is clear that language is only perceived from the outside by the person who is listening; the person who is speaking, who hears his thoughts externalized, knows he is their author and only experiences language as a projection of his thoughts in the way the conscious reverie can be. Neither of them loses their sense of what belongs to them as subjects, whereas in auditory hallucinations voices are attributed to another person who also has the power of knowing their thoughts even when they are not verbalized. The interpretation of these symptoms assumes that there is a splitting of thought-processes accompanied by a projection and a return of what is projected in a hallucinatory form.

The question which arises then is to know whether, in this case too, positive hallucinations are preceded by negative hallucinations, that is, by a denial of the perception of verbalized thoughts, belonging to internal language, without being expressed out loud. This is very probably the case.

Nonetheless, if negative hallucination can exist as an entity apart, without necessarily being followed by positive hallucinations, as is usually the case, we may wonder if we should not refer to it under certain circumstances in analytic treatment. I am alluding here to certain moments in the analysis of borderline cases where the analysand does not understand certain of the analyst's interpretations, or even does not seem to recognize his own words when the analyst reminds him of them. In the first instance, the analyst thinks it is an ordinary resistance or an act of repression. But I have come to think that what is involved here is a real psychic agnosia which stems not only from an attempt to avert consciousness but also from a non-recognition of words, phrases, and propositions, whether they are his own, or whether they are repeated by the analyst or again have recently been expressed by the latter but are too closely related to what has to be disavowed.

Our remarks so far have led us from negative hallucination in hypnosis, encountered above all in connection with visual perceptions, to the analysis of the model of hallucinatory wish-fulfilment which again concerns the sphere of vision and is prevalent in the phenomena of representability [*figurabilité*] in dreams, then to the comparisons between unconscious representations, hallucinations, and perceptions, looking finally at the case of auditory hallucinations and their relations with language and thought. This last approach reconciles, to some degree, the investigation of the phenomenon of hallucination with the conditions of the analytic setting which imply a perceptive restriction, above all visual. Although it is rare for auditory hallucination to be compatible with the practice of so-called classical analysis, it at least has the advantage of refocusing the investigation on speech and language, the subject's internal splitting reduplicating the analysand–analyst relationship in the "classical" cure. In fact, the main interest of such a rapprochement is to shed light on cases involving non-neurotic structures which, when they are the object of analytic treatment within the modified setting required for them, can face the analyst with unexpected situations which he naturally tends to interpret within the parameters operating for neuroses, but which soon make it felt that they call for other types of interpretation evoking not so much the logic of repression as that of disavowal seen from the specific angle of perceptive non-recognition.

The exemplary case of the "Wolf Man"

Most of the issues we have been considering are to found in the case of the "Wolf Man". In an earlier study (Green, 1977),[8] I made a detailed analysis of the hallucination of the severed finger which the patient talked about. Let us recall the circumstances: Sergei recollects a scene which took place when he was 5 years old: "I was playing in the garden near my nurse, and was carving with my pocket-knife in the bark of one of the walnut trees that come into my dream as well. Suddenly, to my unspeakable horror, I noticed that I had cut through the little finger of my (right or left?) hand, so that it was only hanging on by its skin. I felt no pain, but great fear."

At this point, Freud inserts a note to report another version given by the patient on a later occasion in which he says he has confused this recollection with another, "hallucinatorily falsified", in which he made a cut in the tree with his knife and had seen blood coming out of the tree. The recollection of this passage in the "Wolf Man" calls for a number of observations. Little Sergei says that he cannot bear to cast a glance at his finger. The fear of seeing the fantasy materialized, which would be confirmed by the sight of the finger, results in his refusing to look. Moreover, he manages in his hallucination—that is, at a time when perception is replaced by its equivalent—not "seeing" the blood which the cut causes. In other words, at the moment when the hallucination occurs, the fantasy of blood is negativized.

Equally, no pain is felt. Nonetheless his state of dejection is so intense (and the impression of reality apparently so convincing) that the child does not try to reassure himself immediately by telling himself his senses are tricking him. The observation at the heart of this "moment of hallucination" which rarely occurs in states of confusion or of clouded consciousness but, on the contrary, occurs in a context of play and in the presence of the nurse, of traces of negativization, makes it possible to construct a symbolic matrix: a woman-mother ... turning his eyes away from ... feeling blood running from a cut ... causing an intolerable pain (through the *jouissance* it brings) ... making me think about [the tree in] my dream. The rest of the associations show the numerous ramifications which such a memory can have. Of all these, let us simply mention the one Freud (1918b [1914]) refers to in a note as a "correction" of the patient: "I don't believe I was cutting the tree. That was a confusion with another recollection which must also have been hallucinatorily falsified, of having made a cut in a tree with my knife and of blood having come out of the tree" (p. 85). Somewhat surprising here is the phenomenon of *déjà raconté* evoked by the account of the recollection and contested by the analyst.

In the case of the "Wolf Man", the childhood object of denial returns by means of a temporary hallucination and also as an anxiety-provoking repetitive dream. But the work of the negative, so patent in the cure under the mask of rationalization which Freud, admiring his patient's intellectual qualities, is taken in by, suggests that there is good reason to question the nature of this repression and to assume that foreclosure is at work. Moreover, a reading of Freud's reflections on anal eroticism suggest the possible link—which he himself, however, does not make—between the Russian and Schreber.[9] Instead of enabling us to clarify unconscious desires, the hallucinatory connotation of the association results in a negativizing potentiation of the psychic work which carries out their elaboration.

So, "I was cutting the tree . . ." is denied secondarily in order to make room for another recollection in which the bark was indeed cut "on" the tree itself, after which there was no hallucination of the severed finger but instead blood was seen coming out of the trunk. Apparently, one hallucination is simply being replaced by another. The rectified version even seems preferable to the initial version because there is an essential semantic element in it which is clearly visible: the link between the cut and the blood. *For us*, the previous semanteme is still present—that is, the allusion to the severed finger. And it is probably here that we miss the essential point: namely, that for the "Wolf Man" the correction does not complete the previous memory by adding a meaning which was lacking. On the contrary, the fact of drawing nearer to consciousness, which is expressed by the explanation of the semanteme "blood", giving us the illusion that there is a closer link between the wound and the sexual member, in fact has the function of trying to invalidate the unconscious link between the cut finger and the sexual member. In the same way, what the recollection allows us to infer from the trauma about the nature of hallucination which, surpassing the boundaries of fantasy, emerges in the surprising context of an unexpected and apparently very "real" event, plunging the subject into a state of collapse and leaving him without reaction, has now been trivialized during the reporting of the story by the familiar innocuousness of the *déjà raconté*. To this may be added the hypothesis of a repressed thought ("and nothing terrible happened"), thereby neutralizing a transferential reliving of the fantasy of a castrating Freud, in contradistinction to the Rat Man (1909d) leaping off the couch at the mention of the rat torture.

Such a way of thinking leads to the hypothesis of a disconnection of causality similar to that evoked by obsessional neurosis. But in this case the manipulations of representation must be interpreted, not in terms of the semantic links of representations—or at any rate not in terms of them—but in terms of the relation between investments and representations. In other words, the links only refer to the relations of meaning in so far as these relate to *claims,* that is, to the quest of the drives in which relations to the other and to oneself are rooted. Let us look again at the successive versions of the hallucinated memories.

One the one hand, a severed finger without blood; on the other, blood without a severed finger. Now we know that if there is some liquid oozing from a tree, it is very likely that the *first* thing it will conjure up is seminal liquid. The blood is thus linked to the denied thought and to the negativized representation of sperm, and therefore to the penis. We should bear in mind, however, that what instigated this hallucination, according to the patient, was the story that a relative of his had been born with six toes, and that the extra one had been chopped off with an axe.[10] Recognition and denial: there is indeed a cut connected with a violent bodily amputation, but it leaves bodily integrity intact and even makes it more "normal". We are not far from the idea: "yes, women are castrated because the *extra* penis they have is taken away from them, which however does not suggest in any way the idea that a consequence of castration might be that I have a member *lacking,* since in fact castration makes her the same as me and means we are constituted in the same way".

This is a good example of what I (Green, 1982b) have called the "Wolf Man's" dual-logic. It is worth pointing out that the manifestations of this logic are not based solely on representation. Furthermore, due to the evasive possibilities which are created by the conjunction and disjunction of conscious and unconscious thing-representations, negativization is at work and, what is more, is deeply rooted in drive activity. We are reminded here of the contradiction between the different "trends" concerning castration which gives Freud the opportunity of describing the (attitude) "I won't have it", since designated as foreclosure by Lacan and as rejection by Laplanche. This blunt refusal blossoms into affective and intellectual ambivalence, as those who worked with Sergei Pankejeff after Freud had every opportunity to experience.

The case of the "Wolf Man" is exemplary in more than one respect, but how? In the first place because negative hallucination goes unnoticed, being covered over by the recollection of a positive hallucination in which it is hidden. Second, because the patient's serious thought disturbances did not lead to the development of the hallucinatory potentialities he possessed. On the other hand, in his case, when regression takes a form which is evocative of psychosis, it manifests itself as a quasi-delusional, if not delusional, hypochondria. Lastly, this hypochondria is focused on an organ—the nose—which is the object of a symbolic contraction, a real short-circuiting of representation. This leads to constant perceptive verifications, with all the possible gains to be had from eroticizing care to breakdown—which is a repetition of the hallucination of the severed finger—when the patient learns that his lesion is definitive. In a previous analysis of this fragment of "The Wolf Man", I (Green, 1977) concluded as follows:

> The hallucination of the severed finger is preceded by the negative hallucination of the extra finger overshadowed in the hallucinatory content; the latter simply positivises, on the basis of this negative hallucination, an amputation which has already been carried out on the level of thought. [Green, 1977, p. 650]

We cannot overlook the relation between this radical investment of the part of his body which is perceptible as much as it is exhibited, and the total absence of perception of the changes in his wife's state of mind—their union was one of the issues at stake in his analysis with Freud, who did not hesitate to give his imprimatur to this project of marriage after having met Theresa. These changes led her to commit suicide, which, according to the Russian, came as a total surprise for him.

Freud probably underestimated with the patient the part played by psychic work in the subject's relations to perception, for he was entirely preoccupied with the analysis of representations (dreams), the memories of infantile neurosis, and finally the reconstitution of the primal scene. The latter mobilized the whole of Freud's energy in the search for proof (against Jung) of his perception of things which was more than likely true. It distracted him from addressing the relations between the internal and external world from any other angle than of amnesia and memory, to which he would have to return at a later date.

In a word, the exemplary nature of the "Wolf Man's" case resides in the fact that for a long time the patient, who had served as a first case for the demonstration of infantile "neurosis", made us overlook the fact that his psychopathological structure in adulthood could no longer be envisaged satisfactorily from the angle of neurosis. This was a fact which the analysts involved had difficulty in integrating with their theory, believing that they were thereby respecting Freud's work—a negative hallucination, no doubt, which concerned both Freud's text and the perception of the case which gave rise to it, as well as the relationship which bound them to each other. In describing *Verwerfung*, Freud implicitly supported the hypothesis—which would be considered impossible today—that the transference could be spared this very "rejection". In fact this implicit assumption burdens Freud's entire theoretical construction. The discovery of the "primal scene" was coloured by it, as the "Wolf Man's" remarks, after his analysis, would show.

Hallucinatory wish-fulfilment revised

The way in which Freud's work lends support to the idea of a work of the negative has left us in no doubt as to its interest. Furthermore, its study shows the original way in which this notion can be enriched by psychoanalysis. But that is not enough. One hopes a better model will be put forward to account for clinical experience and to give a more satisfying picture of the human psyche.

In what ways are the Freudian models no longer satisfying for the psychoanalyst today? As far as I am concerned, it is not Freud's most daring concepts which I would want to call into question. I accept the fact that they are often conjectural in character because—given our present state of knowledge—it seems to be to be inevitable. To my mind, it is not much a question of rejecting Freudian concepts as of emphasizing their shortcomings. To be more exact, we need to uncover the implicit assumptions on which they rest.

Let us take, for example, the model of hallucinatory wish-fulfilment. It supposes from the outset the prevalent and sufficiently assured inscription of residues of an experience of satisfaction which serves as a point of reference, "in case of need", through recourse to the representation (hallucinatory fulfilment) of the said experience of satisfaction, as an aim to be achieved if a state of calm is to be regained. This means that the experience of satisfaction took place and was repeated sufficiently often to give rise to a referential inscription without contrary effects—that is, without unpleasure, anxiety, or pain which contest its prevalence. Equally, the models of the psychic apparatus, and notably the one Freud puts forward in the article on "Negation" (1925h), rely on the efficiency of the psychic apparatus to get rid of what it feels is bad by expelling it outwards, a process I have proposed to call excorporation. This is so that incorporation, and then introjection, lead to a purified pleasure-ego, the structural core of the psychism whose constitution is a prerequisite for any development. Now, we may recall Freud's note concerning the pleasure–unpleasure system in the "Two Principles" where he hints at the need to include maternal care if the system is to work. We can say as much here: in order for hallucinatory wish-fulfilment to occur, and for the pleasure-ego to establish itself, it is necessary that the system of functioning which they imply benefits from maternal coverage.

Hallucinatory wish-fulfilment is grounded, as it were, in drive activity always in search of satisfaction. The role of quasi-object which hallucinatory wish-fulfilment offers the psyche leads us to stress this dependence of the constitution of imaginary objects on the real primary object evoked by hallucinatory wish-fulfilment. Consequently, while it is necessary to implicate the subject's drive structure which pushes for the creation of these formations, it should not be forgotten that it is based on the traces of real experiences which imply the action of a *real* object. This quality of being real [*ce réel*] should not be taken into account so much for its nature which is opposed to the imaginary as for its influence on the production of the latter and for its relations with the psyche's other modes of functioning.

The development of Freud's work culminates in the final drive theory. The model of hallucinatory wish-fulfilment is contemporary with a drive duality which opposes preservation and sexuality. It proves itself to be perfectly adequate in this theoretical context since hallucinatory wish-fulfilment is a response to hunger (thus to self-reservation) and to sexuality (the pleasure of sucking). Hallucinatory fulfilment will not be affected by the introduction into the theory of the destructive drives, which is rather surprising.

In certain of his late writings, Freud (1939a [1937–39]) often speaks of the importance of very early experiences and of those which are opposed to them. Manifestly, he is alluding here to the "opposite" of experiences of satisfaction. Now, taking into account the equilibrium or the antagonism of the experiences of satisfaction with those of pain (or of unpleasure) brings in the function of the object. Whereas in the experience of satisfaction it plays above all a protective role confining itself to guaranteeing the conditions which make satisfaction possible, in the experience of pain, its deficiency, leaving the subject exposed, has the effect of provoking a forceful destructiveness which gradually spreads. It does not succeed in preventing a hallucinatory fulfilment of pain or of unpleasure and is responsible for the creation of a "bad" breast which the subject can end up identifying with (I am the breast), or for the destruction of any representation which signifies the loss of all hope of a hallucinatory wish-fulfilment (satisfactory).

It is clear that such a rectification of the Freudian model, based on the need to take into account the effects of the destructive drives and the object's role in the production of experiences of satisfaction and pain, sheds light on the paradigmatic value of the model of the setting and of the cure, and, consequently, the function of the object in the work of the negative.

This reformulation has given us a better understanding of the two aspects of the work of the negative: the function of hallucinatory wish-fulfilment on which dream theories are based and neurosis, both of which can be linked up with Winnicott's function of illusion and the negativism in borderline cases where it takes on the forms of moral masochism, the negative therapeutic reaction, the "negative side of relationships" (Winnicott), and the experience of beta-function with Bion. In the first case, the life or love drives imply an attachment to an object based on hope which will allow other objects to be invested and prohibition to be recognized. In the second case, the reference to the destructive drives explains the negative attitude towards the object which paradoxically aims at a state of parasitical clinging which in most cases is mutually sterilizing. A lot of patience, endurance, stoicism, and tenacity are necessary to be able to stand this in transference. Here the work of the negative oscillates on the one hand between the analysis of negative transference and destructive projections towards the analyst and, on the other, states of non-representation, emptiness, and blankness in which thought becomes anaemic against the background of the negative hallucination of its own psychic productions. This process of turning the cure into a desert is the work of the destructive drives. This situation enables us to understand the extent to which the function of representation is more an acquisition than something given.

The reference to consciousness, in a negative form (the unconscious), was not far away due to the spirit of intentionality which certainly did not disappear from the new context of the psychic apparatus of the second topography but broke with the idea that there is a causality which is fully intelligible. There remains the idea of a wilful accomplishment: this is not inspired by the model of a projected action but one which has not been carried out, finding a way to realize itself in the mind and through this internal fulfilment to acquire a status which makes it close to an idea. Even the reference to action would be improper here, and I think there is a need to make a slight distinction between action and acting. And yet we would be betraying the spirit of the concept if we were to see its content as a blind force, predestined, unmotivated, and "soulless", if I may put it like that. It is here that one realizes that the drive is a borderline concept and one can understand Freud's choice in favour of the id. "Id" can be neither me nor another; id cannot be a thing either, and still less the manifestation of a spiritual power. Id is an indeterminate determination. It is a determination because its effects are controlled by a number of factors which are inherent to the structure of the human being. It is indeterminate because no subject is able to give a clear and unambiguous idea of it. But on the other hand, id claims to be the source of all later intentionality whether one calls it ego, subject, or other, these being bound up with an action which is called desire, wish, intention, project, and so on. There can be no doubt whatsoever that for Freud the id has an equivocal position in relation to the natural organization. It depends on it, but cannot be reduced to it, and has no independent identity from it. In fact, the id is neither part of the natural organization nor outside it. It is by means of it that the sense that such an organization exists is manifested and that it is necessary to make good its imperfections. When the psychic apparatus is functioning smoothly there is scarcely any reason to refer to it. But the integration which removes the sense of its individuality, dissolved through operations in which the various agencies collaborate, obscuring the fact that they exist separately, is quick, at a time when its unifying power is failing, to remind us of its determining weight and of the difficulty in seeing its influence wane in the presence of more differentiated psychic forms. Id is an inchoate pre-form, an early form which detaches itself from physiological functioning without yet being able to apprehend it, not to mention feel it, but is perhaps able to feel there is a connection and to seek to establish a state in which this impression of constraint disappears, either by eliminating the confining tension or by freeing itself from it. One can see here the cross-roads, whose paths are sometimes indiscernible, between the avenues of drive exigency and those of the object capable of satisfying it, from which an ego can emerge in both cases.

What does this change mean? In the first topography, hallucinatory wish-fulfilment is based on a postulate—that is, that there has been an experience of satisfaction, that this has been registered, and that its inscription serves as a reference and model guiding later experiences. This is the reason for adopting the criterion of representation as a basic fact of experience and as an issue at stake in satisfaction. It is up to the latter to transform this exigency for satisfaction into wish-fulfilment, the condition for the emergence of the pleasure which is sought after. Pleasure arises from its roots in need. Desire is a pivotal concept, for one cannot overlook the fact that it is the satisfaction of need which sets it in motion. This happens in such a way that it appears to be concerned about the vital protection of the satisfaction of need, whereas it is aiming in a more hidden way (because covered by need) at the reproduction of pleasure. We are now in a better position to understand the function of pleasure. By procuring pleasant sensations, which are the essence of its manifestation, and by establishing an object to dispense them, pleasure binds the ego to the object in such a way that the attachment is not confined to providing for need (owing to the immaturity of the organism), but continues, in another form, ceasing to be determined by the fulfilment of aims dependent on biological conditions. It is by this means that the operation of searching for a transferable aim is carried out. Not simply from one aim to another but also from one object to another within a generational, historical, and temporal dimension. Furthermore, the object is necessary for pleasure; pleasure is the relation of the ego to itself and can, under certain restricted circumstances, find an object-substitute in the subject's own body. It is clear that the main importance of these ideas is that they enable us to imagine the interlacing of the various registers and the pattern of certain functional circuits.

We are now in a position to understand the function of the *double link* of pleasure. By attaching to itself an embryonic ego (which perhaps only emerges after the relation has occurred) it binds this something, which does not yet exist, to something else which is not itself and which can only be a double "without". At the same time, however, by finding within itself the means to procure a substitute pleasure, it divides this ego (through auto-eroticism) thereby constituting its internal double "within". The ego is thus born from this double division "without" and "within". It is only pleasure which can accomplish this—that is, which can constitute the mediation needed to oblige the subject to place himself "between" in order to avoid the confinement of the inside and the decentring solicited from the outside.

We can understand that "it" relates to this pre-ego designation which is bound up with both that (without) and this (within). And "it" becomes "id" as a prelude to an ego.

The difference with the initial model of hallucinatory wish-fulfilment is that under these conditions, which vary in function of the parameter of satisfaction derived from the object, nothing is less guaranteed than its "later fulfilment". It is likely that the set-up provided by the species seeks to tip the balance towards the hope of fulfilment which the wishful hallucination satisfies, so that the purified pleasure-ego can constitute itself in a wide range of situations. But by envisaging the passage from need to pleasure, and thus to desire (which will construct its hallucinatory satisfaction), by linking pleasure on the one hand to the object (that) and, on the other, to the erogenous zone (this), it is assumed that, whereas need limits itself to the elimination of tension, pleasure seeks in turn a similar elimination of tension. It achieves this not simply by obtaining pleasure in the erogenous zone but, given the divided

The work of the negative and hallucinatory activity

status that the ego has acquired, by means of the relationship between the pleasure of the erogenous zone *with the projected reflection of this pleasure on the object*. The fact that this elimination (of tension) is accompanied by the bonus of pleasure which is the plus-value of the operation explains why this modality is preferred, but it does not however eliminate the aim which it continues to pursue—that is, getting rid of unpleasant tensions. In this way the ego has found a way to link itself with the erogenic zone and to be sure of the object's attachment in the first stages of the apprehension of time, in anticipation of future experiences in which the object will be needed.

Now while the pleasure of the erotogenic zone comprises an element of automaticity due to the natural organization, the part which is projected and reflected on the object must receive from the latter, for want of satisfaction, a response which does not contradict it at least. In other words, if the projection is not confirmed—that is to say, in the case where there is a clear contradiction between what is experienced and what is perceived—pleasure emerges which is torn between its strengthening in the ego and the aggravation of its hiatus with the object. In these situations hallucinatory wish-fulfilment is conflictualized; the outcome is either the aggressive version of pleasure (owing to the object's disappointed expectations), or the masochistic reflection of the object's pleasure on the erogenous zone, or finally the attempt to eliminate pleasure through the impossibility of warding off extreme unpleasure—that is, a blank, aphanisis.

The foregoing remarks are an attempt to show that the second topography coincides with a modification of the status of representation. The latter is no longer uniform (a drive-invested thing or object representation) but divided into psychic representation of the drive and thing *and* object representation; it is no longer a given for the construction of the psyche but an accomplishment of it; it is marked by the body and at the same time it accentuates, in spite of appearances, the object's practicality as a necessary complement. Speaking of the drive means speaking of the division of the object (internal to its organization and external to the drive). And this is what explains the paradoxical nature of the final stage of the theory—that is, a psychic apparatus which, grounded in the id, seems more solipsistic than ever, whereas the matrix agency of the psyche, comprised of destructive drives and of life or love drives, makes the object indispensable in the latter case.

The work of the negative will no longer involve psychic activity as it can be imagined independently of the positive aspects of consciousness; it will concern itself with the relation to the object caught in the cross-fire of the destructive drives on the one hand, and the life or love drives on the other. The work of the negative thus comes down to one question: how, faced with the destruction which threatens everything, can a way be found for desire to live and love? And reciprocally, how should we interpret the results of the work of the negative which inhabits this fundamental conflict—that is, the dilemma which we are caught in between the anvil of absolute satisfaction, to which omnipotence and masochism bear witness, and the hammer of renunciation for which sublimation is a possible outcome? Beyond this conflict looms detachment, a step towards the disinvestment which is supposed to free one from all dependence on anyone or anything, so as to be able to encounter oneself at the price of murdering the other person.

These remarks which study the effects of the conditions determining hallucinatory wish-fulfilment should not be considered as relativizing its importance. It remains the natural aim of the psychic apparatus: nightly oneiric activity shows this. But we have also learnt that nocturnal hallucinatory activity is not limited to dreams. And if it was possible for Freud to save this theory by a brilliant interpretation of anxiety dreams—as hypocritical dreams—psychoanalysts today generally agree that nightmares should be considered separately. This confirms our belief that there is a tendency for unconscious psychic activity to create hallucinations, wish-fulfilment only applying to a part of its production. We might mention here the reasons which pushed Freud to replace the unconscious by the id. The substitution of psychic forms (representational) by drives (of life and death) may have led Freud to neglect to take into account certain forms of representativeness in which the capacity for representation finds itself, so to speak, overwhelmed by a dynamic coefficient with a more or less disorganizing effect on representation or, more precisely, capable of breaking the link of representation with wish-fulfilment. Either the dynamic quality takes it upon itself to invest the representative potential by enacting a destruction of the relation to the object, or this destructivity turns against the representative power itself. These are many of the points which work against the vocation, which we have called "natural", of representation to compensate for the obstacles which reality puts in the way of wish-fulfilment. Perhaps we can go as far as to affirm, on the contrary, that through representation reproducibility offers the increased possibility of shifting the motifs which underlie this preferred mode of functioning towards wish-fulfilment. It was reflections of the same order which led Freud in *Beyond the Pleasure Principle* (1920g) to the conclusion that its institution must be preceded by an inaugural mode of concatenation, the establishment of which is a pre-requisite for the sovereignty of the pleasure principle. Binding is the first operation: pleasure, by maintaining its rich variety of effects, invests it, as it were, with a supremacy which will make it its herald. It would be worth looking again at the object's status, doubly divided between its participation in the drive set-up and its position outside it. We are now in a position to express this differently by distinguishing between a desiring-object and a caution-object. Our hypothesis is that the latter may only be apprehended within the "framework" of maternal care and is neither perceptible nor capable of being represented—its function being to facilitate the production of hallucinatory wish-fulfilment. This contributes to the construction of the fantasy-object as well as to the object objectively perceived, in so far as it is the *guarantor* of the fantasmatic object. Coming full circle, but without it being possible, however, to make them meet up, the real object represents the form of the caution-object which can be conceptualized. Thus hallucinatory wish-fulfilment and object caution are closely linked without, however, becoming one, for hallucinatory fulfilment can only occur with the object's caution and even with the object's desire which the ego (of the infant) desires, and which desires it too. But this cannot be represented. The paradox then is that Freud goes to extreme lengths to defend the solipsistic hypothesis of a death drive, whereas everything suggests that what he is describing is explainable in terms of the vicissitudes of dependence on the object. Conversely, it would be an error to attribute the latter with the accomplishments performed by the psychic structure considered in the light of its intrinsic properties. At this point it is necessary to distinguish between the position of hallucinatory fulfilment which gives prevalence to the intrapsychic (Freud), and that of the object relation (from Melanie Klein to authors describing early interactions) which favours a relational, or better, an intersubjective approach. The aim here is not to come up with some sort of fallacious synthesis, but to show the point of view offered by each of them, the analyst needing to alternate between them by examining the characteristics of the theoretical field to which they belong.

But if this is the case—that is, if binding is to be given pre-eminence—the relation to hallucination then appears as an exigency for repeatability, reproductiveness, representability, and reorganization subject to the pleasure principle. In other words the ego, left to its own devices in sleep, is driven to verify the validity of the object's caution, the latter being an integrated part of its internal organization. At the same time it tests the validity of the accomplishments of the introjections which made its constitution possible. Let us not lose sight of the fact that Freud takes traumatic dreams as an example to justify abandoning any reference to the pleasure principle as the first organizing factor of psychic processes. Nightmares, which have a very similar structure, enable us to follow the evolution of the modifications which Freud deemed necessary. The child's nocturnal terrors fit into the same scheme of things. What is important in these oneiric structures which do not fall within the sovereignty of the pleasure principle is not, as is the case with dreams, the preservation of sleep, but waking, which frees the dreamer from a situation in which he is threatened by dangers. We can draw a parallel here between the end of the nightmare which comes with waking and the intervention of negative hallucination to suppress a perception, insufficiently protected, of the boundaries which make it possible to keep the latter well away from unconscious representations—or separated from them by a certain number of filters. When one thinks of the nightmares in stage 4 of sleep which are accompanied by a re-somatization of anxiety and by a lifting of the motor inhibitions which normally occur during sleep, causing a disorganized state of agitation, there are good reasons for supposing that, under the influence of pathogenic factors, it is the system of boundaries as a whole which is unable to ensure that the different registers of physical life are kept apart: so it is also the somato–psychic boundary, the preconscious and the protective-shield which seem to be subject to threatening infiltrations. Claude Janin (1990) has described the collapses of the psychic topography which occur in a less obtrusive manner and which are valuable indicators of the movements taking place in classical psychoanalytic treatment. It seems to us therefore that negative hallucination fits in with Freud's remarks on perceptive activity. It is not so much that these represent a theme which has been insufficiently explored, and which needs to be cleared up, as that they command attention because the problems raised by certain psychic phenomena have not been resolved. But we must nonetheless bear in mind that here, as elsewhere, it is the dependence of this activity on the pleasure principle and its acolytes, the binding of repetition and the reality principle, which will serve as a guide for reflection.

Rediscovering the world and reflexive constraint

No view of perception can afford to overlook the issues raised by studies ranging from neuro-physiology to experimental psychology. Faced with the precise nature of the data which the scientific approach offers, it is difficult for clinical practice to obtain the recognition it deserves. The wide spectrum which extends from *Méconnaissances et hallucinations corporelles* (Hécaen & Ajuriaguerra, 1952) to agnosias following cerebral attacks of various kinds is a source of perplexity. But it is also true that clinical work sometimes presents us with facts of incomparable richness, inviting us to speculate further on the basis of experience which may teach us much more than we can learn from years of experimenting.

At this point I wish to relate the story of a shoemaker who was blind from the age of 10 months and came from the lower-middle class. He liked his job which he was able to do almost perfectly in spite of his amblyopia. He had never lost hope that scientific progress would one day enable him to recover his sight and he consulted doctors over a period of thirty years requesting an operation to this end (a graft of the cornea). In other respects he was a confident, open, and cheerful person. After his requests had been turned down several times owing to the uncertainty of the prognosis, an operation was finally carried out when he was 52 years of age. This case, reported by Gregory and Wallace (1963), is of considerable interest on several accounts, but I shall just focus on the aspects which seem particularly relevant to my purpose. When he was examined forty-eight days after the operation, there was already astonishment that as soon as his long-awaited wish to see again had been satisfied, he showed no surprise upon rediscovering the world. It is easier to understand that, in spite of recovering his sight, his world of blindness persisted in many ways. If he was asked to make a drawing of objects, he could only make a correct graphic representation of the parts which were accessible to his blind-man's faculty of touch. To acquire a new capacity for seeing, he had to be able to transfer experiences related to touching. He was unable to learn to read.

For six weeks he lived in a state of euphoria, but soon his mood changed. He became gloomy and no longer enjoyed looking at his wife, whose appearance displeased him, any more than he liked looking at his own face. He was forced to admit that he found the world disappointing: it was different from how he had imagined it. He would start at anything which smacked of imperfection or degradation and developed a phobia for dirt. When the sun was setting, he seemed preoccupied. Worse still, whereas when he was blind he had been well-adapted to his daily tasks, now that he had got his sight back again he was incapable of carrying out ordinary tasks and felt handicapped compared with people who could see. In the home where he lived, he would sit at night in front of a very large mirror with his back turned to his friends. He became progressively more depressed and died two and a half years after the operation. In retrospection, the surgeons believed that the operation which had given him his sight back had been a mistake.

There are many things to be learnt from this case, and it is a crucial experience for perceptive knowledge because the lesion affected neither the retina nor the visual brain but the extreme periphery of the eye, at the most superficial point of the perceptive organ. Gregory and Wallace point out that the dangers encountered by individuals who have regained their sight concern the non-optical properties of objects. This draws our attention to the fact that, according to existing models of vision, the interpretation of the cerebral cortex makes information meaningful when it applies to the non-optical properties of objects. The fascination for mirrors remains a puzzle, since the image they reflect is disagreeable. The spectacle of the world is only bearable if one turns one's back to it and if one receives a reflected image of it. The mirror image, far from supplying more information, is an attempt to turn away from reality. When he was shaving and had to take care not to cut himself, he found closing his eyes more reliable than seeing. In his *Traité de la peinture*, Leonardo da Vinci recommended that painters who were worried about the quality of a painting should look at it in a mirror, saying they would then be able to get a better idea of it, as if it had been painted by another master.

It is well-known now that perception goes hand in hand with a questioning of internal models which is just as active as the investigation of the external perceptive field. Such an "internal view" is a component of all visual or cognitive movement. Diffuse exploratory activities—scanning—complete the information coming from the specialized focusing of touch or sight. In this way the latter are able to communicate more fully, nothing occurring without the aid of the detection of symbolized features, identifiable in the external world, during an activity which is not only quite active but in which searching is concomitant with creating information.

Perception and memory are perhaps mutually exclusive in the way they appear to consciousness, but external view and internal view mutually reflect each other in their task of ensuring immersion in the present, grounded invisibly in the quest which links what is currently relevant with what is not.

The phenomenal field of negative hallucination

If "reflection" is the basis—imperceptible—of the most general theory of perception, hallucination is equally fundamental to any psychoanalytic conception. The analysis of the occurrences of negative hallucination shows that it can occur in the most ordinary situations as well as in the most extreme pathological states. Once one is no longer surprised by the psychic plasticity which hypnotic suggestion reveals, it is in the manifestations of everyday psychopathology, or during fleeting impressions which are out of the ordinary and contain something strange about them, but which are of very short duration (*déjà raconté, déjà vu, fausse reconnaissance*), that one can discern in people who experience these manifestations the very marked presence of mechanisms of denial. Periodically, then, everyone may resort to the mechanism of negative hallucination without there being any serious consequences for their psychic functioning.

However, the fact that this is possible obliges us to reconsider the theory of the virginity of the receptors of the perceptual system. In fact, what most of the examples show is that the negative hallucination which occurs in non-pathological states vouches for the proximity of unconscious thoughts and external perceptions, with an unconscious representation having the value of a figuration of a primal fantasy or, better still, serving as a bridge of communication between several of them. Whereas psychic functioning offers unconscious representation the possibility of separating into its elements, of displacing or condensing certain aspects of this decomposition, or even to subject the investments of affects to the same treatment, the occurrence of negative hallucination reveals subsequently—that is, after restoring either eclipsed perceptions or, failing that, reconstituting the continuity of perceptive sequences—the more or less complete series of thought associations. In an almost identical but inverted mode, this amounts to quasi-material *proof* of the interpenetration between unconscious representation and external perception without any diversion being possible. What I mean is, in contrast to the hypothesis which, in order to render more intelligible a sequence of psychic phenomena considered complete from the point of view of consciousness, consists in proposing the insertion of an unconscious representation, which as a result is conjectural and dubitable, in the case we are considering it is the quite noticeable lack of something perceived which makes it necessary, in order to reconstitute the completeness of the sequence it is part of, to relate this lack to a representation whose unconscious character does not raise the same doubts concerning its existence, because the assumption that it participates in the advent of perceptive negativization takes on a more compelling character when the interrupted continuity is re-established. The connection which thus exists between perception and its suppression makes it quite clear that it needs to be accounted for in terms of the unconscious representation whose previously hypothetical character now looks more convincing. Why is this the only solution possible? The answer may lie in the fact that the unconscious representation is invested by the drive motion but in such a way that the affective aspect remains entirely unconsciousness, only manifesting itself through the meaningful connotation marked by the unconscious representation. Such a connotation denotes a mere marking of the unconscious representation, without an affective quality capable of entering consciousness, but manifesting itself through the difficulty of displacing such a representation—replacing it by another which is not so immediately meaningful. From then on, the collision with the external perception gives the situation a traumatic dimension in the shape of "an excessive perception" which is intolerable, dethroning the submission to external material reality, in order to lend credibility to psychic reality without modifying the former. Now Freud always distinguished internal excitations from external excitations by saying that while it was impossible to free oneself from the former by means of motricity, this could be achieved with the latter. It really seems as though a "motor image" were mobilized in the opposite direction from that which is normally the case in the experience of satisfaction, contributing to a withdrawal of the investment of the perception. In these cases, rather than speaking of a real denial, it would be better to speak of an *inadmissible recognition* (rather than disavowal). Of course, the main interest of these phenomena is to show us the range of the possibilities for the intervention of the defences which show that even external reality cannot escape their influence.

Two other cases remain to be considered. The first is that of the psychoses in which there is a powerful hallucinatory investment. Without going into details, we shall simply mention the two major examples of amentia and paranoia. As far as the first of these is concerned, we shall elucidate the oneirism which occurs in it by the following observation from the "Revision of the Theory of Dreams", in which Freud writes:

> The state of sleep involves a turning-away from the real external world, and there we have the necessary condition for the development of a psychosis. The most careful study of the severe psychoses will not reveal to us a single feature that is more characteristic of those pathological conditions. In psychoses, however, the turning-away from reality is brought about in two kinds of way: either by the unconscious repressed becoming excessively strong so that it overwhelms the conscious, which is attached to reality, or because reality has become so intolerably distressing that the threatened ego throws itself into the arms of the unconscious instinctual forces in a desperate revolt. The harmless dream-psychosis is the result of a withdrawal from the

external world which is consciously willed and only temporary, and it disappears when relations to the external world are resumed. [Freud, 1933a, p. 16]

The comparison of dreams with psychosis is an indication of the attention which Freud now pays to the latter, in spite of himself, no doubt. We therefore need to be alert to whatever leaves the psychic space vacant, allowing the ego to throw itself "into the arms of unconscious drive activity" and to understand that it is not so much unpleasure which is involved as whatever causes intolerable pain. This can only be accounted for by what he called the repression of reality. He was not specific about the mechanism he was referring to, but it has now become partially more intelligible.

In this case, it is not only inadmissible recognition but disavowed reality which prevails. And if hallucination is proof of the psyche's almost unlimited capacity to carry out transformations even to the point of creating the neo-reality required for its accomplishments or of rendering the intolerable perception innocuous, the same result can be achieved by the mere thought which is satisfied with ignoring the world instead of constructing a new one. In short, if negative hallucination negativizes itself by being covered over by positive hallucination, we may assume that in purely interpretative paranoia potential hallucinatory activity is negativized. Thus disavowal will not have to apply to the materiality of a perceived reality—the "intolerably excessive perception" which we were speaking about—but this would, as it were, be "let be", becoming the object of the ego's perceptions, whereas it is the relation of perceptions to representations which would be altered by the investment coming from drive motions acting on the links between representations. The relations between drive motions, unconscious representations, and representations of reality would then be modified. In the case of paranoia, we can understand Bion's remark that hallucination is the obstacle encountered by that which cannot be. It is around the pivotal point of preconscious representations, whose major role in thought processes needs to be kept in mind, that the intervention of the negative comes into play in the relation between thing-representations and word-representations. This is how we can imagine psychotic functioning becoming perceptible. For word-representations have two essential functions. On the one hand, it is by means of their activity that our thought processes can become perceptible—they are, so to speak, their principal, if not exclusive, material support, their signifier—and, on the other hand, they are closely linked with thing-representations (themselves originating in perceptions). There is therefore a contrivance which unites thought, language, and the perceptive–representative sphere. Furthermore, as conscious thing-representations are themselves inter-connected with the unconscious representations energized by the drives which have not been integrated by the ego, we can observe the subversive production of thing-representations. This is how the infiltration of drive motions tends to spread to the whole of the chain we have described, having its strongest effect on the weakest link (unconscious representations), bringing drastic defences into play which are mobilized under the circumstances to the detriment of perceptions, where the external world is concerned, and of judgements and ideals representing reality in the ego—that is, the activity of thinking, where the internal world is concerned. The "abolition" which Freud speaks of, namely, the withdrawal of investment, throws the whole system out of balance, for what is involved is a "local" rather than a global mechanism—the latter corresponding more to amentia. This "hole", or this vacancy of the unconscious psyche, does not bring about, as it does in repression, a cut or an amputation on the basis of which the system then reorganizes itself to disguise this alteration. On the contrary, in this case, what is left "suspended"[11]—at least provisionally—creates a space weakened by this evacuation which initially makes it necessary to exclude whatever is liable to awaken the memory of this action, undermining psychic integrity. This has two serious consequences. The first is that external excitations, meeting resistance, tend to surge into the hole left by the abolition of key signifiers, disrupting what remains of the organization of representations which cannot cope with handling the invested sensory information. On the other hand, however, the disorganization of the relations between the different types of perception (external and internal) leads to a somatizing psychic disinvestment, receiving a sensory influx from within the body (regressive recorporation). Without manifesting itself as such, its main effect will be to increase the burden of the psychic task (already burdened by the weight of the least psychically invested bodily narcissism confronted with the ego's grandiose fantasies), having to ward off the experience of internal chaos. Each time the capacity of the representative system to deal with symbolic structures is affected, it is compelled to make greater use of projection. Language then becomes the object of a struggle, which means it can no longer be conceived, as Freud thought, solely as a restitutive process, but it seems to be the locus of disavowing thought, subverting judgement, and creating another ego—a second ego for the ego—where its reflective capacity, instead of taking shape through its relation to the object, splits itself, dividing the ego not only from itself but from the other ego it has created. Denial is then essentially the negation of affirmation making negation possible, along with the substitution of the ego united by its splitting. The relation to the object is marked by the need to ward it off, making it possible to substitute it—denying its negative hallucination—with the mortal struggle between the two parts of an ego at war with itself and blind to its own division.

The memory-system (and thus the system of object-representations too) is crushed by the weight of a pure present invading all the figures of temporality so that a reserve of traces is never formed which is capable in one way or another of being reunited with the lost object. There is nothing to be found again: that's just how it is . . .

Just as the perceptivo-representative "unchaining" will not leave intact the drive–action equilibrium, paradoxically psychosis erases all consideration of the id as a simple result of the mechanisms we have described as disavowal, splitting, and the doubling of the ego to ward off the object. And if the reserve of temporality happens to be lacking, it is the emerging awareness of repetition compulsion which is threatened, not only by unconsciousness which is its usual state, but also by an inaptitude (in the juridical sense) for awareness. This is not through a sense of a lack or inadequacy but through a proclamation of non-qualification rather than disqualification; in other words not so much a lack of suitability as unsuitability, as if the demand for awareness were addressed to the wrong person.

What I have just described in psychosis would not be intelligible without an experience of borderline cases, without it being necessary, however, to adhere to the outmoded idea which conceives of them simply as structures on the borders of psychosis. In the psychic mode of functioning which is specific to these structures we can observe the perpetual movement back and forth between the spheres of representation and perception. Here there is a broadening of the function of negative hallucination which obliges us to formulate its relations with repression more clearly. This leads us to cast our minds back to familiar ideas concerning the defences, which are more readily accessible to the experience of the psychoanalytic process.

Repression and negative hallucination

We have a sufficiently clear idea already of the mechanisms at work in repression, which remains the prototypical form of defence. But repression is employed against the internal processes of drives, affects, and representations, whereas negative hallucination is carried out against perceptions. Whether it is an external or internal perception, we should not confuse representation and perception, and it is the role of reality-testing to make the distinction between the two. In this respect we shall see that language poses a particular problem.

What happens when there is a negative hallucination with respect to an external perception? I shall look at things as follows. When a negative hallucination occurs, two scenes unfold almost simultaneously on two different stages: on the one hand, between preconscious thought and unconscious representation and, on the other, between preconscious thought and perception. It is this situation which is not understood, because what must be avoided above all is the meeting of an unconscious representation and a perception, as if the perception were to acquire the value of a hallucinatory wish-fulfilment. In the internal theatre (of fantasized activity), thought or preconscious preoccupation is connected with the unconscious representation but the latter is repressed. For example, preconscious thought may express an annoyance or a fear without being more precise than that, or even be accompanied by a conscious representation which is very subdued in comparison with the unconscious representation. But there is a flow of investment in both directions. Against this psychic background, the perception which appears and which is interpreted according to the current state of mind, that is, in function of preconscious preoccupations, crosses these, as it were, and prepares to encounter an unknown psychic phenomenon, just as two trains going at full speed on the same rails are heading for a collision. This time the two trains are the repressed unconscious representation and the conscious perception overwhelming the precarious link between the preconscious representations. This is what gives the perception the value of a hallucinatory wish-fulfilment, but such a fulfilment always carries with it the danger—directly or indirectly—of undermining the subject's narcissistic integrity (threat of castration carried out, of implosion, or of disintegration). As a result the only means of fending it off is cutting off the perception, because the drive motion which is at the basis of the unconscious representation cannot be curbed and has got through the censorships. This is especially so in that the unconscious representation becomes incapacitated due to the prohibition against making representation function as a source of thought. On the contrary, it has to be dried up to prevent the meaning of the unconscious representation and its connection with its essential synchronic and diachronic connotations from emerging.

In reality things are not straightforward because the link between unconscious representation and perception does not bring together two equivalent psychic forms. It seems therefore that an intense and extremely rapid piece of psychic work is carried out between representations stemming from the central fantasy and its core, as well as between perception and the associative memories it evokes.

It is also noteworthy that negative hallucination is not limited to non-perception but is completed by the unconsciousness of non-perception. Equally, it is possible for the work of disconnection to be completed internally by the displacement–replacement of the unconscious representation onto a related unconscious representation, as in the mechanism of fetishism where the missing perception (of the mother's penis) is covered by that of a piece of clothing near to the sexual organs or by that of another part of the body having some resemblance or close connection with the penis. Of course, the negativization applies essentially to the encounter between interior and exterior, namely between the unconscious representation and the perception. The negativized perception can give way in the psychic investment to a displaced substitute representation which occupies the subject's mind at this moment, providing rationalization with the excuse of "distraction". It would be more appropriate to speak of "*dystraction*"—that is, traction caused by a difficulty, a state which is deficient when it comes to repressing a psychic event destined to be suppressed or conserved, because the fact that it is part of the repressed, far from shielding the latter, exposes it to danger by making it run the risk of an implosion–explosion. Now such an event would be alarming on several accounts. Dynamically, it goes without saying, owing to the loss of ego organization which leaves it exposed to the risk of chaos. But topographically as well (that is, in view of the formal regression), because such an implosion–explosion would inevitably make the ego aware of what it seeks to hide from itself; namely, that its functioning is threatened by its relation to primal fantasies, the meaning, origins, and aim of which it is unaware of. Negative hallucination seems therefore to be a radical and extreme defence—even in those cases where it is of short duration—because it carries out a condensation of denials in connection with the sideration of the usual capacities for de-condensation: displacement-substitution, repression–rationalization, repression–affective reversal, and so forth. If hallucinatory wish-fulfilment is capable of occupying the space of the internal world, the de-realization of the latter as a mode of the ego's functioning, accomplished without any trace of its negativizing intervention, may be tempting. And it is in this respect that, from the point of view of the unconscious ego, negative hallucination is indeed the representation of the absence of representation, as I maintained in *The Fabric of Affects and the Psychoanalytic Discourse* (Green, 1999).[12]

As for the destiny of such a defence mechanism, it is subject to multiple personalities one of which (but it is neither the most frequent nor the most inevitable), as in the case of the "Wolf Man", can give rise to a hallucination whose destiny is itself subject to a number of factors which will determine the subject's psychic future.

It is clear that negative hallucination cannot be linked solely to disavowal or denial, depending on the terminology. The disjunction can probably not be adequately explained by avoiding the encounter between unconscious representation and perception; the phenomenon no doubt needs to be interpreted in terms of what Freud designates as "ideas and judgements which represent reality in the ego". There are, in fact, four terms in question:

preconscious thought and perception, each in direct contact, and, further towards preconscious thought, unconscious representation, and the non-specular representation of reality (judgement). Thus in situations which give rise to negative hallucination, reality then gives unconscious representation a dangerous pre-eminence which, limiting its appearance in consciousness, nevertheless deems it absolutely necessary to cut off its links with perception and strives to disavow the latter. In analysis, we do not often have the opportunity of observing the presence of negative hallucinations although they do sometimes occur: for example, when the analysand meets his analyst outside a session, or even when he suddenly spots some detail in the setting which seems to be new, although in fact it was always there. The importance of these observations lies less in the content of what leads to them than in the fact that they invite us to bear in mind the possibility that they may occur in contexts related to central aspects of the patient's conflictual organization.

I would like to dwell a moment here on the case of the non-perception of thoughts through language. I am thinking of those patients whose difficulties lie on the level of thinking, as Bion has described. For my part, I have tried to understand the mechanisms involved in blank thought. I think that we would be able to understand it if we could imagine thinking, not only without images—without representation—but also without words to perceive what one thinks. It is in this respect that language is both a representation and a perception; it represents the relation between things and the relations of thought relations making it possible for the latter to be perceived. The negative hallucination of thought also manifests itself in the analytic situation in the inability to express oneself with words. This is not the silence of an absence of speech but that of the formation of words as tools for thinking, or of the relation between morphology and semantics of words. Words can in this case just about be perceived on a sensory level, but what is lost is the relation of the words to their meaning in accordance with the reference to the unconscious. I am not of course speaking about the unconscious which remains as such, but to that part of it which has already been the subject of an analytic interpretation. At other times, there is evidence that this has been heard, but the patient suddenly seems to be unaware of it again. It is not so much forgotten as treated as if it were something new or something which related to the state which existed prior to any interpretation. In regard to this, there exists in the patient a combination of amnesia (of what was said at the last session or a few minutes before) of aphasia, an inability to speak because words fail, and of agnosia, when the analyst recalls words already spoken by the patient at an earlier time in the analysis, without succeeding in making the patient recognize them. Of course, I am only making use of this terminology, borrowed from psychoneurology, to give an idea of what is happening on a psychic level.

Hallucinatory negativization and unconscious representation

While we see negative hallucination as a prime example of the work of the negative, we may ask ourselves how it fits into it as a whole. And it is true, as the case of the "Wolf Man" shows, that it is not always easy to differentiate between an unconscious representation and a hallucinatory negativization. We cannot just oppose "representation of the absence of representation" and repression of a representation. Let us take the case of dreams defined by Freud as a deployment of hallucinatory activity in relation to wish-fulfilment, or let us consider it (according to the later definitions of it) as an *attempt* to fulfil a wish. When relating a dream it is frequent for the dreamer to say: "At this point the dream is unclear and I can no longer see the person I have just been talking about, although I can sense their presence", or again, "Such and such a person appears but I can't see their facial features". Should we accept that censorship, whose task is it to disguise meaning, is responsible for this deletion at the heart of representation, when the latter is both omnipresent and when the mechanisms of dream work ensure that the necessary disguises exist? Is there not a failure of representability and/or a failure of wish-fulfilment, incapable of making use of the disguises at its disposal? What else is there to say other than that this deletion can be understood as a marker of negativity designating, through a lack of disguise and representation, that which, invested by drive motion, exceeds the limits of representative plasticity and no longer seems content to resort to hallucinatory vividness in order to signal its importance. Ordinarily, this hallucinatory vividness gives the dream its feeling of reality, thus attracting attention to what is said during this moment of dreaming, inducing one to look for an interpretation which will make the unconscious fantasy, which is the source of dream, accessible. Here, the deletion simultaneously sharpens the details and suppresses their existence, as if to draw attention as well to the danger that it is thought to be the cause of this deletion. Which is one way of saying: "You're dreaming!" In the language of dreams this would be: "You're not really dreaming about it!", just as in waking life one would say "You're not really thinking about it!"

Or again, to use analytic language, translating: "I hadn't thought about it" (which is an admission negatively of the contrary—i.e., "that is what I was thinking but I shouldn't have been") into the dream dialect by, "I didn't dream that", reveals that even in dreams, even in the "fulfilled" reality of the oneiric hallucination, there can be no place for such a thought which has "come to mind" in this way.

Already in *L'enfant de ça* describing blank psychosis—in which the concept of negative hallucination accounts for thought disorder—J. L. Donnet and I insisted on the difference in patients' discourse between the statement "I can't remember any more", or "My memory's failing me", and the seemingly similar statement "My mind's gone blank". It might be worth pointing out that Z, the patient who was the subject of our study and who we thought was suffering from thought disorder—which was confirmed by other colleagues who had examined him themselves without our knowing it—did not know how to express, did not possess the words to sustain affects which, moreover, he could hardly name. Here, once again, it was representation which was involved.

It is important therefore to understand the difference between negative hallucination and negativization at the heart of representation. The negativization of representation always applies to a representation, a return (of the repressed) or of some mental trait which has already undergone a form of elaboration within the psyche. The only case which might escape this characteristic is the perception of internal sensations and feelings, but we may suppose that it is less these feelings as such which are at stake than the associations which they establish with representations. On the contrary, we have seen with negative hallucination that what is involved is the status of external reality which, as an actualized presence, is shaken and reveals nothing of its resonance with the roots, whose negativization destroys any possibility of conjecture. The link with the unconscious representations in the violence of the encounter cannot be reduced to a wish-fulfilment, a mode which psychic reality is used to, but can be ascribed to a "realizing" response from reality which indirectly marks the prohibited or impossible status of the wish and thereby increases the potential danger of materializing the primal fantasy.

The question which arises, then, is to know how the perception of thoughts through language is to be understood. For while perception is a mode of being of presence, it always refers to a couple formed with another partner which defines the field in which the problem arises—that is, there is a gap which is at times unthinkable in its link with hallucination, or problematic in its relation to representation, or again, as we have just seen, has to be reduced by means of the link with unconscious representation. With internal perceptions, this gap is dislocated between two extremes: the first, through internal sensations, concerns the sense of existence through its bodily grounding which adapts poorly to any sort of division or reflection; the second, on the contrary, can only be apprehended in the reflexiveness of language which, in its very manifestation, implies the existence of dual polarities, whether it speaks of the world or of itself, whether it forges links between a speaker and an addressee—sometimes distinct, sometimes confused—or again whether it must face the alternations between presence and absence (Lacan). In the case of psychoanalysis, the dimension of transference has led us to distinguish between transference onto the object and transference onto speech (Green, 1984), forming a meeting point for all the issues we have been discussing.

The change of paradigm and its Freudian sources

From the moment psychoanalytic thought was faced with the need to acknowledge the shortcoming of Freudian theory with regard to problems posed by non-neurotic structures and of remedying them, it was not just a new chapter which needed adding to the traditional corpus, but a change of axiological orientation. It went unnoticed by many that the need for this new orientation, which would have to be defined in the light of contemporary experience, had already been sensed by Freud, who knew that it would soon be necessary to determine the direction it would take, although the length of his own life would not permit him to accomplish this himself. Very briefly: the main preoccupation of psychoanalytic theory was to reveal the unsuspected continent of internal psychic reality, being content to consider external reality—dealt with extensively elsewhere—from the angle of the favour or disfavour accorded to unconscious wishes and to the absolute necessity of taking them into account, Freud having declared cases marked by a repression of reality as unanalysable. We know that this prescription—which was also a proscription—did not prevent some analysts (Freud included) from hitting upon observations of great interest concerning psychic functioning based on investigations of certain psychotic states. Certain disciples disregarded the master's oracles. Many of them followed in the wake of Melanie Klein, a courageous pioneer who no doubt counted on there being better chances of reversibility with children, whose continuing growth was supposed to make it possible to get libidinal development moving again along quite ordinary paths. In my view, this approach led to an increase in misunderstanding to the extent that, necessarily, the study of psychotic states in childhood could only accentuate the polarization of research into the internal world. Now, when we read Freud, we see clearly that while his disinclination for tackling psychotics was not modified in any way, after the "turning-point of 1920" it was no longer perversion which was opposed to neurosis (as its opposite) but melancholia on the one hand—a pure culture of "death drives" under which the category of narcissistic neuroses is exclusively subsumed—and, on the other, the psychoses, which no longer belonged to the same denomination but continued to be defined by their relation to reality. Furthermore, interest in the perversions did not diminish, but there was a change of focus. Indeed, the consideration of pleasure sought after by the component drives in the prevalence of erogenous zones, aims, and objects seemed to give precedence to the mystery of the threat of castration being set aside. It was fetishism which now took on a paradigmatic function. It might be helpful to point out that splitting serves as a defence, allowing a link to be made between perversion and psychosis, as the *Outline* of 1938 indicates 1940e [1938]. Over and beyond that, Freud has a premonition (in the study of the same year; 1940e [1938]) of its central role in the processes of defence. Now the novelty of the discourse introduced in the article "Fetishism" (1927e), which Freud was to pursue until the end of his life, lay in a thoroughly original approach towards perception and the possibilities of denial which were opposed to it, comparing classical repression (henceforth linked to affect) with disavowal (or denial, whose action is directed at perception). This is what analysts did not grasp in reading his work, either because they tried to be faithful to the explicit Freud, consecrated by the psychoanalytic tradition known as "classical and orthodox", by continuing to link his thought to perversion only, or because they were attracted by the new paths opened up by Melanie Klein, tracking down unfathomable archaisms.

Now what Freud was saying, in fact, was that it was becoming impossible for psychoanalysis to continue along the path which had claimed the interest of his contemporaries—that is, its revelations of psychopathological forms adjoining normality; henceforth, progress could only come from research into the relationship between psychic reality and external reality. It was not until the impasses of Melanie Klein's thought had become apparent that this message, which had gone unheard at the time, was understood. This was in turn put to the test at the heart of the Kleinian movement by Bion who reviewed the Kleinian vision of psychosis, dethroning the archaistic interpretation of unconscious fantasy, replacing it with a new dimension accorded to projective identification—this being closer to the vicissitudes of Freud's drive motions. To this was added the innovation of a theory of thinking (completely absent from Kleinian writings before him) at the basis of psychosis. Winnicott, moreover, who was at first seduced by the Kleinian approach, eventually had to break away from it in order to give the environment its rightful place, its position having been underestimated hitherto. In addition, he enriched it by making allowances for the relation between the internal and external world through the discovery of the intermediate area. These two complementary orientations relativized the assumption of Klein and Isaacs that unconscious fantasy was the equivalent of drive functioning, a hypothesis brought forward during the polemical context of the discussions between the adversaries and partisans of Melanie Klein in the years 1941–45 (King & Steiner, 1991).

Nonetheless, the drift away from Freudian thought would prevent the re-interpretation of it by Hartmann's ego-psychology from gaining much ground in spite of the fact that it enjoyed a certain success. Negative hallucination is evoked, for example, in the works of his disciples Arlow and Brenner, in relation to the psychoanalytic approach to psychoses. M. Mahler alludes to it in passing, in child observation and in connection with autism, but the phenomenon never gave rise to reflections going beyond observable facts. And Lacan was only too happy to play on the short-sightedness of American authors in order to attract his readers to his conception of the ego alienated in its specular identifications—a hypothesis based on the perception of the coupled image of the subject and the other in the mirror, leaving his abstruse theorizing on the Real until much later (Lacan, 1936). The late introduction of the tripod Real, Imaginary, and Symbolic—RIS—carefully eschewed making a link in any way, as in Freud, between reality and perception. And as the name of Merleau-Ponty cannot be overlooked in evoking the cultural context in which French psychoanalysis developed—his *La phénoménologie de la perception* (1945) was regularly quoted in any work on hallucination—we shall recall his brief intervention at the Bonneval Colloquium in 1960 in which he expressed his astonishment at seeing language taking up the whole stage without any mention being made of the relation to the world which perception reveals (Ey, 1966). Let us add for good measure that, on the other hand, the theory of representation has been developed further in French psychoanalysis than elsewhere.

Interest in perception was rekindled in an unexpected way. Generally, the only time psychoanalytic thought came to speak of perception was in relation to conscious errors, following the famous example of Swann's tormented imaginings while watching from the street the lighted window of a certain inaccessible Odette, until he realized that he was looking at the wrong floor. Now the study of certain patients, whose symptoms occur on the somatic stage, provides the analyst who is talking to them with the opportunity of observing a *perceptive hyper-investment* which is quickly seen as the sign of an irregularity in mental functioning attributed to a vacillating permeability of the preconscious (Marty, de M'Uzan, & David, 1963). Thus it was no longer the study of the psychoses—in which elaborations on the relation to reality[13] were of limited theoretical interest, merely describing the manifest with psychoanalytic vocabulary and lacking the necessary instruments for laying bare the underlying organization—which opened up new horizons, but the study of somatic illnesses. It would have been better to follow the path which treated what is perceived not only as the object of a displacement, as is indicated by psychosomatic patients, but probably also as the object of a return to an external world which the subject must cling to. This is because he lacks moorings from which the libidinal reflux can organize lines of defence to cope with the complex products of regression. The psyche appears more clearly in those configurations in which it is endangered; that is, where it finds itself crushed between soma and reality.

A critique of the Freudian theory of perception and the reference to representation

One could not help noticing that either the Freudian view of perception had not been sufficiently understood or it lacked something which placed limits on its usefulness. What was without doubt in question was the Freudian postulate of the indefinitely reviewed availability of the perceptive surfaces of reception, the need for which was accepted in a situation where there was an exclusive opposition between perception and memory, but which nonetheless contained many obscure points. How, then, were perceptions and representations to be related, given that the latter are derived from the former? Where, then, was the meeting-point for investments coming from without and those coming from within? Of course, the idea of an interface seemed fairly essential, but was the complexity of these relations compatible with the image of a flat mirror, even if it was endowed with the properties of a two-way mirror? We have been keen to point out the successive corrections which Freud was obliged to make concerning his early ideas that perception provided evidence of a reliable relation to reality.

If we just take the example of visual perception, the source of 80 per cent of perceptive information, how are we to reconcile the idea of its receptivity, which is always ready to take in new data and to link it to consciousness, and the existence of a *visual drive* whose scopic aim is guaranteed by drive motions implying a dynamism necessary for achieving a purpose which goes hand in hand with the search for the object capable of satisfying it, and which is scarcely compatible with the serenity required for a "faithful" registering of information coming from the external world? And if we have good reason to deplore Freud's destruction of his article on projection, it is also because the lack of it has left us poorly equipped to develop a theory of perception.[14]

We are justified in affirming—I have done so on several occasions—that the reference point of psychoanalysis is representation, a concept which is deployed in several registers, including that of the representations of reality in the psyche. We find ourselves embarrassed on two scores here. For while we are hard pushed to go beyond this summary observation which notes the inescapable character of such a notion, we cannot go much further unless we are able to say what such representations represent—in other words, without establishing a psychoanalytic concept of perception.

It would appear that the solution is easier where representations, corresponding in the internal world to perceptive reality, are concerned. Is the space of consciousness only inhibited by thing-representation, with the verbal complement which is connect with it, or is it not conceivable that the thing thus represented might also be accompanied by what still shows through of its relation to the unconscious thing-representation, by resonating with the preconscious, without the unconscious part being discernible as such? This last aspect can be inferred because language is not confined to its reference to the conscious thing-representation, but also bears the trace of *relations* between conscious and unconscious thing-representations. Better still, by means of affect and beyond it, the drives or their more distant derivatives infiltrate language. In other words, while it is undeniable that the word-representations are related *directly* to conscious thing-representations and cannot entertain relations directly with the unconscious, indirectly they bear the trace, not of unconscious representations alone, *but of the relations between unconscious representations and conscious representations,* the nature of the latter permitting an intricacy with the language of words, even though this dominating mark wavers at times.

Although the theory of perception obliges us to couple it with representations, and preferably conscious representations, it nonetheless implies the potentiality of an indirect infiltration by the unconscious. So the theory of perception is disappointing from the point of view of psychoanalytic research. Its analysis involves introducing parameters which are both more rigid and more disconcerting than the mechanisms discovered by unconscious functioning. One major fact stands out: unlike representation whose properties—whether they concern drives, images, or words—are always liable to fragmentation and then all sorts of operations of combination and re-combinations (with certain elements being suppressed and, of course, the extensive transformation of primitive forms, etc.), *perception, for its part, does not split.* It can be eclipsed—partially or wholly—but not divided up. Perception can be envisaged in terms of different factors including quality (comprising rhythm, intensity, etc.), clarity or confusion, focalization or diffusion, distinction or fusion, to which can be added the features observable in the configurations of experiences of depersonalization, projection, denial, negative and positive hallucination, but it lends itself neither to being divided up nor to being combined. There is a "linearity" which it is difficult to shake off in the analysis of the phenomenon of perception. Before Lacan discovered an unexpected way out, offered by the promotion of linguistics to the rank of a pilot-discipline, he exhausted himself tracking down the forms of the imaginary in the concave and convex interplay of mirrors, engendering the illusions of an inverted vase. They have had little influence on his disciples.[15]

One notable exception was the unexpected encounter with Winnicott who, inspired by reading Lacan's paper "Le stade du miroir" (1949), put forward the idea of the mother's face having a mirror role. The dilemma perception/representation was thus elegantly transcended by the idea that what the baby sees in the mother's gaze is himself. It was also affirmed that excessive dependence on the impressions perceived in the maternal face created a premature disillusionment prior to the experience of omnipotence which is indispensable to the baby's capacity to create a good subjective object.

Negative hallucination and speech

When negative hallucination is not simply an accidental or even isolated phenomenon—when, for instance, the psychic apparatus seems to be caught unawares and it reacts to the unexpected situation in ways which are not customary for it—then it seems that the analytic situation scarcely has the means of identifying such a defence or of understanding in detail how the processes which trigger it work, any more than the consequences that stem from its employment. As we have seen in the case of the "Wolf Man", it is with subjects whom we suspect demonstrate modes of psychic work which are different from those found in the neuroses that we expect to encounter its expressions. But since it is in relation to reality that these manifestations are most easily identifiable, the analyst is not well placed to interpret them, particularly as, by a kind of reduplication of the phenomenon—in those cases where the analysand notices, which is not frequent—when it is reported in the session, the fact is treated as trivial and does not arouse the curiosity which generally takes hold of the neurotic subject when he becomes aware of a parapraxis through introspection. In short, with the neurotic subject there is a "bias of intentionality" which, when it is not very clearly sensed before the cure, is set in motion as soon as it has got under way, for this is the sign by which transference can be apprehended, in all sense of the term. To be sure, the analyst preserves the setting, but in so far as it is amplified by the meaningful potentiality of the subject. The setting is the space–time allotted to the subject for deploying speech which he addresses to the object who is supposed to hear. It is clear that the operation is not without risk when the double understanding of the discourse is insufficiently protected from the dangers to which it is exposed. It seems that negative hallucination then becomes a regular process and not just occasional, in all the cases where reality as a whole (bodily reality and reality of the world)—and not only through one or the other of its representatives placed in a symbolic position—is experienced as hostile. This may be perceived directly, but solely by means of hysterical identification. In any case, the purpose of negative hallucination is to deny the subject's fear of the consequences of his own hostility, in fact of the pleasure that the expression of it would give him if he had the power to exercise it freely. In contradistinction to what occurs in the psychoses, there projections are not due to a desire (foreclosed) placed outside, as is regularly the case in paranoia, the existence of which can be sensed in foreclosed homosexuality. Although we may also suspect this to be a demand lying behind complaints about other people's cruel indifference, it is also a projection of the subject's narcissism, a narcissism which denies the object's existence, found merely to be disappointing, treacherous, and unreliable. There is no need to dwell at length on factors we have already emphasized: pregenital fixations, the fragility and vulnerability of the ego's defences which are both rigid and in danger of breaking down, the prevalence of splitting mechanisms and projective identification, a lack of auto-eroticism, the foreclosure of symbolic formation for want of a reference to the paternal law, an absence of capacity for representation, object relations marked by an intolerance of separation, an incapacity to mourn, and so forth. We place these various descriptions under the heading of processes which are closely related to negative hallucination. The analytic setting—notably when the face-to-face situation places the analytic partners in the field of perception—creates excitation which makes the subject anxious about his insufficient capacity for holding. He fears this will be overwhelmed when the object is no longer there and that he will be deprived of its help, even if, when this help is available, it is threatened by a kind of hallucinatory realization (acting) which affects the quality of the transference. Negative hallucination is brought into play by the anxiety provoked by the return of the repressed, which is not perceived as such but as a fulfilling actualization. The connotation of restitutive repetition is not recognized in the transference which seems to unfold with the atmosphere of a trauma in full swing. In other words, it is more a question of a return (one-way) of a psychic event needing to be exhausted (rather than repressed), although the means to achieve this are uncertain, faced with an object which is both powerless to cope with the situation and sometimes prompted to contribute, by doubtful inadvertency, to what is involved in the trauma. We therefore have to go much further than this. And since unconscious representation cannot offer the psyche a meaningful potential which can be elaborated, that is, which can be displaced, condensed, and so forth, and because the latter finds itself, as it were, dogged by the demands of drive motion, the ego finds no other solution than to reverse the course itself of psychic events by situating this point on the nearest surface of what confronts it—that is, towards speech.

It makes use of speech just as repression makes use of drive motion or its representatives by striving to neutralize it. However, since it cannot bury it—as it would have done with unconscious representation, leaving it free to offer the preconscious only censured, filtered products, in other words, sufficiently purified to be "thinkable"—the crux of the conflict shifts to the chain of word-representations. And it is equally important that negative hallucination corresponds as closely as possible to the familiar expression "no one'll be any the wiser" which, if it is to be fully understood, should be taken as meaning "not seen, not caught", which is tantamount to saying: "not known, cannot be caught". Thus it is necessary, while maintaining things as they are, to apply the work of the negative to the perceptive function of thought provided by language, in the hope of stopping the associative flow at the level of word-representations, "horizontally", if one may put it like that, and to immobilize the relations between representative systems of words, of things, as well as of the body (drive as "psychic representative") and of reality (judgement of existence) in the direction of depth.

It is clear that in order to apply its action to speech, which is after all the aim, it is the relations which are formed with the body and with reality which are involved. In order to understand this better we must cast our minds back to our hypothesis which requires that we distinguish between the psychic representative of the drive (as the representation of excitations from inside the body reaching the psyche, a delegation which cannot be represented) and object- or thing-representation (as a representable representation stemming from perception), the conjunction of the two forming the ideational representative, the famous *Vorstellungs–Repräsentanz*.

> The coaptation of the psychical representative as a bodily demand, but unrepresentable (*infigurable*), the movement of this unrepresentable bodily exigency, coming to invest an earlier trace left by the object which has brought satisfaction consti-

tutes the inaugural moment of thought. And it is this primary binding which is the starting-point for the possibility of analytical work by means of transference as a relation to fixation and displacement. [Green, 1988, p. 493][16]

In other words, the relation word-representation–thing-representation, characteristic of conscious activity, is dependent on such a coaptation because the latter governs the relations of the repressed and determines dynamically, economically, and topographically the regime of unconscious representations throughout the entire extent of their domain, and therefore through the preconscious, with what is represented there of the relations between words and things. If, as I maintain, thing-representation is situated between drive and language, we can say equally that word-representation is situated between the objects represented and thought. But while each element of the preceding notions referred to a representational support which was bound up with that of a higher level of organization, thought offers the particularity of only disposing, at the heart of the psychic apparatus, of the material support of the level which is adjacent to it—that is, language. Presenting a psychoanalytic view of language would be going beyond the scope of this study, but it is clear that our understanding of the nature of the psychoanalytic process cannot evolve without clarifying a minimum number of ideas.

The Saussurian distinction between speech and language or between message and code, indeed seems necessary and indispensable. More recently, Atlan (1983) has proposed that language be approached from two directions, namely the relations between the brain and language and those of language and thought. However, we cannot overlook the paradox that we are required to use language to know thought, even though the investigation of language can only reveal to us what belongs to language itself, and despite the fact that we do not possess any other means of knowing thought than through language. And yet there is more than one reason for believing that thought exists independently of language. The fact remains that Freud's idea, which sees in language the possibility of *perceiving* thought processes, is loaded with consequences. It is less a question of isolating this level from the others than to see it as a continuation of the activity of representability. Listening to the speech of a patient is to "imaginarize" it [*l'imaginariser*]—that is, to carry out an imaginary conversion of speech in order to draw out, not only a representation but also a network of operations raised to this level of intelligibility by referring to what can be represented, starting from a situation which cannot if one continues to adhere to the drive basis of psychic activity. But in turn this representability may make way for operations of another nature which no longer have recourse to what can be represented. What is important to understand is the preservation "even under different aspects" of investment which permits meaning to be constructed at each stage.

The pair of concepts perceptual identity–thought identity has existed since the earliest days of psychoanalysis. But what becomes of thought identity if it depends on a language-perception of thought? There is no reason to believe that negative hallucination—which we have seen may affect the experience of bodily existence—stops at the gates of language, because the latter consists of verbal matter. On the contrary, there is every reason to suppose that language, owing to its relational vocation, may be the preferential target of negative hallucination. Language indeed is, on the one hand, hyper-invested by the very conditions of analysis—analytic speech takes the grief out of language, as we have written elsewhere—and is open, on the other, to the return of the other person's speech. Thus the action of language not only exposes itself by communication with the other but is exposed to such communication. The source of language is thus endo- and exopsychic; its exercise becomes sensitive to the perception of that which has the same nature as its own thought. It is the interface which is always in danger of being surprised by oneself and by others and so becomes an object of excitation and surveillance, an opportunity to excite the other and elude his watchfulness.

In those structures where the various systems of functioning are the object of confusion and/or splitting, we may, upon identifying these mechanisms and having long attributed them to repression, regard repetition compulsion or the absence of change to be the product of processes which we had hitherto overlooked. The same is true for the non-perception of the identity (of thought) between material produced by the analysand and its interpretation by the analyst. Admittedly, one can always challenge the pertinence or exactness of the interpretation. But there is more to it. On some occasions, reminding the patient of what he has said before—and this cannot date back very far—meets with no recognition on his part. In this case, the non-identity of thought involves first a non-recognition of a perceptual identity which is scarcely open to question. And the analyst would be wrong to think this is simply forgetfulness—that is, resistance through a repetition of repression. I think, in fact, that we should not hesitate to refer here to a negative hallucination of borrowed forms to express the meaning of words which could not be separated from their formulation before they were recalled. There exists a whole graduated series of denials going from the non-recognition of spoken words to the non-comprehension of their meaning and from there to the associations related to this understanding. But apart from this, negative hallucination may involve the affect (connotation of transference) which served as a marker for what was said. It can also direct its potential for denial at the object's presence. Sometimes, too, in a more complex way, the object which is difficult to think about is not only resistant to representability but presents itself as a presence which cannot be represented, making the excess weight it brings to bear on the subject and the ease with which contact with the latter is lost alternate (and coexist!).

But why are we speaking here of negative hallucination rather than representation—and its vicissitudes? It might be thought that we were complicating matters unnecessarily if we were not to draw attention to the fact that what needs emphasizing here, due to the difficulties connected with the act of thinking, is not so much the domain of psychic activity within the patient as the domain of his relation to that which makes him sensitive to perception, as a phenomenon of actualization, of "realization". In other words, not so much the re-presentation as a new event to be considered in the absence which enables us to see what it refers to, as the presentation of that which, by its very presence, leaves no other alternative but its hallucinatory negativization.

It is the analyst's task to offer the patient a different approach to the psychic events which are witnessed in the setting, namely to treat them as products to be preserved through transformation, thereby conferring on them the status of transference representations, available for transferring representations. Things will continue in this way until the representation itself can take leave of them, that is to say, to the point where anxiety, rage, impotence, ideas of hate and death—in short, negativism—can one day find their expression in the formula which we no longer expected to hear. "No doubt you will think that my intention was to . . ." And here, really, the analyst had not thought of it . . . or had ceased to think that it could be thought about like that. No doubt he knew, more or less unwittingly, that he would thereby be relieved of his functions by the patient's thought alone, allowing himself to dream of something else.

Review of a conceptual development

When I tackled negative hallucination for the first time,[17] I put forward a model of double reversal (Green, 1983).[18] In an effort to conceive of a construction based less on the ideational representatives of the drive than on drive investments—today I would say on the psychic representatives of the drive[19]—and on the assumption that a system of functioning exists before repression comes into effect, I assumed that the combination of the turning round upon the self and the reversal into its opposite—the double reversal—created an enclosing circuit, demarcating opposed spaces (internal and external) which could be regarded as a structure providing a frame for psychic space capable of gathering and inscribing representations as well as making them interact. I added that, in addition, there was a need for a mechanism which I called decussation:[20]

> In this reversal by means of decussation it is as if the response expected from the object found itself carried along in this movement in which the extreme positions of the inside and the outside are exchanged in the drive flow. . . . What arises in this way is a circuit which does not have repercussions on the characteristics of the object but on its response which, while preserving the object in its absence, delegates it to the subject *as if* it were the object which had brought about the realization. One might see a metaphor at work here.

I continued by comparing the protective shield and repression, stating that

> there is no correspondence, as there is between an inside and an outside, but . . . something between them is crossed so that

what is inside may be treated in the same way as that which comes from outside provided that the inside can be perceived as if from the outside, *without their merging*. This clarifies and extends Freud's formula according to which the id is the ego's second external world. [Green, 1983]

What is lacking therefore in the psychoanalytic theory of perception is the need to include it in a space of reversal[21] which we have described for drive investments by including a part linked to the mother's response, for which we have suggested a figuration which helps one to understand the transit external–internal. Nonetheless, the specific problem of perception still needs to be identified. A few indications should suffice for the time being, but their importance should not be underestimated.

To begin with, it must be remembered that for Freud perception does not come first. What comes first is attributing the object with connotations of pleasure and unpleasure, with the consequences we are familiar with of incorporation and what I have called excorporation (Green, 1986b). If something is perceived, this is caught in a configuration in which the information conveyed by what is perceived is included in what is transported by the drive motion where the dominant feature is constructed around the modality *contact-movement*, whose speciality in touching and kinaesthesia will benefit. Perception stands out from this conglomeration which includes the relational spheres touching/touched, in movement/at standstill, held/released, in symbiosis/in distress, and so forth, all covered by the contrasting pair pleasure–unpleasure, coupled with the pair which I can only describe very vaguely as "with–without", a preform of the future distinction between presence–absence. These considerations are only important in that they help us to understand what ensues. *Perceiving is not knowing, but re-cognizing; re-cognizing means following once again the path of a movement defined by its substitutive value for touching what is described as desirable or undesirable, or, failing that, acceptable or unacceptable.*

These points may shed light on the remarks I made in 1967:

> The mother is caught in the empty framework of negative hallucination and becomes a containing structure for the subject himself. The subject constructs himself where the nomination of the object has been consecrated in place of its investment. [Green, 1966–67]

With this definition I am enlarging considerably the sense of negative hallucination. It is no longer restricted to the more or less regressive register of the manifestations of denial, from the psychopathology of everyday life to hallucinatory confusion. Its basis is no longer internal perception but hallucination in the primary process which Freud sees as being equivalent to perception. This hallucination must not be confused with a representation, although there is some justification for doing so. What matters is to distinguish the manifestations of the work of the negative, that is, repression directed at representations or affects, and negative hallucination which is related to the attempt to *create* something perceptible or to thwart what is perceived, even where internal psychic manifestations are concerned. The effect of negative hallucination is to prohibit direct access to representation encouraging the subject to take into account a certain reality which is expressed in the discourse of what can be represented, as an instance of a psychic event to be thought about. The responsibility is not, however, attributed to the vicissitudes of the phenomenon and to what happens to representation, as is the case where the defensive measure has confined itself to the condemnation and/or the distancing of what is conscious (repression). This is why I speak of it as representing the absence of representation, to emphasize its future relation with thought. This is also why it is not surprising that we speak about it by pointing out its effects at the very heart of representation to the extent that, in contradistinction to repression, which only leaves open the possibility of differed knowledge through the return of the repressed, it is in the present that it carries out its informative function by making us aware of how its object "is blanked out" and leaves a mark by the very manner in which it disappears.

There is no more vivid example of this than the negative hands found on the walls of Neolithic caves. A hand which is drawn never gives the same sensation of its prehensile power and the elusive nature of its grip, of the lure of perception, and of the mark which the latter leaves on our body at the point where it perceives.

In this sense, it matters little that the distinction between the supports of negative hallucination sometimes makes us hesitate between perception and representation, for what really matters is to understand that "the negative hallucination" (of the mother) has made the conditions for representation possible (Green, 1983, p. 127).

Prospects for future research

The review we have just made of these earlier developments leads us to realize that they operate on two fronts. By including the object's "response" in the constitution of the double reversal, we are considering the overall picture from two points of view: one which strives to apprehend what is usually called "mental functioning" and the other which implicitly postulates an "object relation" (even if it is regarded primarily from the angle of primary narcissism). These two approaches echo each other constantly. For, to come back to the containing structure, how are we to image its formation without considering what depends on the perceptive sources in the conditions which exist when it is established? The internal context in question cannot be explained solely by negativizing the primarily visual representations of the maternal presence, evoked by the mnemic traces of what can be "looked at" in it, but also by the transformation of non-visual data, tactile and kinaesthetic among others, which provide this closure with the necessary means to "withstand" and which relate to that in the child which feels (depending on whether we use Winnicott's or Bion's terminology) "held" or "contained". And it is this very impression—or this effect, if you like—which is scarcely "perceived" in a concrete way which can be represented, but which means that everything which occurs on the psychic scene will be "held" together—that is, bound and capable of creating what is binding. Of course, the possibility and even the inevitability of unbinding is included in this binding but comprises the prospect of an eventual rebinding. We can see then how the containing structure is not perceptible as such, but is only perceptible through the productions arising from the setting, which remains silent, invisible, and "imperceptible" in a different way than through a reference to the dimension of latency. Here, then, we are faced with the aporia of the symbolic matrices of thought.

We are bound to say that it is here that the essential justification for the analytic setting lies—that is, its necessity as well as its function of revealing the internal context which governs what happens in the perceptive and representative spheres. For it is very much in the relation perceived–represented that the whole dimension of what Lacan called the non-specularizable unfurls. This, of course, is nothing other than the act of thinking.

The inside and the outside must be thought about in terms of their relations which are sometimes mutually exclusive, sometimes subject to reciprocal interpenetration, and sometimes only tangential. These are all hypothetical situations enabling us to escape the linearizing fatality of the relations which usually link perception and its object. The link which ties the fate of perception to consciousness is equally strong, even in Freud's writings. Now we need only to pause a moment to realize its inadequacy, whether one points to the levels of psychic activity below consciousness (and one thinks here of the "apperceptions" from Descartes and Leibniz to Husserl) or whether one attempts to integrate perception with the beginnings of understanding. Is this not another way of doing justice to Freud's grouping which covers the field extending from internal sensations to thought processes? It is also no doubt true that modern phenomenology has preferred to structure the question differently by giving preference to the idea of "appearances" (in consciousness) which does away with the barriers between perception, representations, and even hallucinations. Are these terminological distinctions entirely without foundation? Going beyond the criterion of conscious activity, we propose instead to consider the perceptive quality from the angle of "making present to oneself",[22] which infers a form of existence unrestricted to consciousness, implying a change of state and a plurality of modes of existence, each of which can take over from the other, without linking these to a "conscious" phenomenon. It should be clear then that Freud's central statement is confirmed and rejected at one and the same time. It is confirmed by the fact that it is indeed the postulation of a latency which is indefinitely renewed so that the presence to oneself can occur in a sufficiently full way to present an exteriority which is definable as such, and rejected by this manifestation which also relates to an interiority, always ready to come and "join in on the conversation". "Presence to oneself" is necessary to explain this transformation which makes it possible to judge what exists, not only because of the dimension of absence which underlies it implicitly and to which it necessarily refers, but also because this "presentation" convokes the elements which are at play in the elementary forms of knowledge and particularly the division between what is to be known and what makes knowledge possible (see Green, 1991).

We shall thus be freed from this aspect of immediateness which perceptive experience comes up against in contrast to the discursiveness of understanding. Perception is discursive, just as thought needs to become perceptible to be thought about. And this is no doubt the explanation for the renewed interest in perception—considered from the point of view of investment—whether it be in psychiatry (Angelergues, 1969) or in psychoanalytic theory (S. Botella & Botella, 1990).[23]

These directions of enquiry are of great consequence since taking perception into account involves several essential considerations. Certain of these are very familiar and are only mentioned here for the position they have within the overall picture, which alone makes them intelligible. Let us recall for memory's sake the findings which concern the distinction ego–non-ego, inside–outside (so eloquently rendered by the Botellas' formula "only inside, also outside"), subjective–object, and so forth. These oppositions underlie what is involved in the theory of the relations perception–representation by implying the questionable precedence of the former over the latter. This is what underlies the link with the insistent materiality of the reference to the object of perception, as opposed to the impalpable evanescence of representation. To these classical notions, psychoanalysis has added new properties. First, there is the dominant "mimetic" characteristic of psychic activity which is expressed in the perceptive–hallucinatory "equivalence". Then the negativizing property, which can modify, transform, and even suppress the perception which is liable to arouse unpleasure. And lastly the convertibility not only between the various registers of perception (external–internal, relating to the body or thought) but also between perception and representation. This is the idea we have been developing throughout the preceding pages. When all is said and done, it is *"investment"* which provides the basis for perceptive activity, for it alone explains both the ego's perceptive fascination for the object attracting its activity, because it discovers in it the lack which is met by the object's very existence,[24] and the way in which pain can, to use Freud's expression, "pull the psychical apparatus away from perception". This very striking image of "pulling away" gives us a sense of the importance of the bipolar vision of psychic activity. This is not only shared between the ego and its other (the object, the id, the superego) but sees this sharing repeated at the heart of the deepest immediateness which inhabits ego experience, as the reference to "presence to oneself" implies. The relation to the object indicates, although it is not named as such, the complementary polarity which makes it possible to think about a relation—a specific reflexivity between perceiving and perceived, just as there is between representative and represented. Here we find all the implications involved in the definitions of the psyche, provided that we do not confuse the products of the division with representation in the classical sense resulting in a theory of the illusory which can only end by recognizing the futility in its own approach. An illusion into which, for example, someone like Winnicott, who defends the idea of the unavoidable paradox which divides (and unites) the subject between subjective object and object objectively perceived, does not fall. Finally, this will enable us to understand the function assigned to language in psychoanalytic treatment, which speaks of the thing and of itself at the same time. This is linked to consciousness and its representations and extends—without ever succumbing to its direct influence and always with the help of the detour of the conscious thing-representation—the resonances and harmonies of the latter, or of what can be transmitted through the functioning of such a structure: that is to say, representative emanations of the unconscious which enable us to identify—another form of presenting to oneself—the surges coming from the id and even, beyond that, from soma, just as consciousness reproduces in its very functioning a part of reality.

The subject's division is grounded in the diversity characterizing the psychic apparatus. Perceptive experience, which seems to be the most undeniable basis of immediateness, does not escape the solipsistic and unitary illusion which underlies its apparent reality. While lacking a clear conception of its constitutive division, it nonetheless has experience, through its negativization in negative hallucination, of what keeps the subject divided between affirmation and denial, presence and absence, investment and disinvestment.

Notes

1. He does not give the same meaning to the phenomenon, emphasizing its characteristic of absence.
2. We know that this "later" never came, as Freud destroyed the study of projection which was to appear in his "Papers on Metapsychology", without coming back to the subject to study it in depth.
3. The possibility of an investment of desire producing a hallucination provides Freud with his first intuition about the nature of a primary process.
4. This has been amply explored and developed in the studies of Sarah and Cesar Botella (1990).
5. If reality-testing is considered as the third crucial experience alongside those introduced in the "Project", satisfaction and pain, it is clear that negative hallucination is located between pain and reality.
6. Freud (1917d [1915]) states that "such a withdrawal may be put on a par with the processes of repression" (p. 234).
7. The quotation marks are Freud's.
8. Actually, it was not the first time that I "had attacked"—to use Freud's expression—the question. I had already expressed my views in 1965 and had proposed a model for it in "Le narcissisme primaire structure ou état" in 1966–67 (included in Green, 1983).
9. In the reflections on the relations between "Shitting on God" and "Shitting something for God" (Freud, 1918b [1914], p. 83).
10. An association which concerns an extra toe and which appears in the context of another story (*déjà raconté*); is this a reduplication of disavowal?
11. *Les choses laissées "en plan"* [translator's note].
12. Originally published as *Le discourse vivant* in 1973.
13. We cannot overlook here Henri Ey's (1973) monumental *Traité des Hallucinations*, the crowning achievement of his work and the sum of knowledge of his era.
14. We have put forward a model—based on hypothetical inferences—for the origins of the perceptive function in our study "Méconnaissance de l'inconscient" (Green, 1991). We wish to refer the reader to it.
15. See in the *Ecrits* the remarks on D. Lagache's paper.
16. See also Green (1982b).
17. This was shortly after I had emphasized its importance during one of Lacan's seminars on 21 December 1965. See Green (1965).
18. This vicissitude of the work of the negative gives me a chance to

point out that I had used a similar expression ("negative moment") for the first time in 1960 in the discussion of the report by J. Laplanche and S. Leclaire on "The Unconscious" at the Bonneval Conference of 1960; see also "Méconnaissance de l'inconscient" (Green, 1991).

19. See Green (1987).
20. From the Latin *decussare*, "divide in a cross shape" (*The Concise Oxford Dictionary*).
21. A study by Guy Lavallee, "La bouche contenante et subjectivante de la vision", postulates a comparable process based on the view of introjection and projection (personal communication).
22. French: "*rendre présent à soi*" [translator's note].
23. That the former (Angelergues) made a long detour through psychoneurology before returning to psychiatry lends even more weight to his approach. And the fact that the latter (the Botellas) strive to understand what underlies the concept of *representability* [*figurabilité*] as a "figure" which is common to representation and perception should be noted.
24. See S. Botella and Botella (1990, 1992) papers given on 17 January 1991 at the study day organized by the Centre R. de Saussure in Geneva. Personal communication: "The perceiving subject is for ever affected by the failure of the hallucinatory solution, by the mark of his own existence in the lost object of satisfaction."

5

The Oedipus of the id: the unrepresentable negative and the transformational processes of analysis

César Botella & Sara Botella

In 1919, Freud discovered the existence of neuroses that had their origin neither in the child's sexual cathexes nor in the Oedipus complex: these were traumatic neuroses (1919d). At the same time, he had to admit, when his patient the Wolf Man returned to Vienna, that his treatment had failed, even though he had thought of it as a brilliant success when it ended in July 1914 (1918b [1914]).[1] In *Beyond the Pleasure Principle* (1920g), Freud put forward the hypothesis of the death drive; then, in *The Ego and the Id* (1923b), he envisaged a second topography with an agency that he characterized as chaos, the id, thereby recognizing the metapsychological insufficiency of the notion of the system Ucs. of the first topography, consisting in repressed ideas [*représentations*]. The second topography consists in "instinctual impulses" [*Triebregung*], whose nature is essentially kinetic, without a psychic ideational representative. The id is "what is non-personal", whereas the Ucs. is considered throughout Freud's texts as constituted from the repressed ideas of childhood. This change opens up the possibility of broadening out the theory of analytic practice. We are interested in its repercussions on the notion of the Oedipus complex.[2]

The organization of the relationship to the object according to the Oedipus complex represents a major axis of reference for analytic work. In spite of the fact that the discovery of the Oedipus complex dates back to 1897 (in his letter to Fliess of 15 October, Freud speaks of the revelation of the "gripping power of Oedipus Rex" in each of us), and that the expression Oedipus complex [*Ödipus Komplex*] had become, around 1910, a familiar notion for psychoanalysts, the first time that Freud offered a precise description of it, stage by stage, was only in 1923, 26 years after the letter—in fact, in *The Ego and the Id* (1923b), with his introduction of the second topography. Why was there this necessity, just when the theoretical upheaval of the second topography was underway, to stop and clarify the Oedipus complex? Perhaps because, with the introduction of the id, the conception of the Oedipus complex could no longer be confined to the notion of wish inscribed in the history of the individual and in the unconscious ideas characteristic of the first topography.

The murder of the father

"Parricide", Freud repeated in 1928, once again referring to *Totem and Taboo* (1912–13), "is . . . the principal and primal crime of humanity as well as of the individual. It is in any case the main source of the sense of guilt . . ." (Freud, 1928b, p. 183).

There is no disputing the existence in Freud's work of the idea of a "primal state"—here the idea "*primal murder of the father*"—"of humanity as well as of the individual", especially as, to this can be added, among others, the notion of *primal repression* [*Urverdrängung*] as an effect of "quantitative factors such as an excessive degree of excitation and the breaking through of the protective shield . . ." (Freud, 1926d [1925], p. 94).

Our hypothesis is that this *primal murder of the father*, this "principal and primal crime of humanity as well as of the individual", this disconcerting assertion, would be less disconcerting if we thought of the *primal murder of the father* as inseparable from the drive, in its origins—the drive [SE: "instinct"] being understood here in the sense of *instinctual impulse* as in the second topography. The realization of this impulse without mediation can only be experienced by the mind as the destruction of what opposes it. The development of the psychic apparatus and the cathexis of the object would mean that this destruction of every obstacle carried out by the violence of the instinctual impulse would take the form of a *visual or pictorial representation* [*Darstellbarkeit* (Freud, 1900a); *Figurability* (C. Botella & Botella, 2004)]: the *murder of the father*.

The metapsychological value of the *murder of the father* may be said to proceed, then, not so much from a phylogenic historical reference, from a model of self-preservation, or from primitive instinctual violence, close to the theories of the ethologists, as from the more intimate nature of the "instinctual impulse" of the id "which confers on certain aspects of the life of the soul a demonic character". The notion of primal parricide referring to an unmediated act, without a cathected object, belongs neither to the order of the representable and the repressable, nor to that of the perceptible. It is neither fantasy nor—even less so—thought.

What Freud calls primal parricide is the reverse side of primary identification [*primäre Identifizierung*][3] *with the father of personal prehistory. And, like the latter, it is prior to any object-cathexis.*

The two sides of the Oedipus complex: Oedipus of the *Ucs.*–Oedipus of the id

A fundamental difference characterizes what could be considered two sides of the Oedipus complex: that of the history of the individual, envisaged from the standpoint of the unconscious of the first topography (positive and negative Oedipus, or early Oedipus of Kleinian theory), and that of the individual's own prehistory, envisaged from the standpoint of the id. On one side is the representation of the *living father*, accessible to the system *Pcpt.–Cs.*; on the other, the representation of the primal parricide proper to the instinctual impulse of the id, unrepresentable and inaccessible to the system *Pcpt.–Cs.*

This difference implies the existence of two categories of causality: the psychic causalities change, depending on whether one turns towards the effects of an act that is still effective, an act that is *already accomplished, though without memory traces*—namely, the parricide specific to the id—or (b) towards the dynamic of the system *Ucs.*, with the wish to murder the father who is the mother's object of desire.

(A.) A primal impulse which, paradoxically, is already accomplished but still effective—that of a primal murder—refers to Oedipus, who, before arriving at Thebes, where he falls in love with the queen, kills his father in the guise of an old man who tries to push him aside at a junction where three roads meet. Under the effect of "the excessive degree of excitation and the breaking through of the protective shield", more than killing the father, Oedipus gets rid of an obstacle on his path—without fear and hate—which in no way represented a third party preventing him from loving an object.

So if we consider that the primal parricide of the id is the foundational event of the Oedipus complex, this implies the idea of the primal predominance of the impulse [*Regung*] of the instinctual impulse [*Triebregung*], without measure, without limits, without frontiers. Although it operates by erasing any difference between the intrapsychic and the external world, between determinism and chance, particular and universal, rational and irrational, the *realization* of this impulse has not left any marks.[4]

(B.) The psychic causalities change with the classical Oedipus complex of psychoanalysis, which implies the precedence in both sexes of incestuous sexual desire over the wish to kill. It is specific to the causality of every neurosis. Freud's genius was to understand the tragic destiny of the myth as the manifestation of the blind force of unconscious desire. Unlike in the tragedy, the foundational event in Freud's work is not murder but incest: "Oedipus kills his father because he loves his mother." Since our analytic theories and practices are based on the model of neurosis, they generalize this causal value of the Oedipus complex. It is this incestuous causality that classical interpretation brings to the fore. Classical interpretation has the dynamic role of offering clarification in the sense of the Kantian *Erklärung*—that is, the role of presenting something by its explanatory limits: "You are suffering from this or that thing because . . . the Oedipus complex". In this context, incest is the limit of every explanation.

The causality of *primal parricide* goes beyond these limits; it is close to a dynamic of causation[5] in which cause and effect do not follow on from one another but are simultaneous. Its metapsychological value resides in the fact that it makes the Freudian idea of the *universal* character of the Oedipus complex conceptually possible, beyond the "concrete universals" of structures and historical contents. Unlike the Oedipus complex of the unconscious in the first topography, and the thirdness sustained by Western cultural constructions, here the issue is one of psychic death.

In our hypothesis of a double oedipal causality involving two contradictory definitions of the Oedipus, we argue in favour of the coexistence of a double logic: one takes account of the Oedipus on the basis of reality-testing; it judges the existence of the father, in conformity with the *ambivalence* towards the *living father*. The other confronts the existence—without judgement, without the value contributed by the experience of the sense-organs, without memory—of the madness of instinctual realization. For the first, we will speak of the *Oedipus of the Ucs.*, and for the second of the *Oedipus of the id.*

The primal content of the Oedipus of the id, on account of its existence outside any object relationship that qualifies and attaches the drive to the representational and fantasy-based logics and causalities of oedipal triangulation, necessarily remains traumatic. The reality of the primal impulse represents a deep source of negative potential that permanently threatens representational psychic reality.

On the vast theoretical horizon of the Oedipus complex, we situate our hypothesis of an Oedipus of the id as an event lacking in psychic quality. The accomplishment of the motional drive, which has no object and no desire, will become comprehensible only under the condition that a transformation into a figurability takes place, the content of which is that the *murder of the father* has occurred. This *"figurability" of the murder of the father* constitutes the traumatic source of the content of the Oedipus complex, marking it forever with the stamp of guilt which no analysis of individual guilt will really be able to transcend. *In psychoanalysis, the third function pertains to a transformational evolution, which ranges from the instinctual fulfilment of the Oedipus of the id to the most avowed links of Eros in the triangular configuration of the oedipal drama.*

Nonetheless, we want to stress the fact that the "chaotic" reality of the id's energy can neither evolve nor be exhausted, that the *murder of the father*, as primal potential of the Oedipus of the id, referring indistinctly to the cause and effect, to the fulfilment and effectiveness of the instinctual impulse, persists and continues throughout life to exert pressure on sexuality as well as on the Oedipus complex as a permanent source of an unqualifiable unconscious state for consciousness. The debate on the cultural character of the Oedipus complex needs to be reconsidered in the light of the notion of the Oedipus of the id, whose foundation is the imperious vital need to achieve visual representation [*darstellen, figurer*] in order to restrain the immediacy of the motor discharge of the id's instinctual impulses, of naming it so as to be able to think.

The notion of Oedipus of the id thus makes it possible to think differently about what Freud called, successively, the "feeling of unconscious guilt", the "negative therapeutic reaction", the "resistance of the id" or the "biological bedrock" [*Gewachsener Fels*], which he always refers to with the idea in mind of a structural and even a biological limit to analytic treatment. The idea of the existence of an Oedipus of the id would facilitate the approach to what, in the negative therapeutic reaction, pertains to the negative potential of the infantile trauma (C. Botella & Botella, 2004, p. 109; Freud, 1939a [1937–39), which cannot present itself to consciousness.

The negation of the murder: transformational primal processes

The notion of *primary processes*, referring essentially to a circulation of energy between ideas [*représentations*] governed by displacement and condensation, is insufficient to account for the field of action of instinctual impulses, or of the "chaotic" dynamic of the a-representational id and of its immediateness. The id neither memorizes nor represents; without temporality, without desire for an object, "im-personal", it is only capable of discharge. So how are we to conceive of the processes which have their origin in the id?

We are resorting to the Freudian terms of *primal* [*Ur*] and of *precipitate* [*Niederschlag*]. The prefix "*Ur*"[6] is usually translated in French as *originaire*, and as *primal* in English. Although it usually covers what is in the order of a remote temporality, such as *the primal, the prehistoric, the primitive, the archaic*, in Freud's thought it refers just as much to the sense of what is fundamental, constitutive, primordial, irrespective of any reference to time. In addition, by associating it with the idea of *precipitate*, Freud goes beyond and in any case adds complexity to the notion of the temporality of the *primal*.[7]

By the formulation *primal process* [*Urvorgang*],[8] which appeared in *Civilization and Its Discontents* (1930a)—and, to the best of our knowledge, this is the only time it appears in Freud's entire work—Freud means a process ranging from the trace of the murder of the primal father [*Urvater*] to the latter's elevation to the rank of divinity. He then compares him with the figure of Jesus Christ, who is killed and then deified—notably, as Bruno Delorme has recently shown, thanks to the evangelists, whose form of Greek rhetoric brought its power of persuasion to the content of the narrative (Delorme, 2009). The narration and its form transform the person of Jesus into the divine figure of Jesus Christ.

Following this interpretation, we are putting forward a hypothesis concerning individual psychic life: the process from the instinctual impulse to its *visual representability* [*mise en figurabilité*] in the form of the *murder of the father*, is a *primal process* [*Urvorgang*] whose successive narrations can lead to transformations in which the original form disappears in favour of a new creation. This would be the case for the Oedipus of the *Ucs*.[9]

The *primal processes* engendered by the id may be said to be *transformational*, conveying both its kinetic energy and precipitates of constitutive elements of infantile prehistory.

We know that, in the emerging psyche, the blind force of the "untamed" [*Bändigung*][10] instinctual impulse of the id, lawless and object-less, will, owing to the successive failures of the hallucinatory process of satisfaction, be "tamed" and obliged to undergo a progressive transformation, leading to recognition of the existence of the object. It may be assumed that a series of moments exist in which the infant alternates between recognition of the object—and pleasure will become dependent on its presence—and moments when he makes do without its presence in moments of hallucinatory satisfaction—an alternation that is equivalent to successive "murders" of the object (Winnicott, 1969). The *murder of the father*, which Freud located at the dawn of humanity, may be understood, in fact, as the production of a transformational process belonging to the emerging individual psyche. In order to become drives of the *Ucs.*, linked to object-representations, the instinctual impulses of the id are involved in successive "murders" of objects, culminating in the progressive idealization of the object that was killed in the past. Winnicott clearly identified this process, and Freud had already had an intuition of it 1915:

> At the very beginning, it seems, the external world, objects, and what is hated are identical. If later on an object turns out to be a source of pleasure, it is loved, but it is also incorporated into the ego; so that for the purified pleasure-ego once again objects coincide with what is extraneous and hated. [Freud, 1915c, p. 136]

In other words, for Freud, the object is born in hate. He was to pursue this theme in 1925 in his article "Negation": "The first and immediate aim, therefore, of reality-testing is, not to *find* an object in real perception which corresponds to the one presented, but to *refind* such an object, to convince oneself that it is still there" (Freud, 1925h, p. 237).

We would add: the energetic negation that we inflict on it. Then, when Freud says: "What is unreal, merely a presentation and subjective, is only internal; what is real is also there *outside*" (p. 237), he leads us to think that reality-testing operates according to a double contradictory conviction—namely, that the object exists "Only inside—Also outside". There is, then, a double psychic movement containing an incompatibility that is nonetheless complementary: an indication of animism that is inconceivable at the level of secondary thinking. It is out of this psychic work, similar to a magical technique, that the sense of existence and of reality will emerge.[11] It corresponds to Freud's conception where perception is envisaged as a "confirmation" of a presentation, itself a "reproduction" of the perception which is a continual transformational primal process: the murder of the object (only inside), and its recognition (also outside), requires "simultaneously" an "only inside" . . . In fact, reality-testing is far from being a simple objective observation; it would be truer to say that it is a permanent process of negation and abandonment of negation, without temporal succession, of simultaneity that is incomprehensible for our secondary processes.

For a general theory of transformational processes

Three Freudian ideas could underpin such a theory.

1. At the same time as he was developing the notion of the id, Freud developed from 1923 onwards the notion of *Eros* whose raison d'être is to "complicate life by bringing about a more and more far-reaching combination of the particles into which living substance is dispersed . . ." (Freud, 1923b, p. 40). He was searching, in fact, for a better notion to combat the death drive than that of the life drives; his aim was to clarify his thinking concerning the *means* and the *manner* of combating the death drive introduced in *Beyond the Pleasure Principle* (1920g). To the first part of this question—that of knowing which *means* (*or force*) is involved—he had already given an answer, but the term of life drive, forcing a conflictual duality that is non-specific to psychoanalysis, was too vague, and even speculative, whereas with the introduction of the notion of *Eros* he found the answer to the issue of the *manner* of combating the *death drive*. In 1938, in the *Outline of Psycho-Analysis* [1940a [1938], Freud used the same formulation as in 1923, concluding that "The aim of Eros . . . is, in short, to *bind together*" (p. 148). He is just as assertive as he had been in 1920: the *binding* of instinctual impulses is "one of the earliest and most important functions of the mental apparatus . . . a preparatory act which introduces and assures the domination of the pleasure principle" (Freud, 1920g, p. 62). We can get an idea of the intensity and complexity of the work of the transformational processes of binding characteristic of Eros if we recall an analogy Freud makes in a passage of *The Interpretation of Dreams* with reference to some lines from Goethe (Faust I). To describe the multiple combinations which occur in the dream work, he compares the latter with that of the weaver: "a thousand threads one treadle throws . . . and an infinite combination grows" (see Freud, 1900a, p. 283).

2. On several occasions throughout his work, Freud uses a chemical metaphor to capture the essence of transformational processes more clearly. It is explicitly formulated in the lectures given at

Clark University in 1909: the experience of the transference is compared to a chemical process in which the analyst plays the role, Freud says, borrowing a phrase from Ferenczi, of a *catalytic ferment* (Freud, 1910a [1909], p. 51). He refers to it again in his intervention at the 1918 Budapest IPA Congress (Freud, 1919a [1918], p. 161). Analytic treatment is envisaged as the result of "chemical precipitations"; which means that, under certain conditions, a change in the state of quality can trigger processes transforming various elements and creating a new product. This leads us to think that Eros and the imperative of binding act permanently on the mind and its transformational primal processes.

3. But nothing is simple with Freud—for, taking up an old idea, which he had first set out in *The Interpretation of Dreams* (Freud, 1900a), in *Totem and Taboo* (1912–13), and also in his *New Introductory Lectures on Psycho-Analysis* (Freud, 1933a), he warns us of the limits of his chemical metaphor and explains the need for a law to regulate the endless swamping of the capacities of *Eros*: there is a *function* in us which demands "unity, connection and intelligibility"[12] (Freud, 1912–13, p. 95).

Basing ourselves on these three ideas, we proposed some time ago the notion of a *Principle of Convergence-Coherence* (C. Botella & Botella, 1992, 1996), which governs psychic life, complementing the pleasure principle and the reality principle. It involves a global tendency, governing the totality of the dynamics of psychic functioning. Its aim is to oppose any form of psychic heterogeneity, to clarify by *making intelligible* all the heterogeneous elements present at a given moment. The processes of transformation will then allow a certain unity to be formed that is as coherent as possible. When psychic conditions are favourable, the outcome is an original creation, sometimes at the price of not responding to the demands of reality—the model being the manifest content of the dream.

Transformational processes resist the tendency to discharge and contribute, through contact with the primary object, to delimiting erogenous zones. Maternal reverie and the instinctual impulse thus "tamed" will support in the child the intelligibility of everything that his developing psyche suffers.

For a broadening of the theory of analytic practice

By taking into consideration the traumatic sources of the Oedipus complex and *transformational processes*, there are grounds for broadening the theory of analytic treatment in such a way that its dynamics would not be limited to that of representational psychoneurosis; analysis would not simply be seen, following the spirit of classical analysis, as a quest for a repressed historical past or, following a tendency of post-Kleinian analysis, as a means of getting in touch again with early object-relations. These objectives, while being necessary and indispensable, can neither make intelligible nor explain the complexity of the analytic process in its full scope. Beyond these objectives, and complementarily, an analysis must resolve other problems. This other dynamic concerns the *binding capacity of transformational primal processes* capable of producing links where representational deficiencies have left points of rupture or gaping holes, and of modifying structural configurations.

Two major paths could be distinguished in analytic practice.

1. One corresponds to the *classical procedure* (Freud, 1923a [1922]), p. 235)—mainly preconscious, with a progressive aim, and, in a certain way, not without a touch of voluntarism, seeking to discover what is already there but buried. The usual Freudian metaphor for it is that of an *archaeological procedure*. It constitutes the regular and ongoing work of the analyst whose model is the analysis of the dream narrative. Free association takes place under the pressure of *purposive ideas* [*Zielvorstellungen*] that have remained hidden, of repressed unconscious wishes, and of unconscious fantasy. The interventions and interpretations of the analysts are made within the framework of the first topography. This *archaeological path* is particularly necessary and effective in the treatments of psychoneuroses in order to bring to light repressed memories.

. Another path of access to the patient's unconscious reality is, in our view, possible: we call it *transformational*. It represents a complement to the classical, *archaeological* procedure. This *transformational path*, a terrain on which the activity of *primal processes* occurs, opens up more easily in the regressive–retrogressive conditions of the dream and up to a certain point in the regressive–retrogressive situation of the session, where a hybrid psychic state can occur which we call the *state of session* (C. Botella & Botella, 2004, p. 80): semi-daytime, semi-night-time. Free association and purposive ideas lose their power there, to the extent even that there may be a rupture at the representational level and a transition to another level dominated by sensory experience, through a *quasi-endopsychic hallucinatory state*, visual or auditory, sometimes projected onto the space of perception.

The objective of this *transformational path* coincides with that of the dream-work which Freud clarified in 1932 by rectifying what he had said hitherto. In fact, the concluding lines of Lecture XXIX (1933a, pp. 7–39) teach us that the fulfilment of an infantile wish as the first objective of the dream-work is, in the final analysis, in the service of a primordial function "which prepares and introduces the pleasure principle", the function of *binding*, the principal aim of Eros. Just as during the dream-work, where the different heterogeneous elements that are simultaneously present, including the *negative* of unrepresented traumas, are transformed into a new formation possessing a new quality, into a hallucinatory content, similarly, in the *state of session*, the analyst's thought-activity, having taken a backward, retrogressive direction, can also acquire the possibility of *binding*, of *transforming* the different heterogeneous elements of the session into a unity, bringing intelligibility to the *negative* of infantile traumas that the patient has neither been able to think about nor represent. In other words, it is a matter of creating coherence where before there was only *memory without recollection and the negative of psychic trauma* (C. Botella & Botella, 2004, p. 109). Nameless suffering can thus acquire meaning and be integrated into the patient's history. Let us say that if the so-called archaeological interventions of the analyst operate on a vertical present–past axis, then so-called transformational ones operate on a horizontal axis in the present of the session: the meaning that emerges reveals not a past but a negative that the patient has never been able to think about, picture, or form a conception of.

With the clinical case that follows, we present a session with moments of *retrogression* in the analyst's thinking and in that of the patient, leading to ruptures in the flow of free association. We can see how a transition from the representational mode of intelligibility to a quasi endo-hallucinatory state opens up the path to transformational processes, to a *"work of figurability"*—that is, of depicting the unrepresentable *negative* in the patient.

A clinical illustration

In the last session, which is the one we are concerned with here, the patient told a dream: *"You are going to have a shower . . . but I do not follow you."* He did not say anything about the dream, and the analyst, somewhat surprised by such a short account whose violence could be sensed in the rough, imperious, abrupt manner of stating, *"I do not follow you"*, opted for an attitude of waiting. The following day, having just settled onto the couch, the patient exclaimed: "I saw you this morning . . . You were on the Boulevard St Michel." The analyst had not seen him. Unlike the dream of the previous session, this purely coincidental encounter immediately took a central place in the session, beginning with the fact that the patient had had a negative hallucination of the analyst's wife, who had been with him. But very quickly the patient began to doubt his recollection: "It was you that I saw, wasn't it?" Interspersed with intervals of silence, the doubts continued, becoming more insistent, and the patient seemed increasingly uneasy: "I think I saw you . . . It's true, isn't it? I'm no longer certain I saw you . . . You were wearing dark glasses, weren't you?" He became increasingly tense, and uneasy: "I don't know any more if I saw you or not . . . You had dark glasses on, didn't you?" During this time, the impressions arising from the patient's doubts aroused in the analyst a sense of uncanniness. Surreptitiously, an image began to emerge in his mind, accompanied by a word that had not come from the analysand and was not one he himself usually used: this word was "hieratic". His *"work of figurability"* could be summed up by the phrase: "Me hieratic with dark glasses". Vague thoughts came to him, also shrouded in doubt: "Dark glasses . . . but do we say dark glasses? Don't we say sunglasses? Dark glasses—the glasses used by a blind man . . . ? It's strange, dark glasses. . . ." Suddenly, the analyst had the impression that he had understood, that he had made a discovery: "Ah, glasses for mourning!" But his thoughts continued to be permeated by doubt: "Hieratic? What does hieratic mean? Solemn? Or rigid, perhaps? Me rigid? dead?" And once again there was a sense of discovery: "Ah, a living–dead!"

While he was having these thoughts, the patient became silent. It was a heavy silence, longer, more pregnant than usual; the analyst had the impression that something important was happening in the patient. Practically without realizing it, the patient interrupted the silence with a questioning mumble, "Erm? I don't know any more if I saw you or not . . .", said the patient, and he then added the astonishing formulation: "I can't see any more if I saw you . . . I'm looking for you in image, and I can't find you any more." With the same violence with which he had made the analyst's wife disappear in the street, he now made the analyst disappear in his recollection of the encounter. The patient had now calmed down again. He had needed to adopt extreme measures to fight off unrepresentable anxiety.

Feeling calmer, the patient changed register and mentioned the dream of the last session. The analyst had forgotten his nightmare. The patient interpreted: "If in the dream I don't follow you into the shower, it's because something prevents me from doing so." He was baiting the analyst who, quite naturally, was on the verge of making a comment on the subject of homosexuality. The session had suddenly become ordinary, with the possibility of repression returning, a discovery of memory-traces, of repressed ideas: the usual oedipal configuration in an inverted form. But simultaneously, almost imperceptibly, the analyst had a vague feeling that his patient wanted to attract him towards this context of homosexuality and of an inverted Oedipus complex, but that this was superficial, covering up another problem that corresponded to the violent movements before he had calmed down. The analyst kept quiet. The patient did not have anything else to add about the dream and didn't know what to say. Perhaps he felt frustrated by the fact that the analyst wasn't saying anything. "Shall I tell you about my duty period? (he had been on duty at the hospital] . . . Since I have nothing else... There were three deaths." The words came out suddenly, bluntly, and the forgotten nightmare came back to the analyst equally suddenly: three deaths... three weekly sessions.... Then the patient spoke about an elderly couple, former deportees; the widow had particularly irritated him because he felt that her husband's death had come as a relief to her; but, as he had cancer it was perhaps better for him that he had died. And when the patient added: "It was obvious that she didn't want to follow him", a striking link was established in the analyst's mind, leading to the idea: "Ah! The thing is, he didn't want to follow me into the shower either... into death!" The analyst then had the impression that the entire session was falling into place, acquiring meaning, and becoming coherent. "Following me into the shower", negative hallucinations, and "Living–dead" were thus all connected by the notion of a violent death. The analyst now understood his intuition that the analysand's homosexual transference had the function of covering something up. Murder was the kingpin. It was against this world of ego-disorganization, of terror, of an act carried out before it could even be conceived of that homosexual investments in the analysand were functioning as a lifeline. And while the patient was speaking again about deportation camps, the idea of death in the shower took on a terrifying dimension for the analyst. As the patient returned again to the dream, the analyst heard himself saying: "The shower is a gas chamber." The intervention triggered liberating and violent sobbing in the patient, which he was unable to control for the rest of the session and only with great difficulty once he was standing up again.

We will confine ourselves to discussing the elements that closely concern our hypothesis of an Oedipus of the id and the role of transformational processes in the session. We will take the dream as our starting-point. Roughly speaking, it indicates homosexuality towards the father and its rejection, in order to go towards the mother: the two sides of a classical Oedipus complex in the boy. However, these oedipal investments are so fragile and unstable that they are unable to constitute a lasting oedipal configuration. They represented a measure of protection against anxieties of another order than castration, whose nature became progressively clearer after this session.

The patient's dream was simple, direct, more perceptive than hallucinatory; primary processes were of a rudimentary nature, there was a short displacement of the father onto the analyst in the context of an undistorted reminiscence of a daily scene: his father, because of his job, had to take a shower as soon as he got home from work at the end of the day. The dream is thus limited to the repetition of a scene from the past, almost without disguise. Is there a prohibited wish that is fulfilled in the dream? Do the words, "I don't follow you" really mean "I wish my mother . . . "? And if our reply is negative, what force can be said to have triggered the dream? We did not have an answer at the time when this analysis took place;[13] now an answer has become possible. The retrogressive course of the patient's thinking, as well as of the analyst's, has thrown light on the matter.

In the regression of the session, an actualization of instinctual chaos specific to the id was created, annihilating any form of object-representation, paternal or maternal, including that of the ego as well. The nature of the violence of the words "I do not follow you" had now been elucidated by the statement, "The shower is a gas chamber", whose metaphorical power brought meaning to the unnameable suffering, to the gaping hole that governed the patient's representational networks. But the statement, "The shower is a gas chamber" remained enigmatic for the patient for a long time, because it did not possess the virtues of clarification of an interpretation. The quality of the intervention lay elsewhere. It provided an immediate link endowed with transformational power giving meaning to an infantile terror whose content, rather than having been repressed, had been erased, leaving no memory-traces. Starting out from such a *negative of trauma,* from a trauma that took place but that had never been represented or thought (Winnicott), the analytic work progressively constructed representations of the past equivalent to the return of memories: in his early childhood, at around the age of 3 or 4—it's impossible to be more precise—the family, of modest origin, had to frequent the public baths. There was one side for the men and another for the women and children. Mother and child were both naked under the shower; a demonstrative mother with sensual gestures washed the excited child, who was pressed against his mother's body, his face at the level of her sexual organs. With the father eliminated, the oedipal triumph, under conditions of the extreme *jouissance* of accomplished incest, surpassed the child's capacities for integration. The panic of the ego transformed it into unrepresentable and unthinkable terror that could not be inscribed as a memory trace and become a recollection to repress. Only the retrogressive movement of the dream, first, and then that of the state of session mobilizing transformational processes was capable of making accessible the "site of the crime" committed, which had remained unnameable.

So, in the case of this small child, the repetition of the conditions of the shower, and its violently incestuous character, meant that the elimination of the paternal object acquired the unconscious value of a realization of a *murder of the father*. This *murder* could neither be represented nor generate a sense of guilt accessible to representational systems. Without representation, without guilt, the murder could not give rise to repression, nor to realizations disguised in dreams. It was the representational gaps and the violence characteristic of the id that would mark the patient's mode of relating. The violence of the words, "I do not follow you" was equivalent to saying, "I eliminate you"; it was the same violence that was present in the negative hallucination eliminating the presence of the analyst's wife when he saw them in the street; and the same model of *murder* is present in the statement, "I cannot see you any more in the image of the recollection."

The insufficiency of the constitution of the Oedipus complex of the *Ucs.* means that the eruption of an Oedipus of the id will occupy the foreground. However, the few minor displacements that occurred in the course of the session are signs of an attempt at elaboration. But these attempts at elaboration, with the help of primary processes and following the conflictual dynamic of the first topography, fail. The primal processes of the id impose their mode of actualization: the *murder* of the analyst attested by the word "black" ("*lunettes noires*": dark glasses)—which the analyst tries to understand by means of the *figurability* that emerges in his mind: "living–dead".

Thanks to this, the analyst is able to give an intelligible form to the effects of the Oedipus of his patient's id, which thus become representable and can enter into a network of associations characteristic of the Oedipus complex. Once temporal succession and individual causality have emerged, the acts link up in a lasting way in the order of the narratives: incest at three years of age, the father's showers at home, transference onto the analyst . . .

One more point. For the practitioner of analysis, neither an analytic conception referring solely to a practice of psychoanalyst as an "archaeologist" of reminiscences, nor a practice that is exclusively centred on the model of the object relation, are sufficient to explain the complexity of all the many changes and transformations that occur during an analysis. The treatment of so-called borderline patients has meant that analytic practice has progressed faster than theoretical knowledge. A broadening of the theory of analysis has become urgent. We hope to contribute to this with the hypothesis of the Oedipus of the id and the idea of a transformational path.

Notes

Translated by Andrew Weller.

1. Warning: editorial limits have obliged us to make choices: thus we have chosen to confine ourselves to certain Freudian foundations. But it is clear that we have also drawn inspiration from other authors, such as Winnicott, Bion, Viderman, Marty and Green.

2. Laplanche & Pontalis (1973, pp. 282–283): "Organised body of loving and hostile wishes which the child experiences towards its parents. In its so-called *positive* form, the complex appears as in the story of *Oedipus Rex*: a desire for the death of the rival—the parent of the same sex and a sexual desire for the parent of the opposite sex. In its *negative* form, we find the reverse picture: love for the parent of the same sex, and jealous hatred for the parent of the opposite sex. In fact, the two versions are to be found in varying degrees in what is known as the *complete* form of the complex."

3. Freud (1923b, p. 31): "an individual's first and most important identification is with the father in his own personal prehistory". But Freud adds in a footnote: "Perhaps it would be safer to say 'with the parents'; for before a child has arrived at definite knowledge of the difference between the sexes, the lack of a penis, it does not distinguish in value between its father and its mother."

4. Oedipus kills an old man who represents no investment but is merely an obstacle on his path. The legend does not say that Oedipus desired Jocasta, nor that he fought to be the King of Thebes. It is because he resolves the enigma that the sphinx poses him that he is named king and

consequently marries the woman who is already the queen. The whole tragedy occurs "because of this power that the city gave me without my having asked for it", says Oedipus (Sophocles, *Oedipe Roi*; Dreyfus, 1967, p. 658). "The subject of Oedipus Rex is not the fulfilment of the destiny of Oedipus, but the discovery by Oedipus that his destiny has been fulfilled" (p. 629).

5. "Causation designates the very operation of the cause, the effectiveness of the production of the effect" (Jacob, 1990). Causation seems to us to be constitutive of primordial psychic processes (C. Botella & Botella, 1995).

6. It can be found on many different occasions in Freud's work: *Urphantasien* [primal fantasies], *Urszenen* [primal scenes], *Urvater* [primal father], *Urtriebe* [primal instinctual drives], *Urtrauma* [primal trauma], *Urfixierung* [primal fixation], *Urhorde* [primal horde], *Mutterbild Urzeitlich* [primal mother image], *Urverbrechen* [primal crime] *Urverdrängung* [primal repression], *Urworte* [primal words], *Urmensch* [primal man], and others.

7. Here are its best-known formulations: "The form is the precipitate of an earlier content". "Symptoms ... are the precipitates of earlier emotional experiences" (Freud, 1910a [1909], p. 14); "On the other hand, these forces which act like dams upon sexual development—disgust, shame and morality—must also be regarded as *historical precipitates* of the external inhibitions to which the sexual instinct has been subjected during the psychogenesis of the human race" (1905d—note added 1915, p. 162). "There is naturally nothing to prevent our supposing that the instincts themselves are, at least in part, *precipitates of the effects of external stimulation*, which in the course of phylogenesis have brought about modifications in the living substance" (1915c, p. 120). "The superego is in fact a *precipitate of the first object-cathexes of the id* and is the heir to the Oedipus complex" (1926e, p. 223). "*precipitates from the history of human civilization*. The Oedipus complex ... is one of them" (1918b [1914], p. 119).

8. Similarly, on several occasions Freud felt the need to refer to the idea of *primal instincts* [*Urtriebe*] (1937c, pp. 243, 245–246; see also 1910c, p. 72; 1915c, p. 125).

9. Various Freudians notions are similar to the notion of transformation: psychic working over/out [*Verarbeitung*], working-through [*Durcharbeiten*], work of mourning [*Trauerarbeit*], binding [*Bindung*] and Eros.

10. As *Untamed Memory*. "*Only after this is* [the] *memory a tamed memory like any other*" (Freud, 1950 [1895], p. 382).

11. We understand "outside–inside" not in the bodily sense, but as signalling the boundaries between "ego and non-ego", which are not only always hypothetical and constantly in need of being reconstituted, but also constantly menaced by the possibility of animistic regression. Moreover, defining the sense of reality as a consequence of a magic technique is

a considerable problem. This idea becomes more acceptable if we take account of the fact that all evolution in the psyche is based on what the latter is at this very moment, on the use of what prevailed formerly without impediment.

12. *"Vereinheitlichung, Zusammenhang und Verständlichkeit."*

13. At the time when this analysis took place, we spoke of "working as a double" (see C. Botella & Botella, 2004, pp. 71–77).

6

The negative in dreams

Joachim F. Danckwardt

Negation in the analytic situation

"Now you'll think I mean to say something insulting, but really I've no such intention" (Freud, 1925h, p. 235): this is an example of negation in the analytic situation representing a semantic "no". Of course, there is also the possibility of a performative–actional or gestural "no" in the analytic situation—for instance, in the form of the analysand's shaking his/her head. But such an example would not conform to Freud's notion of the content of a repressed image or idea making its way into consciousness on condition that it is negated. Freud's negation would actually be a way of taking cognizance of what is repressed and thus would imply a specific way of perceiving.

Unlike in the waking state of the analytic situation, there is no semantic negation to be found in dreams, "whereby the subject, while formulating one of these wishes, thoughts or feelings, which have been repressed hitherto, contrives, by disowning it, to continue to defend himself against it" (Laplanche & Pontalis, 1973, p. 261). This only applies to negation in the psychoanalytic situation. Negation as it is conceived of by Freud is probably the most common negative therapeutic reaction we meet within the mental frame of the psychoanalytic situation. In this specific state of mind, as a characteristic of the analytic situation, preconscious–imaginative thinking prevails, and in this regard it differs principally from any discursive-logical forms of thinking. Terms such as daydream-thinking, daydream-work, and daydream-life may best tally with this state of mind in the analytic situation.

Negation between analytic sessions

But how does negation manifest itself outside the analytic situation—that is, between analytic sessions? Suppose, the analysand was actually dreaming and in an altered state of mind—that is, in a state of primary process thinking! And then the analysand brings his/her dream into the following psychoanalytic session, recollecting and recounting the dream! It is true, the analysand in the analytic situation may make use of semantic negation: "You ask who this person in the dream can be. It's *not* my mother" (Freud, 1925h, p. 235). And in the session the analysand might pretend: "It's true that my mother came into my mind as I thought of this person, but I don't feel inclined to let the association count" (Freud, 1925h, p. 235). However, during the actual process of dreaming the analysand could only replace his mother in a visual–hallucinatory symbolic form with the figure of another person and thus negate her.

Freud does not explicitly deal with the issue of "negation in dreams" in a special article. The topic also does not figure in any of the various editions of *The Interpretation of Dreams*, the term is not even mentioned in the index of his dream book. There is only one quotation from Du Prel concerning the question, "as to whether consciousness and mind are identical. This preliminary question is answered in the negative by dreams" (Freud, 1900a, p. 612).

Negation in dreams between analytic sessions

As for the issue of negation in dreams, there are only scattered references in Freud's collected works. In "The Antithetical Meaning of Primal Words", Freud states:

We obtain from [the well-known linguist] C. Abel [1837–1906] the astonishing information that the behaviour of the dream-work which I have just described is identical with a peculiarity in the oldest languages known to us. [Freud, 1910e, p. 156]

Freud begins the above article with a quotation from the chapter on dream-work in his *The Interpretation of Dreams* (Freud, 1900a, p. 232):

The way in which dreams treat the category of contraries and contradictions is highly remarkable. It is simply disregarded. "No" seems not to exist so far as dreams are concerned. They show a particular preference for combining contraries into a unity or for representing them as one and the same thing. Dreams feel themselves at liberty, moreover, to represent any element by its wishful contrary; so that there is no way of deciding at a first glance whether any element that admits of a contrary is present in the dream-thoughts as a positive or as a negative. [Freud, 1910e, p. 155]

In the chapter on "Affects in Dreams", Freud explains the functioning of negation in dreams as instigated by the specific nature of the dream-work. The dream-work effects the "no" by means of inhibition of affect, which is achieved by the censorship of the dream. The censorship is responsible not only for the distortion in the dream, but also for the inhibition of affect by creating an antithetical representation—that is, an antithetical affect representation. Freud's dream of the "open-air closet" may serve us here as an example.

Freud's dream of the open-air closet

I will here give as an instance a dream in which the indifferent feeling-tone of the content of the dream can be explained by the antithesis between the dream-thoughts. It is a short dream, which will fill every reader with disgust. A hill, on which there was something like an open-air closet: a very long seat with a large hole at the end of it. Its back edge was thickly covered with small heaps of faeces of all sizes and degrees of freshness. There were bushes behind the seat. I micturated on the seat; a long stream of urine washed everything clean; the lumps of faeces came away easily and fell into the opening. It was as though at the end there was still some left. Why did I feel no disgust during this dream? Because, as the analysis showed, the most agreeable and satisfying thoughts contributed to bringing the dream about. [Freud, 1900a, pp. 470–471]

Freud's associations to the dream reveal him as a great man—for example, as Hercules sweeping the Augean stables, or as Gulliver extinguishing the great fire of Lilliput with a stream of urine, or as Rabelais' superman Gargantua taking revenge, and so on. Freud's associations include the day-residues that caused the dream in first place. What made the dream exciting was Freud's day-time mood of revulsion and disgust about his grubbing about in human dirt in his lecture on the connection between hysteria and perversion in which he cleared up the errors and prejudices in his former theory of the neuroses (Anzieu, 1986; Grinstein, 1980).

According to the theory of wish-fulfilment, this dream would not have become possible if the antithetical megalomanic train of thought (which, it is true, was suppressed, but had a pleasurable tone) had not emerged in addition to the feeling of disgust. For what is distressing may not be represented in a dream; nothing in our dream-thoughts which is distressing can force an entry into a dream unless it at the same time lends a disguise to the fulfilment of a wish. There is yet another alternative way in which the dream-work can deal with affects in the dream-thoughts, in addition to allowing them through or reducing them to nothing. It can turn them into their opposite. We have already become acquainted with the interpretative rule according to which every element in a dream can, for purposes of interpretation, stand for its opposite just as easily as for itself. We can never tell beforehand whether it stands for the one or for the other; only the context can decide. A suspicion of this truth has evidently found its way into popular consciousness: "dream-books" very often adopt the principle of contraries in their interpretation of dreams. [Freud, 1900a, pp. 470–471]

In his paper "Negation", Freud elaborates that in waking life negation allows the content of a repressed image or idea caused by painful experiences to enter into consciousness only on condition that it is negated. The result of this is merely an intellectual acceptance that avoids unpleasure, because what is essential to the repression (its affective component representing the repression of the instinctual wish) persists. Secondary process thinking indicating the transition from the pleasure-ego to the reality-ego "can only cathect an idea if it is in a position to inhibit any development of unpleasure that may proceed from it" (Freud, 1900a, p. 601). This can be achieved by negation only in waking life, not in dream-life. On these premises negation in waking life has to be considered an indispensable driving force in the development of mental functioning, along with the generation of symbolic systems.

> With the help of the *symbol of negation*, thinking frees itself from the restrictions of repression and enriches itself with material that is indispensable for its proper functioning. [Freud, 1925h, pp. 236; italics added]

> But the performance of the function of judgement is not made possible until the creation of the *symbol of negation* has endowed thinking with a first measure of freedom from the consequences of repression and, with it, from the compulsion of the pleasure principle. [Freud, 1925h, p. 239; italics added]

Since the dream cannot produce a *semantic no*, there can therefore in the dream be no autonomous *function of judgement* emerging out of the former. Nevertheless we come across a number of dreams that contain judgement, criticism, and affirmation. Here is Freud's relevant statement on the matter:

> Everything that appears in dreams as the ostensible activity of the function of judgement is to be regarded not as an intellectual achievement of the dream-work but as belonging to the material of the dream-thoughts and as having been lifted from them into the manifest content of the dream as a ready-made structure. [Freud, 1900a, p. 445]

Today this view is no longer shared by psychoanalysts belonging to the various Kleinian or Bionian schools of thought who further developed Freud's dream theory. Donald Meltzer, for instance, in his re-examination of psychoanalytic theory and technique in his book *Dream-Life* (1988, p. 114), argues that because of the interaction of visual and verbal language in the dream, dreaming generates a different grammatical mode of thinking that could be conceived of as unconscious affect-thinking.

Negation, function of judgement, and drive theory

Upon a closer reading of Freud's statements concerning the topic of negation and the function of judgement in the dream, certain indications can be found of an issue that in Freud's paper "Negation" is only implicitly referred to here and there. In elaborating the issue of negation, Freud lays out some elements of his theory of thinking by making certain assumptions concerning the development of the intellectual function of judgement as well as reality-testing. The function of judgement affirms or disaffirms the possession by a thing of a particular attribute and it asserts or disputes that a presentation has an existence in reality. The capacity of affirming or disaffirming of the possession of attributes—that is, the capacity to say "yes" and/or "no"—Freud traces back to the earliest stage of ego development dominated by the workings of an archaic pleasure-ego. This is an implicit echo of his earlier paper on "Instincts and Their Vicissitudes" (Freud, 1915c, 136 pp.). In this paper Freud develops his first theory of the drives according to which the pleasure-ego wants to introject into itself everything that is good and to eject from itself (project) everything that is bad. Thus introjection and projection can be said to represent the most archaic form of judgement, respectively, of saying yes and/or no. What is the next step in this development in the Freudian line of argumentation? It is the intellectual (higher level) capacity of judgement:

> Judging is a continuation, along lines of expediency, of the original process by which the ego took things into itself or expelled them from itself, according to the pleasure principle. The polarity of judgement appears to correspond to the opposition of the two groups of instincts which we have supposed to exist. *Affirmation—as a substitute for uniting—belongs to Eros; negation—the successor to expulsion—belongs to the instinct of destruction.*
> [Freud, 1925h, p. 239; italics added]

Freud conceives of the "instinct of destruction" as the death instinct directed against the external world.

> But the performance of the function of judgement is not made possible until the creation of the *symbol of negation* has endowed thinking with a first measure of freedom from the consequences of repression and, with it, from the compulsion of the pleasure principle. [Freud, 1925h, p. 239; italics added]

What is manifested as negation is nothing but the *transformed action of expulsion*. In other words, the death instinct undergoes transformation towards higher level thinking. "A negative judgement is the intellectual substitute for repression" (Freud, 1925h, p. 236).

Freud's implicit further development of his hypothesis of the life and death instincts

The paper "Negation" contains, according to Joseph Sandler (1983, 1992) an implicit further development of the hypotheses already outlined by Freud in "Instincts and Their Vicissitudes" and in *Beyond the Pleasure Principle*. Thus "Negation" belongs in a certain sense to the series of works based on the hypothesis of the life- and death instincts, including "Instincts and Their Vicissitudes" (1915c), *Beyond the Pleasure Principle* (1920g), *The Ego and the Id* (1923b), and "Negation" (1925h). In this context, two things are noteworthy. First, Freud dispensed with any of his controversial biological hypotheses or any references to organic matter on which he had based his earlier line of argumentation. Now, Freud focused exclusively on the psychological aspects of his theory of the drives: "Its source is a state of excitation in the body, its aim is the removal of that excitation; on its path from its source to its aim the instinct becomes operative psychically" (Freud, 1933a, p. 96), in attaching itself to an object or by the lived relation to it (Freud, 1915c, p. 118). Instincts manifest themselves through their constant pressure and are mentally represented by affective and ideational representatives: "If the instinct did not attach itself to an idea or manifest itself as an affective state, we could know nothing about it" (Freud, 1915e, p. 177). Thus affects are the "qualitative expression of the quantity of instinctual energy and of its fluctuations" (Laplanche & Pontalis, 1973, p. 13).

Second, Freud was no longer concerned with finding evidence for the biological existence of the death instinct as such but was primarily concerned with making full use of *the theoretical and explanatory potential inherent in his hypothesis of the death instinct in regard to the development of the function of judgement and the capacity of saying yes and/or no*. Yet for a long time no one seemed to have noticed it. What also went unnoticed for a long time is the fact that Freud left open the possibility of future synthesis of his various ideas and findings pertinent to this topic. And this conspicuous ignorance accounts for the fact that the entire discourse concerning Freud's hypothesis of the death instinct—unlike that of its opposite: the life instinct—got somehow stuck and came more or less to a standstill. A close and deep reading of the abovementioned series of Freud's articles, especially "Negation" as well as the pertinent chapters in *The Interpretation of Dreams*, distinguishes the more relevant from the less relevant lines of thought. As a result this also allows a connection to be made between implicit subtexts as well as an integration of bits of theory embedded in different semantic contexts. This strategic method helps to overcome a discourse where any discussion of the hypothesis of the life- and death instinct is reduced to a mere discussion of the death instinct and where the workings of the death instinct are exclusively deemed as an isolated futile destructive phenomenon—save its admitted homeostatic effect. Already in the 1990s, J. Laplanche had postulated that Eros and Thanatos should not be regarded as mere opposites (Laplanche, 1984, 1996; Reiter, 1996). Grotstein argued along similar lines (Grotstein, 2000). The separated and not synchronized [*dissoziierte*] development of the life–death instinct hypothesis contributed considerably to the tentative and controversial reception of the concept; people as a consequence expressed serious doubts as to its *theoretical value* and *clinical usefulness and applicability*. What in all of this unfortunately got lost is *the developmental aspect*—that is, *the vicissitudes of the instincts* (which includes *the death instinct*) as originally developed by Freud in his seminal paper *Instincts and their Vicissitudes*. Nevertheless, upon a closer reading of Freud's work one can identify implicit hypotheses and assumptions concerning the ideal or presumably normal function of the death instinct in terms of development and workings of the life–death instincts. Such a function he had already postulated for the early phase dominated by the pleasure principle. Here Freud attributes to the death instinct a *particular task*:

> ... the task of which [Thanatos] is to lead organic life back into the inanimate state; on the other hand, we supposed that Eros, by bringing about a more and more far-reaching combination of the particles into which living substance is dispersed, aims at complicating life [=combine organic substances into ever

larger unities; Freud, 1920g, p. 43)] and at the same time, of course, at preserving it. Acting in this way, both the instincts would be conservative in the strictest sense of the word, since both would be endeavouring to re-establish a state of things that was disturbed by the emergence of life. The emergence of life would thus be the cause of the continuance of life and also at the same time of the striving towards death; and life itself would be a conflict and compromise between these two trends. [Freud, 1923b, pp. 40–41]

A close and deep reading of "Negation" and the relevant chapters of *The Interpretation of Dreams* makes it possible to extricate from these works Freud's new and implicit "speculations". If the developmental process of the life- and death instincts evolves relatively undisturbed, the death instinct conceived of as a psychic agency interacting with other psychic regulatory systems makes profound sense. "By 'sense' we understand 'meaning', 'intention' and 'position in a continuous psychical context'" (Freud, 1916–17, p. 61). In that sense, for Freud *negation is the manifestation of the death instinct* on a higher intellectual level and is regarded by Freud as *the successor to expulsion*. Freud also makes the assumption that the pleasure-ego separates itself off from the object which means that it may not only destroy its link to the object but also attack the function of linking as such, in case the object proves to be not only incapable of providing complete *satisfaction* but also turns out to be a source that is incapable of *pacifying* the ego. Such detaching or attacks on linking are, however, not only destructive but they must also be thought of as acts of creation and re-creation, which means that, by way of splitting and projection, the developing ego, in a next step, becomes capable of re-constituting the object anew "outside". The capacity to distinguish between "inside and outside" and the process of "object-formation" has thus been set in motion. Freud calls this stage after the purely narcissistic stage has been given up "object-stage" (Freud, 1915c, p. 137). This means that the workings of the death instinct originally play an essential part in the process of object-formation and in the development of the capacity to distinguish between inside and outside, between subject and object. Thus the successful functioning of the death instinct must be ascribed a decisive role in the development of the various modes of mental functioning and the processes structuring the psyche. Therefore, it can be said that the death instinct and the life instinct are not only to be conceived of as complementary but have to be seen as functioning as a dialectical unit (Dorey, 1985, p. 98).

All this considered, it seems justified to make the assumption that there is a normal development of the functioning of the death instinct and on the basis of this premise to investigate the conditions that might compromise the functioning of the death instinct, rendering it pathogenic or pathoplastic. Although Freud did not explicitly make this distinction in his writings, it nevertheless is possible to infer it on the basis of a close reading of Freud's written work. Freud observed that the death instinct, unlike the life instinct, is much more elusive and difficult to grasp. The death instincts seem to do their work "unobtrusively" (Freud, 1920g, p. 63), virtually "mute"(Freud, 1923b, p. 46). According to Freud, the death instinct only becomes "powerful"(Freud, 1923b, p. 59) in its representative—that is, in the "instinct of destruction" (Freud, 1923b, p. 42).

By introducing the *symbol of negation* in his article "Negation", Freud points to another developmental stage in linking symbol formation explicitly with negation. The *formation of the symbol of negation* represents for him a new transformed nature of the work of the death instinct (Danckwardt, 2011), although Freud does not elaborate further upon this. Lilli Gast (2008) provides this contemporary reading of Freud's article, and Elfriede Löchel (2000) elaborates on the relevant issues. With his concept of *negation in dreams* in *The Interpretation of Dreams*, Freud had already provided a missing (i.e., connecting) link in the transformational sequence—that is, between the annihilating action as the expression of the most archaic "no" and the performative-actional or gestural "no" of the "Fort-Da game" in *Beyond the Pleasure Principle* and, eventually, the semantic "no" of "Negation". The connecting link—that is, the concept of reversal into its opposite—is the only negation that dream-work can produce. To that purpose, dream-work, by means of its specific symbolic mode of thinking, reverts hallucinatory-scenic and visual mental images into their opposites. Freud's above-cited description of his dream of the "open-air closet" in *The Interpretation of Dreams* gives a vivid illustration of this. By introducing a new form of symbolization (the symbol of negation), Freud implicitly points to the possibility that somewhere at a crucial point in the course of the developmental process things can go wrong—that is to say, the symbolic function might not be achieved and the development of symbolic systems can be thwarted. Freud also writes (1923b) that through the fusion of the two instincts and with the instrumentality of a special organ, it is possible to direct the destructive impulses against the external world. Hermann Beland believes that concepts like "fusion" or "merging" only bear a descriptive value and are therefore merely makeshift concepts (Beland, 2008). To his mind, such concepts actually obfuscate the fact that the development of symbolic thinking can only come off via projective identification, projection, and re-introjection. According to Bion, symbolic thinking is the result of a functioning basic communication. For this mental achievement Bion invented the concept of alpha function.

Freud wrote "Negation" (1925h) five years after *Beyond the Pleasure Principle* (1920g) and two years after *The Ego and the Id* (1923b), where he developed his second drive theory—that is, the hypothesis of the life and death instincts. In "Negation", by making reference to "Instincts and Their Vicissitudes" (1915c), where he had expounded his first theory of the instincts, Freud implicitly extended his life- and death-instinct hypothesis. On the one hand Freud made use of it to describe a fundamental feature of the *conditio humana* by linking his hypothesis to the achievement of the capacity to say yes and/or no. On the other hand, he made use of his hypothesis to describe pathologies as the outcome of disturbances of the dual system of the instincts. The insufficient reception of these implicit further developments in Freud's theory has contributed to a general denial of the death instinct and the controversies over it to this day. Freud developed his hypothesis to the point of symbolization. Only on the basis of symbolic systems can a sequence towards negation proper evolve: the actual annihilating action—that is, concrete destruction—is replaced with the hallucinatory–scenic mode of symbolic thinking where mental images are reversed into their opposites or transformed into antithetical ideas (as it is characteristic for dreamwork), and further by the performative–actional or gestural "no", and ultimately by the semantic "no".

Summary and clinical vignettes

The concept of negation in dreams and its relevance for the psychoanalytic clinic

Negation denotes a mental process that, like denial or disavowal, belongs to the wide range of defence mechanisms the human psyche develops in its attempt to ward off internal dangers linked to ideational representatives and mnemic images threatening the subject from within. Thus negation can be said to be directed at an ideational content with the intent to avoid the disagreeable implications that go along with the mental recognition of reality. Negation, therefore, must be ascribed a somewhat intermediate or transitional position between denial and disavowal, which have to be conceived as more primitive and rudimentary forms of psychic operation. Repression represents a more highly developed and complex mental process (Eickhoff, 1998). What follows is the description of a clinical sequence that provides supporting evidence for the clinical relevance and usefulness of the concept of negation in dreams. The clinical material is taken from two consecutive sessions of an adult patient's analysis.

The analysand was a former art teacher who had applied for psychoanalytic training in order to become a child and adolescent psychotherapist, but he had, in fact, not been accepted for training. He subsequently became an art therapist instead and eventually managed to work in private practice. It was then that, at some point, he sought psychoanalytic treatment, because he wanted to find out the reasons why he had not been accepted for psychoanalytic training, and also why this rejection had hurt him so much. As a child—from 1 to 10 years of age—he had had to stay with foster-parents during the week, while he used to spend the weekends at home with his parents, who lived in another town quite far from where his foster-parents lived. At the end of the week his parents would come and fetch him home, and at the beginning of the following week would bring him back to his foster-parents' place.

For the purpose of my present discussion I will present a particular incident of a session to which the analysand arrived a few minutes late.

When I come out of my study to greet my patient, he rushes past me with quite some determination and single-mindedness, straight into my consulting room. While passing me in such a hurry, he hardly looks at me but just casts a quick glance towards me in a somewhat condescending manner. It is true that he does shake hands with me, but he is acting in such a conflicted way that, while shaking my hand, he is, at the same time, ruthlessly pushing it aside, literally elbowing himself through me into my consulting room and heading straight onto the couch. I am really taken aback, when it suddenly occurs to me that this sequence of action-dialogue actually reveals some contradictory elements of a nonverbal communication. "Goodness me!", I think to myself, slightly annoyed, isn't his behaviour arrogant today!" I have a sudden notion of arrogance being a way of annihilating the transference–countertransference relationship (Akhtar, 2009b; Bion, 1958; Danckwardt & Wegner, 2007).

Then the analysand begins the session by telling me that he actually finds it very odd that all of a sudden this anxious uncertainty took hold of him when just a moment ago, lying down on the couch, he hadn't felt at all that way. He then comes up with a few ideas concerning the possible reasons for his sudden confusion and anxiety. He appears very absorbed while murmuring his thoughts and ideas, just as if nobody else were present in the room to pick them up. I had the impression of someone being lost in some sort of self-analysis.

The analysand talks about his grand-daughter and says that when he is with her, he always picks her up with a look of disgust, just as if she were merely some alien element. And, in fact, while telling me about these episodes with his grand-daughter, his tone of voice reveals some element of horror and disgust. He now thinks of his lifting her up high into the air— just as adults often do with small children—only to then keep her away from his body, with outstretched arms! And he adds that he feels terribly ashamed when thinking about it now. Suddenly a dream comes to his mind which he had already spoken about in his last session. Which part of the dream? My immediate thought is that my patient probably wants to communicate to me a particular sequence of the dream that refers to an aspect of our relationship that has not yet been worked through and which he now is attempting to use as a vehicle to re-establish contact with me. The analysand promptly says that he is actually thinking of that part of the dream where *he is together with me in my consulting room with another person present as well: a boy*. I ask him whether he thinks that his confusion about his looking for security on the couch might have something to do with the way he treats his grand-daughter—that is, like a stranger. Maybe he treats her, as well as me, in such a way in order to show me how he himself felt treated when he was a child—namely, as an alien element in the family! He thereupon tells me that his grand-daughter is now about the same age as he had been when his parents had decided to give him away to foster-parents during the week. Only at the weekends did he stay at home with his real parents. In fact, his parents had made this arrangement with his foster-parents when he was only 1 year old and maintained it until he was 10. My analysand then vividly recalls a scene that must once have had a terrible impact upon him: both of his parents are sitting in the front seats of the car while he is left alone on the back seat, feeling completely powerless and utterly helpless in face of being taken away, totally incapable of refusing to accept it.

At the beginning of the next analytic session he refrains from using any action-language. Scarcely has the analysand lain down on the couch when he immediately begins recounting his recent dream, which he dreamt since we last saw each other. He shows a certain surprise about the fact that he can recall the dream only "vaguely" and only "some parts of it". What he can remember, though, is that in the dream *he experienced himself being inside an apartment with two rooms and a kitchen. From behind a wall, where he imagines the kitchen with his wife in it, he hears a noise. He walks to the door, switches on the electric light and catches sight of something white in colour which he surmises to be a ghost*. At that point he woke up from his dream in a state of anxiety and realized that he was covered in sweat.

Commentary

The analysand's dream between the two sessions evidences that it was not possible for him to produce a semantic "no" that would have allowed him to avoid shouldering the painful implications of my interpreting his retaliatory feelings towards me and others. Nor was he able to semantically negate me as the one who had caused his painful feelings by offering him an interpretation. All the same, in his dream between the two sessions the analysand was in some respect capable of distancing himself from me with respect to the interpretation I offered. This was achieved by means of the negation in the dream by a hallucinatory-scenic mode of symbolic thinking, whereby the mental image of the first dream is transformed into an antithetical idea—in other words, the "persona" of the first dream is replaced by the "ghost-like figure" in the second dream. Or, put differently, the figure of the "persona" is "de-objectilized" (Green, 1993). Due to the fact of the emergence of the antithetical idea in the dream, the mode of dreaming could be preserved from internal dangers linked to ideational representatives and mnemic images—in fact, the analysand eventually awoke in a state of anxiety and was covered in sweat—and thus protected the dreamer from the recognition of reality. From this perspective the concept of negation in dreams, which lies at the centre of a very dense conceptual nexus within the Freudian model of mental functioning, proves to be still extremely relevant and highly useful for our present-day psychoanalytic practice, not least because it also represents an excellent gyroscopic tool in our psychoanalytic clinic.

Note

Translated by M. A. Luitgard Feiks and Juergen Muck, Nuertingen, Germany.

7

The effects of negation on the analyst–analysand relationship: the paradoxes of narcissism

Jorge Luis Maldonado

In his article "Negation" (1925h), Freud explores three important areas: "no" as a linguistic phenomenon; the concept of judgement and its double function (judgement of attribution and judgement of existence); and the relationship between the subject and reality. Although he considers that negation is linked to the linguistic expression and puts forward the hypothesis that "we never discover a 'no' in the unconscious" (p. 239), Green (1993) maintains that this does not imply an absence of negativity in the unconscious. Green's conceptualization takes into account phenomena that go beyond language. Negation is situated within a broader set of notions, together with repression, foreclosure and disavowal, all of which constitute "the work of the negative".

Despite the impossibility of observing a "no" in the unconscious, the final structuring of the unconscious, which happens as a result of the effects of the Oedipus complex and which culminates in its dissolution, is a consequence of a prohibition that carries an implicit "no". This is the "no" which prevents the consummation of incest, when the subject is faced with the threat of castration, and which generates the desire for parricide. The effect of the "no" contained within this prohibition is seen not only indirectly through symptoms and unconscious derivatives but also, and essentially, in the expression of anxiety.

In "Negation", Freud states that this is essentially linked to resistance. However, in "Constructions in Analysis" (1937d) he broadens the spectrum of meanings that the patient's negation may have in response to an interpretation. In this later article, he considers that the analysand's response is something more than resistance and that the validity of the response to an interpretation, whether this be "yes" or "no", must be found in "indirect forms of confirmation". He places emphasis on the associations which follow on from the interpretation and which include something that is analogous to the formulation previously offered by the analyst. Memories or dreams—"corroborative dreams" (Freud, 1923c [1922])—that occur after the analyst's intervention may have greater value in confirming the analyst's interpretation than the patient's "yes". Thus, the unconscious processes that are mobilized as a result of the analyst's intervention acquire greater significance in terms of the confirmation of the validity of an interpretation than the conscious response that the analysand might give.

Indirect confirmations indicate that, due to an interpretation, something has been transformed in the analysand's inner world, even when the transformation is expressed in a negative form. Such is the case with the negative therapeutic reaction, which Freud mentions in "Constructions in Analysis". In this article, he considers that the patient's "no", apart from signalling resistance, may also reflect other factors and may contain various meanings that derive from the complexity of the analytic situation.

In this chapter I explore some of these factors, which are the determinants of the ambiguous meaning of the patient's "no". A case study is used to illustrate not only how negation reflects a resistance against the content of the interpretation, but also how negativity—implicit in negation—plays a key role in the relationship between patient and analyst. This can be seen specifically in the countertransference when negation is manifested as a constant disregard for the analyst's interpretations. This case study highlights disturbances in the function of the "judgement of existence" that occur in narcissistic pathologies.

The function of intellectual judgement and its role in the distortion of perception

Freud highlights that two essential decisions are implicit in the "function of judgement". These consist in attributing a property to a thing and asserting that a representation exists in reality. These functions are also concerned with decisions that are the converse of the above: to disaffirm the possession by a thing of a particular attribute or to dispute that a representation has an existence in reality (1925h). These two negative functions are essential in the analytic experience as they reveal disturbances in the relationship between the subject and their objects.

The observation of patients with narcissistic disturbances is a rich source of investigation for diverse conditions that come under the conceptual umbrella of the negative, which includes negation. This is particularly the case with decisions of judgement in which the subject disaffirms a property of a thing or disputes the existence of a representation in reality. Narcissistic pathologies, and in particular narcissistic personalities and patients with narcissistic character traits, present clinical pictures that contain these characteristics in an accentuated form. These pictures enable us to observe how narcissistic pathology characterized by negativity is sustained by aggressive aspects of narcissism. This was highlighted by Rosenfeld (1971) as being one of the hallmarks of these patients.

Narcissistic patients, motivated by anxiety, feel the need to organize their mental structure so that it negates their inner reality, which may seem very alien and threatening to them. This negation is directed against the analyst's interpretation and the contents of the unconscious that this may reveal. I would like to focus on the situation in which judgement, motivated by narcissistic rivalry, is used to dispute not only the interpretation but also the very existence of the analyst insofar as it is the analyst who formulates and conveys the "message" about the analysand's unconscious. In this situation, what the subject tries to deny is any evidence to support the existence of an object with whom the subject has established an affective relationship and whose presence and potential absence may cause suffering. This impels such patients to build a defensive system that enables them to disregard the analyst's words by ignoring, dismissing, or invalidating what the object says. This lack of recognition of the "existence" of the other becomes the factor that blocks the anxiety generated by the patient's relationship with the object. Rosenfeld (1964) highlighted how these patients try to negate every situation that reflects dependence on the object. The cost of this defensive system is emotional isolation, which results in a vicious circle, creating a distance between subject and object, with the consequent feeling of helplessness for the patient. Thus, the "judgement of existence" comes into play, as it is the very existence of the analyst that the patient negates.

Case study: judgement of existence in clinical practice

Mrs A came to analysis when she had just turned 30; she sought analysis as a result of her anxiety and depression caused by losses in different areas of her life. Her existence was permeated by tragedy: the death, two years previously, of her father, whom she described as a much admired yet authoritarian and distant man; constant arguments between her husband and her mother about the administration of her father's estate; the recent suicide of her older sister; her concern for her sister's daughter at being orphaned; the psychosis and imprisonment of her brother-in-law, who had committed murder; and the emotional instability of her three sisters. She had one daughter and wished to have other children, but this wish was associated with a fear of losing the child due to her history of numerous abortions and miscarriages.

Mrs A had married a man with whom she had never had premarital sexual relations. Before marrying, she decided to have surgery to restore her hymen so that her future husband would think she was a virgin. It may have been that her unconscious intention was to disavow and negate both the pregnancies that had proved conflictive with her internalized mother, and the traumatic abortions that had predated her marriage. This led me to hypothesize that, underlying the distortions of judgement evident in her concealment of the truth, there existed a need to disavow and to negate a conflictive and unconscious aspect of herself that had caused a splitting of her ego.

A graduate in fine arts, she felt that she had had many failures as a painter, given that she had left many paintings unfinished, causing her to feel extremely frustrated. This inability to complete a task was also true of work-related activities, which added to her sufferings. She found it difficult to absorb new information and quickly abandoned every course of study that she embarked upon. From the beginning of analysis, I realized that behind the façade of hysteria, the narcissistic aspects of Mrs A's personality were accentuated. It was also evident that her defensive structure masked a profound, long-term depression.

Mrs A's situation was utterly desolate. She had lost all feelings of goodness and had no sense of self-worth. Her inner world was peopled by numerous objects whom she experienced as dead or moribund. The main problem that came to light in this analysis lay in her complete loss of confidence and the use of manic defences (Segal, 1952) in a failed attempt to recover her self-esteem. The seriousness of her illness stemmed not only from the plurality of mourning she had to bear but also from the use of these defences, in particular the need to triumph over her libidinal objects, to annihilate them, which prevented the working through of the mourning process.

Initially, work was mainly focused on her feelings of ambivalence, which hindered working through, as well as associated persecutory and depressive anxieties. As her treatment continued, significant negative transference became evident, which was manifested by her constant disregard for any interpretations, with the consequent undermining of any analytic activity. There was also an oedipal rivalry against any people linked to the analyst. This reflected the rivalry she had with her mother and sisters, on account of libidinal feelings for her father reactivated in the transference. However, it was another dimension of her rivalry with the analyst, namely *narcissistic rivalry*, which was the factor that generated the greatest obstacle to progress in analysis. *Oedipal rivalry*, as distinct from *narcissistic rivalry*, contains a specific quality: competition with another—sibling, parent, or competitor—if this other is an obstacle in the relationship between the subject and a libidinal object. The love directed towards a libidinal object is the central axis of the conflict and the source of aggression, implicit in parricidal and fratricidal wishes; this aggression is secondary to the libidinal bond established with an object. In contrast to oedipal rivalry, *narcissistic rivalry* is characterized by hostility that arises because the very existence of the object is the factor that diminishes the subject's feelings of grandiosity. These feelings of grandiosity are based on the illusion of power whereby the subject feels that they can completely do without the external world of objects. The negation of the existence of the other is the fundamental aim of narcissistic rivalry, which configures a disturbance in the judgement of existence.

In the analytic dialogue with Mrs A, one of the ways in which this narcissistic rivalry was expressed was via the constant use of negation in response to my interventions. At the outset, "No" . . . "I don't think so" were the habitual responses to interpretations that made reference to her ambivalence in connection with both her libidinal objects and other conflicts that configured her state of depression. Not only did this negation appear to be directed towards possible meanings of unconscious fantasies suggested in the interpretations, but it also seemed to be directed towards myself.

Gradually, this initial, explicit "no" was replaced by responses that implicitly carried the same negative meaning. This negative response consisted in ignoring my words, such that no interpretation would cause her to deviate from telling her pre-established narrative. These narratives consisted of lengthy descriptions of her arguments with her family, between her husband and her family, or between all parties concerned.

Although her narratives enabled her to express these everyday conflicts, they also kept her in a defensive capsule that isolated her from any interchange of ideas in the analytic dialogue. At times, the countertransference was experienced as sterile, discouraging, and frustrating, given that my expectation was that any interpretation that I might offer would be ignored or dismissed by the analysand. It seemed as if the tension and the hostility that she described in her stories as a result of the arguments between the protagonists were being reproduced in the here and now of the analytic relationship. Money-Kyrle (1956) describes this phenomenon when he highlights how the analyst may unconsciously begin to feel hostility towards the patient if their reparative drives cannot be satisfied. In this clinical case, the creative potential of the analytic experience ran the risk, for both members of the analytic dyad, of remaining undeveloped, as was the case with the creative expression of the patient, both artistically and academically.

I endeavoured to show Mrs A that her unresponsiveness to my interpretations, where she seemed to ignore what I said, was possibly a way of trying to put me in the role of one of her opponents in the family conflicts. I told her that this might lead to an argument and that both of us could end up reproducing the same tension and conflicts that she had described to me. This interpretation, which I made in different contexts, was initially met with indifference. My impression was that this indifferent behaviour was intended to influence the countertransference and to provoke some sort of emotional reaction. I suggested to her that the situation that had arisen was not about whether she felt my words were valid or not, but was about her not acknowledging what I said. Consequently, the absence of any response on her part meant that my words became void of meaning, since it was as if I were speaking into an empty space with no listener.

In the first session of the week, Mrs A would regularly make reference to a recurring theme. Her constant complaint was that her husband would abandon her every Sunday to play polo. Initially, I interpreted this as an expression of early experiences of abandonment, helplessness, and hostility, which were reproduced in the analytic relationship as a consequence of every weekend separation. She gave no indication whatsoever that she had heard what I said and continued her narrative. This seemed to indicate that her complaints were more than just the expression of the abandonment and desolation that she felt on Sundays but, rather, seemed to stem from another determinant: rivalry in the analytic relationship. It seemed that the session had been transformed into a polo match in which each team was trying to triumph over their rival. The characteristics of this sport—the phallic image of the horse between the rider's legs, the intense competitiveness, the skill required—serve as an expression of the features of the phallic–narcissistic character (Reich, 1928). The experience of abandonment was reproduced in the here and now as the patient established a game of phallic rivalry with me. Her way of triumphing was to ignore my interpretations, which could, at the same time, have been experienced as goals scored against her. Her ignoring of my interventions made it impossible to enter into a dialogue that would have allowed me to correct my interpretations if these were felt to be inadequate. This, in turn, made her feel as if she were being abandoned by the analyst–husband, not only on Sundays, but also in the here and now of the session. All of these factors led me to believe that this distancing had aroused feelings of helplessness that were making her suffer. I believe it was the working through of this phallic–narcissistic rivalry that was a key factor in the favourable development of this analysis.

The analytic relationship between myself and Mrs A had a certain similarity to Freud's (1916–17) eloquent description of the treatment of narcissistic patients. He states that the analyst is faced with an "unconquerable wall" as a result of the patient's defensive condition. Analytic experiences shows that this wall enables the subject to obtain spurious gratification by affecting the object's mood, making them feel ignored. Gradually, as a consequence of this emotional isolation imposed by the patient, the analyst feels treated like a thing. At the same time, this unconquerable wall creates an affective barrier between the subject and their object, leading the patient to a state of helplessness and isolation. This was the case with the analysis of Mrs A.

As was mentioned earlier, Freud states that the validity of interpretations can be found by indirect forms of confirmation, which take place subsequent to the analyst's interventions. It is not always possible to uncover fantasies or other unconscious contents in the manifest content that arises immediately after the analyst's interpretations if these are, in fact, adequate. It is often the case that the expression of this confirmation is *delayed,* and sometimes a number of sessions elapse before the patient's associations reveal what is actually happening in the analytic process and in the analytic relationship. This is evident in those patients who have marked schizoid defences, as is the case with the patient under consideration. The validation of the interpretation emerges in the clinical material only when the patient allows the free flow of associations. Abraham (1919) considered that the resistance to free association is particularly marked in narcissistic patients. Other authors (Bleger, 1967; Bollas, 1987; Green, 1983; Lacan, 1953; Reich, 1928) have also contributed to the description of this phenomenon.

Although transference is operating unconsciously at each moment of the analytic session, this does not mean that the patient's discourse always conveys the meaning of the transference fantasies that are active at each moment of analysis. When the patient's utterances are no longer free associations, when they no longer contain unconscious derivatives that reveal unconscious phantasies, this tends to be due to the fact that the patient is using words as a sort of "verbal acting out", as described by Maldonado (1975, 1984), Etchegoyen (1983), and Joseph (1988). When this occurs, the patient's utterances tend to produce an emotional response in the analyst's countertransference instead of serving a communicative function. In Mrs A's clinical material, this effect was achieved by not acknowledging or rejecting any interpretations. This generated in me an emotional void, and my countertransference feeling was that I was being treated as an inanimate object. This reflected what Mrs A had projected in the transference relationship: her loss of vitality, which was the consequence of the stifling of her emotions.

As can be seen in this case study, the pathological form of self idealization that narcissistic patients employ derives from their ability to elicit feelings of worthlessness and vulnerability in the object. The benefit that they gain lies in the fact that their self-esteem is bolstered by the omnipotent control that they exert over the object's emotions. In Mrs A's case, this disturbance is evident in the way she tries to regulate her self-esteem.

Narcissistic patients use various methods to provoke an emotional response in the other, in a way that is contradictory. One of these methods uses negation specifically to make the object feel ignored by the subject's disregard for or dismissal of the object's words. The patient asks the analyst for help, but, by means of a defensive system in which narcissistic withdrawal predominates, this overt request is transformed into something different, which consists in emphatically denying the existence of the object. The narcissistic patient tries, consciously or unconsciously, to make the object feel rejected. This reflects a need to provoke an emotional response in the object whose ability to help the patient is not acknowledged. A paradox is created whereby the patient needs the analyst, this being tacitly understood by the patient's presence at the sessions, but their request for help is transformed into a display of self-sufficiency, showing their ability to do without the analyst's help. The possible consequence of this is that the other feels that their existence is not recognized by the subject. This paradox, which involves the judgement of existence, can be condensed as follows: "Your presence is necessary to demonstrate that I find your presence unnecessary." A second paradox lies in the fact that the subject, in order to do without the object, needs the object to indicate in some way—for example, as an expression of emotion in the countertransference—that they are affected by this rejection (Maldonado, 2003, 2008).

Judging by Mrs A's evolution, she clearly benefited from her analysis, although initially this progress was not explicitly acknowledged by the patient. In fact, the improvement in her symptoms was in striking contrast to the negativity that characterized her responses to my interpretations. It seemed that these not only negated the possible meanings of the interpretations but also had a negative impact on my creativity. Her initial reaction seemed to indicate her disconnection from the interpretations, as if they had not been heard. It appeared that the patient had succeeded in producing a state of isolation and that narcissistic withdrawal had in fact taken place. However, material that emerged in subsequent sessions showed that her narcissistic withdrawal had not in fact been completely established. This could be seen as the acting outs that had previously taken place in the analytic relationship began to be replaced by clinical material that contained symbolic meaning. This allowed me to construct hypotheses about the characteristics of the patient's inner world and to have a deeper understanding of the transference–countertransference relationship previously described.

Mrs A expressed great enthusiasm for a mechanical toy that belonged to her young daughter. The toy was a small clockwork dog, made of metal, that was mounted on a platform with wheels. Once the toy was wound up, it would begin to move while making a barking sound until it crashed into a wall. When this happened, it would bounce off the wall and once again continue barking, knocking into other walls in the room. The material suggested that this toy represented an aspect of the patient that she wanted to be heard, like the barking of the mechanical dog. It seemed that, on this occasion, her unconscious had opened up and that free association had come into play, expressing an indirect form of confirmation. This appeared to be a delayed response to previous interpretations that had highlighted the defensive and hostile nature of her negativity and the isolating effect that this had on her. It also shows how the use of schizoid mechanisms, evident in her attitude of disregarding the interpretations put forward, had caused her to have a sort of mechanical functioning, a reification of herself (the metal toy, the walls that it continually bumped into). This was accompanied by the loss of her vitality, which had had an adverse effect on her creativity. The characteristics of the representations from this material (the clockwork toy) relate to the reification of object relations, implicit in the schizoid mechanisms described by Klein (1946) and later developed by Bion (1963), who highlights the subject's inability to differentiate between inanimate and psychic objects. The material also suggests behaviour aimed at devaluing the interpretations, transforming them into "the barking of a metal dog".

This material, owing to its symbolic value, paved the way for the analytic work that took place over a number of sessions. I pointed out to the patient how her wish to make headway in her analysis and her infantile wish to be heard (the barking of her daughter's toy), were at odds with ("crashed into") her attitude of negativity. I added that this contradiction was detrimental to her own interests and could be likened to the clockwork dog crashing into the walls of the room. When interpreting, I also took into account the countertransferential context in which the material arose. I pointed out that her responses to my interpretations, permeated by her indifference, seemed to be aimed at blocking my words and acted as a barrier, in the same way as the walls of the room were a barrier for the little clockwork dog, blocking its path. Taking into account that her defensive system was configured to counteract persecutory anxiety, I also said that by being transformed into an "inanimate object", my words became inoffensive, and less harmful, like the barking of the toy dog. I added that this was similar to what had happened with her own creativity in that it had become diminished and thus less harmful to her internal objects, but that the overall effect of this only exacerbated her anxiety. Later, more symbolic material was forthcoming, which might be considered a sign of her acceptance of the value of these interpretations.

This clinical material was particularly meaningful as these symbolic representations provided the vehicle for the patient's expression of unconscious communication. This served as a tool to inject vitality into the subject, the analytic process, and the object of transference. The vitality that had previously been lacking in the analytic process due to the clinical material being devoid of symbolic value was now restored by the contribution of material that was highly meaningful. Meaningful clinical material, true free association, which enables the analyst to comprehend unconscious fantasies, is related to the concept of reparation described by Klein (1937). The transference object is "repaired" as it becomes possible to work with representations; the patient "repairs" the analyst by offering material that represents their unconscious fantasies and, as a consequence, allows the analyst to exercise his analytic function (Maldonado, 2003). By providing this meaningful material, Mrs A reinstated me as an analyst, enabling me to construct hypotheses about what had previously happened in her inner world and in the analytic relationship. The material also shows that the patient, by restoring the positive function of the "judgement of existence" and by ceasing to negate the analyst's function, repairs her own self. The libidinal aspects of her personality, her true positive transference, are present in these deferred representations, which are a form of confirmation of interpretations and which contain a greater heuristic value than a "yes" or "no" response.

This material highlights not only the nature of the manic defences contained within the patient's rivalry, but also the offensive condition that these manic defences denote. This coincides with the conceptualizations of authors who have investigated this subject. Rosenfeld (1971), Joseph (1975), and Etchegoyen (1981) have drawn a distinction between "defensive mechanisms", whose function is to avoid anxiety, and "offensive mechanisms", whose aim is not solely to avoid anxiety but also to disturb the object. These offensive mechanisms could be thought of as manic defences that tend to generate a disturbance in both the identity of the object and in communication.

The evolution of this analysis

Mrs A had internalized a series of images of persecutory objects with whom she identified. These were configured as mother and father figures in her inner world and were felt to have vindictive intentions, preventing her from expressing her creativity maternally, artistically, or academically. An important aspect of her anxiety was linked to the paradoxical nature of her creativity: as a consequence of her rivalry, she felt that her creativity was destructive and potentially harmful to her libidinal objects.

Improvements in symptoms, external successes, and the attainment of new skills that one sees in analysis are not necessarily indicators of the positive therapeutic reaction. Some improvements in symptoms—in particular in those patients with whom negative transference is not evident—tend to coincide with the clinical picture of a concealed psychoanalytic impasse, and it is precisely this apparent improvement that masks the real clinical picture. In the light of these reservations, it is important to evaluate the seemingly favourable development of Mrs A's symptoms. The patient was in analysis for 7 years with sessions at least 4 times a week but, for the most part, 5 times a week. Over the course of her treatment, the level of anxiety and the intensity of Mrs A's conflicts gradually began to diminish. This enabled her to strengthen the links with her libidinal objects, to develop academically by enrolling in and successfully completing another university degree—a long-standing aspiration—and eventually to become a very successful painter—a success that she had never envisaged. (Her paintings were sold in different countries and some were bought by a European museum.) Yet it was the patient's contribution of clinical material that provided the most significant indicator of the changes taking place in her inner world, rather than these ostensible improvements in her symptoms. A case in point is the material relating to the clockwork toy, among other manifestations of her unconscious fantasies (such as dreams) that she communicated to me over the course of her analysis. It was the representability of this material that uncovered the patient's fantasies, the conditions of the self, and the analytic bond.

In phallic–narcissistic pathology, the subject identifies with the phallus, which is seen as having absolute value. This makes it difficult to incorporate other masculine and feminine identifications of both parents into the subject's self, and these are rejected as a result of the condition of exclusivity that characterizes narcissism. As a consequence, the subject can only adopt phallic traits of the father figure (as a partial object) and uses these to sustain omnipotent fantasies. This identificatory pathology can be seen in a short dream that Mrs A reported. In her dream, *she was in her father's office, which was in semi-darkness, she and could only make out the blurred outline of a man wearing a tie. This tie stood out in the darkness as it gave off a phosphorescent light.* This dream could be seen as an expression of libidinal fantasies towards the penis-tie of the father, but it also shows, by means of the indistinct silhouette, how unclear other features of her father–analyst's identity were. The dream shows a degree of recognition of the phallic condition of her father, which, in itself, reveals to the analyst the overvaluation of the phallus, which sustained her narcissistic structure. It was this overvaluing of the phallus that prevented the incorporation of other paternal functions.

The desire to change the structure of her inner world was manifested in the patient's intention to modify certain aspects of her body. Although she was aware that she was attractive, with harmonious facial features, she considered having cosmetic surgery to reduce the size of her nose. In addition, she also consulted a number of gynaecologists about reducing the size of her clitoris, which, she felt, was too large, and similar to a penis. The conveying of these thoughts was her form of communicating to me her wish to modify phallic–narcissistic aspects of her personality that caused conflicts with her internal objects—her parents and sisters in particular—and hindered her from realizing her creative potential.

The progress shown by Mrs A allowed me to understand and to evaluate retrospectively the prolonged period during which the patient's attitude was predominantly negative. Although the patient benefited from treatment, she did not acknowledge this progress during the early stages of analysis. However, towards the end of her treatment she not only recognized the value of analysis, she also expressed this recognition in a number of interviews she requested after the analysis had come to an end.

For a long time at the beginning of her analysis Mrs A lived through the drama of the narcissistic patient. Driven by feelings of envy (Klein, 1957) and by means of the wall she had constructed between herself and her objects, she managed to deny the improvement in her condition that resulted from her analysis, and as a consequence these benefits remained hidden. This difficulty in being able to explicitly recognize the benefits that derive from analysis can prove to be a source of great anxiety for the patient.

Conclusion

These observations of the analytic process clearly show that the patient's apparent detachment from the analyst during moments of narcissistic withdrawal is not a clear reflection of the real clinical picture. It is precisely in these moments that the effect on the object is most intense, given that the patient, by means of negativity, influences the emotions of the analyst, potentially causing a disturbance in the analyst's identity. The intense control which the patient exerts over the analyst and which underpins narcissistic withdrawal paradoxically increases the patient's dependence on the analyst, and it is this very dependence that the patient struggles to free themselves from.

In the case of the patient described above, who used extreme schizoid defences, the negative judgement of attribution has a form of double expression: the removal of the attribution of vitality from the analyst, coupled with the attribution of the condition of an inanimate object. The negative judgement of attribution provided the underlying basis for behaviour by means of which the subject, in their omnipotent fantasy, tries to damage the identity of the object, although this may not necessarily be successful in reality.

The notion of "judgement of existence" established by Freud in "Negation" is crucial for the understanding of narcissistic pathologies, as it is the very existence of the other that is the source of conflict. The means by which judgement is used to negate the existence of someone who arouses both love and hate in the subject are evident in the seemingly indifferent behaviour displayed by the narcissistic subject.

The striking contrast between the constant negation of interpretations, on the one hand, and the improvement and progress in the patient's symptomatology, on the other, show that negation and the consequent negativity evident in the clinical material are a visible aspect of a state of transition that culminates in the resolution of the patient's conflicts. Underlying this manifest negativity, the unconscious process of working through and the transformation of conflicts are taking place. At times, almost imperceptibly, there is a transition from the initial negation of an unconscious idea to a state in which the patient reaches a greater acceptance of this idea. The latter is expressed in those moments when the patient begins to convey to the analyst clinical material that is representative of unconscious fantasies that are operating in the analytic process. The material presented shows that the process of working through can remain hidden. Negation is seen here as one of the ostensible factors that occur during the analytic process while, simultaneously and unconsciously, a series of transformations of fantasies is taking place.

Note

I would like to thank Mrs Madeleine Baranger for her very helpful comments on this paper.

8

From psychic holes to psychic representations

Ilany Kogan

Several weeks ago I had the opportunity to visit Berlin's Jewish Museum for the third time. An architectural masterpiece, the museum is a spectacular structure that has firmly established itself as one of Berlin's most notable landmarks. The zinc building is unique in that it ties the museum's themes to its architecture, which is rich in thought-provoking symbolism that makes German–Jewish history palpable.

The museum's architect, Daniel Libeskind, called his conception "Between the Lines"—a name reflecting the tensions of German–Jewish history. In the design of the building, the past takes shape along two lines: one straight, but broken into many fragments, the other winding and open-ended. The intersections of these lines are marked by Voids—empty spaces that slash through the entire structure in a straight line, top to bottom.

The Voids, which are quite separate from the rest of the building, have walls of bare concrete; they are neither heated nor air-conditioned and are largely without artificial lighting. They are an architectural expression of the irretrievable loss of the Jews murdered in Europe. In Libeskind's words, "A Void is *not really* a museum space. It represents "that which can never be exhibited when it comes to Jewish Berlin history: humanity reduced to ashes" (Libeskind, 2000).

Sharing with a colleague my impressions of the Voids as well as Libeskind's remarks about them, and the thoughts they evoked in me in connection with this chapter, in a book on Freud's "Negation" paper (1925h), I was struck by this colleague's brilliant observation: "Isn't Libeskind using 'negation' here? Isn't it clear from his *'not really'* that he was (unconsciously) aware that the Void *is indeed* a museum space? We see the psychic game of negation 'live' in action here!!"

I agree with my colleague's astute observation about the negation in Libeskind's remarks. I would take this one step further: that it is not only Libeskind's statement, but also the Voids themselves that convey "negation". These Voids are museum spaces that represent death and, like "negation", "belong to the instinct of destruction" (Freud, 1925h, p. 239).

Here I wish to examine "negation" from the perspective of the psychic representation of absence. Two of the Voids roused thoughts that relate to this theme. The first Void, the "Voided Void", is a bare, narrow, unheated chamber rising the full height of the building, silent and unlit except for indirect light from a high diagonal slit, dimly echoing the end of a thousand years of Jewish life in Germany. The effect of this empty, hollow space is petrifying. The second Void is the "Memory Void". The floor of this space is covered by a sculpture entitled *Shalekhet* (Fallen Leaves) by Israeli artist Menashe Kadishman. This sculpture consists of over 10,000 open-mouthed faces coarsely cut from heavy, circular iron plates, evoking painful recollections of Holocaust victims. Both Voids represent death, and, in my view, both Voids are full: While the "Memory Void" is replete with open-mouthed faces, the "Voided Void" is replete with emptiness.

These two Voids are reminiscent of the different formulations of the experience of absence that may be applied to Holocaust survivors' offspring: the "empty circle" and the "psychic hole". The "empty circle", a term formulated by Laub, symbolizes "the absence of representations, the rupture of the self, the erasure of memory, and the accompanying sense of void that are the core legacy of massive psychic trauma" (Laub, 1998, p. 507). The "psychic hole" is conceived of as an "absence of psychic structure" (Kinston & Cohen, 1986, p. 338). But in the case of Holocaust survivors' offspring, I define this "hole" as a space that encapsulates all of the unconscious fantasies linked to the parents' traumatic past (Kogan, 1995, 2007a, 2007b). In my mind, the notion of the "empty circle" is conveyed by the Jewish Museum's "Voided Void" and the notion of the "psychic hole" by the museum's "Memory Void". Both the "empty circle" and the "psychic hole" are expressions of "negation", as they represent death and destruction.

In this chapter I explore the term "psychic hole" and compare it with similar terms from the world of astrophysics and terms used in the psychoanalytic literature, particularly the "empty circle" mentioned above. I then present my own conception of the "psychic hole" in cases of Holocaust survivors' offspring. I explain how this "hole" is created and describe a particular aspect of the "psychic hole" that is unique to Holocaust survivors' offspring—namely, the enactments (termed "concretization" by Bergman [1982]) generated by the negated traumatic themes that reside in it. I illustrate these enactments using clinical material taken from case studies of Holocaust survivors' offspring (Kogan, 1987, 1993, 1995). The clinical vignettes reveal the transgenerational impact of the memory hole resulting from negation of survivor parents on the lives of their offspring, up to the third generation. They also show the painful journey from enactments to psychic representations—a journey that exposes the negated traumatic events and facilitates the work of mourning and the eventual achievement of a better integrated self. Finally, I offer technical suggestions for analysts to help patients remove the "negation".

The "psychic hole"

For children of Holocaust survivors, there is no memory of a time when the Holocaust did not exist in their awareness, whether articulated or unconsciously conveyed by their parents. The remembrance of the Holocaust is constructed out of materials or stories—those spoken aloud, told, and retold, as well as those silently borne across a bridge of generations (Auerhahn & Laub, 1998; Axelrod, Schnipper, & Rau, 1978; Barocas & Barocas, 1973; Brenner, 2002; Kestenberg, 1972; Laub & Auerhahn, 1993; Laufer, 1973; Lipkowitz, 1973; Rakoff, 1966; Sonnenberg, 1974). This remembrance marks those who carry it as "secret bearers" (Micheels, 1985). Children who become burdened with memories that are not their own (Auerhahn & Prelinger, 1983; Fresco, 1984) often echo the dramas existing in their parents' inner worlds by enacting them in their own lives (Krell, 1979; Kogan, 1995, 1998, 2002; Laub & Auerhahn, 1984; Phillips, 1978). These often violent enactments intermingle death wishes with potentially dangerous situations (Kogan, 1998). In many cases, they are caused by persecutory anxieties that develop into delusional fantasies of paranoid proportions—anxieties that demonstrate a lack of differentiation between self and others, past and present, inner and outer reality. At the core of the compulsion to enact the parents' traumatic experiences in their offspring's own lives is a kind of identification with the damaged parent, termed "primitive identification" (Freyberg, 1980; Grubrich-Simitis, 1984; Kogan, 1995, 1996, 1998, 2003, 2007a, 2007b). This identification leads to a loss of the child's separate sense of self and to an inability to differentiate between the self and the damaged parent. I find this phenomenon similar to the identification characteristic of pathological mourning, which Freud (1917e [1915]) describes as a process whereby the mourner attempts to possess the object by becoming the object itself, rather than bearing a resemblance to it. This occurs when the mourner renounces the object, at the same time preserving it in a cannibalistic manner (Green, 1986a; Grinberg & Grinberg, 1974). It is this type of identification that is at the core of the offspring's inability to achieve self-differentiation and build a life of his or her own.

The coexistence of the offspring's global identification on the one hand, and the "negation"—defined by Freud as the "cognizance of what is repressed" (Freud, 1925h, p. 235) on an intellectual level, while the feelings connected to it remain repressed—of the parents' trauma on the other, a coexistence that is present in many cases of Holocaust survivors' offspring, creates a gap in the latter's emotional understanding, which I conceive of as a "psychic hole". The "psychic hole" can be regarded as a two-sided coin: one side conscious ignorance of the parents' trauma, the other side unconscious knowledge of it.

I wish to compare the "psychic hole" with a metaphor borrowed from the world of astrophysics—the phenomenon of the "black hole". This term, reviewed by Eshel (1998, p. 1115), is pregnant with meaning in psychoanalysis, as it is in astrophysics.

The "black hole"—in astrophysics and psychoanalysis

In the world of astrophysics, a "black hole" is defined as a body that sucks all the forces of gravitation into it. It is described as a "region of space–time where infinitely strong gravitational forces literally squeeze matter and photons out of existence" (Penrose, cited in Gribbin, 1992, p. 142).

In psychoanalysis, the term "black hole" is used to describe the nature of early traumatizations caused by premature and/or traumatic physical separation from the mother or by troubled symbiosis with her. These traumatizations lead to a premature psychological birth. They propel the infant into a world of precocious separateness from its mother, a sort of shocking infantile catastrophe associated with stark terror, and may lead to primitive mental disturbances.

The concept of a "black hole" was first applied clinically by Bion (1970) in reference to the infantile catastrophe of the psychotic. It was further developed by Tustin (1972, 1986, 1990, 1992), who applied it to psychogenic autism of children. Tustin claimed that adult patients who are prone to autistic ways of behaving have, instead of a psychic core that holds them together, an unmourned sense of loss or "black hole". This "black hole" represents the absence of the mother and is a primitive depressive situation that may occur even earlier than the paranoid-schizoid position (Tustin, 1986). The experience of the "black hole" promotes the use of very strong defences—for example, the autistic shell—to cover over the rupture in the psychic umbilicus and to split away any hint of vulnerability. Grotstein (1986, 1989, 1990a, 1990b, 1990c, 1993) applied this term to schizophrenia. He emphasized that the "black hole" is felt "not just as a static emptiness, but as an implosive, centripetal pull into the void" (1990, p. 257).

While these psychoanalysts applied the term "black hole" to mentally ill patients, Eshel (1988) applied it metaphorically to individuals who seem to function in their social and professional life; in these cases, Eshel sees the "black hole" as the product of the impact of a "dead" parent, particularly the "dead mother" (Green, 1986a).

The "psychic hole" in psychoanalysis

The concept of a "psychic hole" was first mentioned by Freud (1894/1985) who stated, "in melancholia the hole is in the psychic sphere" (p. 104). In contemporary psychoanalytic writing, a "hole" in the psyche connotes a deficit or absence. It is synonymous to psychic concepts such as absence, void, black holes, inner deadness, and being unavailable to oneself or others—concepts that refer to the experiential states of patients who do not "register" their experience, even such acute experiences as trauma, object loss, and separation.

There is a connection between the "psychic hole" and trauma and the mechanism of "negation". Baranger, Baranger, and Mom (1988) suggested that

> we can think of the subject of the "pure trauma" as a subject without history. These are subjects with a history, but a history with a huge hole in it. . . . What is "actual" of the neurosis is not biological, but is the impenetrable wall within the subject which opposes the historicization of some sectors of his existence. [Baranger, Baranger, & Mom, 1988, p. 125]

The "holes" they describe tend to dismantle the survivor's sense of psychic history. The traumatic experience remains, according to them, "present and unintegrable" and antagonistic to structure. Indeed, trauma's ability to debilitate individual psychic structure is perhaps its most definitive characteristic. I believe that the "psychic hole" results from the negation of traumatic experiences that are too painful to be integrated into the victims' cognitive and affective framework.

The "psychic hole" in the case of Holocaust survivors' offspring

In this chapter I apply the term "psychic hole" to a specific population: the offspring of Holocaust survivors.[1] These survivors had undergone massive trauma and often conveyed their feelings of depression and aggression to their children in a manner beyond words.

My definition of the term "psychic hole" is similar to the "black hole" in the sense that it is a body—one that encapsulates all the unconscious fantasies connected to the parents' traumatic past. Thus, it differs from Kinston and Cohen's formulation of the "psychic hole" as an "absence of psychic structure" (Kinston & Cohen, 1986, p. 338). It does not belong to the category of "blankness"—"negative hallucination", "blank psychosis", "blank mourning", all connected to what Green (1986a) calls the "problem of emptiness" or the "work of the negative"[2]—or to Quinodoz's non-existent "hole-object" (1996).[3]

My definition of the "psychic hole" also differs from Laub & Podell's "empty circle" (Laub & Podell, 1995, p. 992), although both these terms apply to a unique phenomenon in the lives of Holocaust survivors' offspring, and both may stem from the "negation" of traumatic experiences. In contrast to the formulation of the "empty circle" as "a space created by the collapse of the imaginative capacity to visualize atrocity" (Laub & Auerhahn, 1993, p. 289), I believe that the "psychic hole", like the "black hole", is not an empty space but, rather, a space that embodies all unconscious fantasies with regard to events that are experienced as an absence. I therefore associate it with the "Memory Void", which is a space filled with sculptures representing death, a concrete expression of this concept.

The origin of the "empty circle" and the origin of the "psychic hole"

Auerhahn and Laub (1998) claim that the "empty circle" in the case of Holocaust survivors' offspring is created by the absence or breakdown of an empathic relationship in the perpetrators that could, under normal circumstances, have contained the affects mobilized by trauma. The "empty circle" is perpetuated through the inherent resistance (or inability) to integrate this "unmentalized" (Fonagy & Target, 1998) psychic spot into the survivor's cognitive and affective framework—that is, through the survivor's inability to possess the experience as knowledge (Laub & Auerhahn, 1993). "In Lacanian terms", writes Lewis Kirshner (1994), "extreme traumas might be defined as experiences producing a tearing of the network of signification that supports symbolic relationships..." (p. 238). We can see this tearing of the network of signification as an expression of "negation". This inherent resistance to signification within the traumatic encounter is responsible for the fact that it is "repeated in behavior, that is, in reenactments of unconscious structures" (p. 238). It is from its unlocalizable place outside the realm of signification and human meaning that the "empty circle" comes to exert a dominating and mysterious force on the identities and lives not only of survivors but of their children as well.

Laub and Auerhahn (1993) explain the origin of the "empty circle" and its impact on the lives of Holocaust survivors' offspring in the following way: For children of survivors, "the enormity and horror of events of massive destruction establish the events as primary, and simultaneously constrain precisely those imaginative processes that must be used if they are to know" (p. 289). Although, typically, their knowledge of the parents' trauma is replete with associations and imagery that the survivors themselves cannot contain (Auerhahn & Prelinger, 1983), at the centre remains a "hole". For these offspring, these "wounds without memory" may compellingly find expression in the very shape of their lives—as a sense of void, terror, vulnerability, and loss that defies all comfort—and may paralyse their ability to start a family of their own. The "empty circle" legacy transmitted to these children thus becomes interwoven with, and often comes to overshadow, their normal developmental conflicts.

In my view, there is no "empty hole" in the psychic structure of Holocaust survivors' offspring. The tearing of the network of signification caused by the traumatization may indeed create a "hole" in the psyche of the Holocaust survivors themselves, expressed through the survivors' inability to integrate trauma into their cognitive and affective framework. However, in the case of their offspring the "hole" does not remain empty but is filled with unconscious fantasies pertaining to the parents' traumatization, which are then often behaviourally acted out.[4] These enactments reveal the "negative" by acting out the negated traumatic themes residing in the offspring's "psychic holes "—themes connected to death and survival.

How is the "psychic hole" created in cases of Holocaust survivors' offspring? Even in those families where a "pact of silence" prevails, a child would still be able to guess some of the details of the parents' severe traumatization. When cognitive development is sufficiently advanced, the child will begin to investigate the parents' past. At this stage, the parents' desire to deny or repress the traumatic events could force them to unconsciously convey to the searching child that the object of his investigation is not something that really happened in the parents' lives—it is, rather, the child's wicked thoughts, a bad dream, something that ought to be forgotten (Grubrich-Simitis, 1984). Thus, the parents' redefinition of the traumatic events in their lives as something horrible that emanated from the child's inner world makes the reality of the trauma unreal for the offspring.

Through the parents' negation or repression of the trauma—a trauma that, by means of "primitive identification", the offspring attribute to themselves—as well as through the offspring's repression of the traces of the trauma, what was known or almost known becomes "unknown". It is the "unknown", or that which cannot be remembered, that creates a "psychic hole", a hole that includes the child's unconscious fantasies about the parents' traumatic past.

Enactment

The body of unconscious fantasies that fills the "psychic hole" generates the compelling need to enact these fantasies in the offspring's current life. As mentioned above, enactment, the projection of denied knowledge by acting out, is an expression of the "negative"—in Freud's (1925h) terms revealed in the denial expressed by stating the opposite. The understanding of the meaning of these enactments that often endanger the patients' lives reveals the traumatic themes that have been consciously negated. This understanding transforms the unconscious fantasies residing in the psychic hole into conscious psychic representations of the traumatic absent events.

I will briefly define and compare the concepts "enactment", "acting out", and "acting in". Freud, who considered psychoanalysis to be a talking cure, regarded nonverbal activity as a problem in analysis. He believed that "acting out" [*"agieren"*] was an expression of resistance to remembering and communicating, thus constituting an obstacle to treatment (Freud, 1905e [1901]; 1914g). However, he also regarded acting out as a way of remembering (Freud, 1914g, p. 150).

Towards the end of his life, becoming more aware of the close relationship between transference and "acting out", Freud indicated that communicating through acting was at least as valid as communicating through remembering: "the patient produces before us with plastic clarity an important part of his life story, of which he would otherwise have given us only an insufficient account. He acts it before us, as it were, instead of reporting it to us" (Freud, 1940a [1938], pp. 175–176).

This newer attitude of Freud's, as well as the more recent attempt in the psychoanalytic literature to give greater legitimacy to acting in psychoanalysis, has led to the appearance of two new concepts: "acting in" and "enactment". These two concepts view acting in analysis as a way of remembering and expressing and as a nonverbal way of communicating, rather than as a way of avoiding painful knowledge, as in the case of "acting out".

"Acting in" is defined as "acting in the transference" or "acting in the analytic situation", which is sometimes the only way for the patient to convey some meaning to the therapist. A problematic aspect of this concept, however, is that it is defined by a local or technical situation rather than by a theory or metapsychology (Etchegoyen, 1991; Laplanche & Pontalis, 1973). Consequently, a further concept—"enactment"—has been coined in the last decade. First suggested by Jacobs (1986), "enactment" was accepted as a far more useful concept than "acting in", which was contaminated by the negative connotations involving resistance to treatment that were attributed to "acting out". "Enactment" differs from "acting out" in that it is primarily an interactive concept, reflecting what occurs in the relationship between patient and analyst and stressing the analyst's participation in the process (Schafer, 1982).

I wish to define "enactment" somewhat differently and apply it to Holocaust survivors' offspring. In the context of the Holocaust, I view "enactment" as a general term that includes some of the attributes of both "acting out" and "acting in". In this sense, "enactment" may serve the purpose of avoiding painful knowledge and memory (similar to the objective of "acting out"; Freud, 1905e [1901], 1914g), while at the same time it is the only way available to the patient to relive an inner experience—as in the process of "acting in" (Freud, 1940a [1938]).

My usage of the concept "enactment" in the context of the Holocaust differs from that of analysts who primarily stress its interactive aspects. These analysts believe that enactment (or "actualization", as it is termed by Sandler & Sandler, 1978) reflects what occurs in the relationship between patient and analyst and the analyst's part in the process (Chused, 1991; Jacobs, 2000; McLaughlin, 1992; Renik, 1993; Schafer, 1982). I define "enactment" as the compulsion of Holocaust survivors' offspring to recreate their parents' experiences in their own lives through concrete acts. Thus, "enactment" is the externalization of traumatic themes from the past that have been negated, and not what occurs in the relationship between patient and analyst in the analytic situation.

The exploration of fantasy, fact, and acting out helps the patient/offspring to "know and then to "feel". By transforming the offspring's unconscious psychic representations of the parent's traumatic past that reside in the "psychic hole" into a cognitive mode, and by linking them to affects that have, until now, been severed from them, the offspring fills the "psychic hole" with knowledge—that is, psychic representations of the trauma. The result is the achievement of "affective understanding" (Freud, 1915e), which takes the place of "negation".

I now present several examples of the enactment of fantasies that reside in the "psychic hole", and how they were transformed into psychic representations of the Holocaust. In these cases, the transgenerationally transmitted mnemic deposits of Holocaust-related memories of the parents are intertwined with independently occurring separation–individuation, oedipal, and adolescence conflicts, which, while interesting in themselves, are outside the scope of this book. Here I focus only on the impact of these deposits on the offspring lives and the negated contents of the Holocaust past revealed through their enactments.

The patients described in the examples below display different levels of disturbance: one is neurotic, and the other two are borderline psychotic patients. In my view, there is not much difference between the "negative" expressed in enactments at the neurotic and psychotic levels. Since the enactments are externalizations of negated traumatic themes from the parents' past, all of the patients below exhibit a withdrawal of their libidinal investment in life and express the "negative" through their self-destructive enactments.

Clinical examples

Gabrielle

Gabrielle, an attractive 35-year-old woman, sought professional help because of her inability to find fulfilment and happiness in her life and personal relationships.[5] Her marriage was on the verge of collapse. She had been married for twelve years, had two daughters (then aged 12 and 8), and worked as a technician in a medical laboratory. At the age of 2½, the younger daughter was diagnosed with emotional problems, thus placing on Gabrielle the burden of raising a disturbed child.

Gabrielle was born in 1946, somewhere near the Polish–German border, to a Holocaust survivor-mother and a handicapped father (he had had a glass-eye since his youth). The family spent three years wandering through Poland before emigrating to Israel, where for the first few years they lived under very difficult conditions. Poor and uneducated, both parents struggled to earn a living. Their marriage was unharmonious and devoid of support and friendship.

Gabrielle's mother was the only surviving member in her family; she had had many brothers and sisters (Gabrielle never knew how many) who perished along with their parents in the Holocaust. The mother, who was then only 17 at the time, managed to flee through the woods and save her own life. She emerged from the forest after the war, limping, emaciated, and suffering from rheumatic fever, which developed into a chronic heart condition after Gabrielle's birth. Though Gabrielle was unaware of it, her mother's past had a great impact upon her life and that of her young daughter.

The clinical material describes Gabrielle's daughter's enactments of "unknown" (negated) traumatic events from her grandmother's Holocaust past. This enactment, which referred to the actualization of her suicidal wishes, was a product of the unconscious fantasies that resided in a "hole" in her own psyche, as well as in the "psychic hole" of her mother, Gabrielle.

> For a long time in the treatment, Gabrielle was unaware of the impact of her mother's past on herself and her daughter. Gabrielle told me how worried she was about her younger daughter, then 13 years old, who seemed to be preoccupied with death and was living in a fantasy world where her fear of death was intermingled with death-wishes. At home, as well as in school, the child told bizarre stories about a family—father, mother, and little girl—who inhabited her throat. Gabrielle's daughter described the little girl as paralysed and confined to a wheelchair. The little girl's mother took her for a walk, pushing the wheelchair ahead of her, and the wheelchair returned empty: the child had fallen out and been run over. In the daughter's story, the child was taken to the hospital where nobody knew whether she would live or die. The daughter's inclination was to think that the girl would die.
>
> During this phase we began exploring Gabrielle's fears about the very special bond between this daughter and herself: "I think that she feels what I feel, and in a way she reads my thoughts." I became aware that there might be a symbiotic relationship between Gabrielle and her daughter and that, through the child, the mother might be expressing feelings of which she was unaware. The daughter may perhaps have been identifying with the aggressive, destructive aspects of her mother and, through her behaviour and stories, was expressing suicidal tendencies that actually belonged to her mother and not to herself. In analysis we discovered that the same symbiotic bond existed between

Gabrielle and her mother, as well as with me in the transference. This was confirmed by the following occurrences:

(1) Gabrielle dreamt a long series of suicidal dreams which reflected her fear of death, intermingled with death wishes towards her daughter and only occasionally towards herself. In Gabrielle's dreams, her daughter was run over by a car or drowned. Gabrielle warned her to be careful, because she felt that the child was fulfilling her own inner wish of disappearing. For example: "I dreamt a dream in which *my little daughter was run over by a car. There was a car full of children, and she fell out of it. I was totally overwhelmed, and by the time I reacted, another car came and ran her over.*" In the associations related to the dream Gabrielle said: "This morning I was watching from the window as my daughter stopped in front of a truck while crossing the road. I saw the truck approaching and I was terribly frightened. I wondered what would have happened had she been run over by it. At the same time, I thought that perhaps my life would be easier."

(2) Gabrielle described her total identification (fusion) with me in the transference. Gabrielle became confused about her own identity and was incapable of differentiating between herself and me. For example, she thought that she saw me walking around the neighbourhood dressed provocatively, and then suddenly realized that those were actually her own clothes that she had recently worn. This confusion of identities, which lasted for about a year in analysis, pointed to the possibility that a similar process of confused identity had taken place between herself and her own mother during an early stage in Gabrielle's development. The dreams and the stories about the Holocaust that Gabrielle reported later in the analysis contained trauma that did not belong historically to her own past, but to the past of her mother. Apparently she had always been entirely absorbed into her mother's feelings and was unable to differentiate between herself and her mother.

Gabrielle herself confirmed the hypothesis of her total identification with her mother during the process of working through her feelings towards her mother: "My black feelings—where do they come from? I know they come from my mother, not because of her illness, but because of the war she went through. She transmitted her depression to me, her sad face was always in front of me, the unhappiness, the quiet despair."

In analysis, Gabrielle recollected a story about her mother's "mythos of survival" (Klein, 1981; Kogan, 1995):[6] "Mother suffered terrible things; she ran away and left her entire family behind. I truly admire her wish to survive; I wouldn't have had the desire to live any more. She told me that she tried to commit suicide twice, and when she put the rope around her neck, she saw her mother's face telling her: "If you've survived up until now, you have to go on living for everybody else."

The longing for suicide, which is typical of many adolescents, is usually mediated by changes in ego functions, the quality of which depends greatly on the structural–cognitive development that takes place in adolescence (Erlich, 1978). Here I focus only on the impact of this young adolescent's unconscious fantasies that derived from the mother and grandmother's negation of traumatic past events.

Gabrielle's ill mother was probably unable to carry the burden of pain and aggression caused by her massive traumatization. She transmitted it to Gabrielle, who unconsciously conveyed it to her own daughter. Thus, in both generations, the mother was unable to help the daughter to achieve self–object differentiation, and hence, the daughters felt the need to live in their mothers' pasts (Auerhahn & Prelinger, 1983; Kestenberg, 1980). The unconscious processes of identification on the one hand, and the negation and repression of the trauma on the other, created a "psychic hole" in both generations. The unconscious fantasies residing in the "psychic hole" in the third generation compelled the child to enact the conflicting emotions and unconscious wishes regarding living or dying—her grandmother's "mythos of survival" (Klein & Kogan, 1986)—in her own life. The child attempted to enact suicide, thus repeating her grandmother's wish to die but also to survive at the same time. She tried to come close to death in order to overcome it.

Hannah

Hannah was a new immigrant living in Israel who sought analysis because of her feelings of derealization and her inability to cope with life.[7] She was the daughter of a Holocaust survivor whose first wife had perished in the Holocaust and who had spent much of the war in hiding. Hannah's father had suffered from masked depression throughout his life, and he never disclosed his past to his new family. But during the first year of analysis, Hannah heard through a cousin about her father's first wife and how she had died. The secret was at long last revealed to his second wife and children, and Hannah's father donated a sum of money to an institution in Israel in memory of his first wife.

Following this, there were many enactments, which expressed Hannah's unconscious attempt to recreate the fate of her father's first wife in her current reality. Moreover, she connected the fact that she was living in Israel, surrounded by Arab hostility, to her fantasies about her father's past. The source of these fantasies was the "psychic hole", the conscious negation of the traumatic past, while unconsciously always knowing about it. A description of one of her enactments follows:

> Hannah rushed back to analysis from a trip to Europe in a state of panic and tremendous anxiety, relating that she was in great danger because "an Arab is after me". It turned out that she had met an elegantly dressed gentleman in the lobby of her hotel, whom she believed to be an Arab spy. Despite the fact that she did not have Israeli citizenship and that she had been living in Israel for only a few months, she immediately told him that she was an Israeli citizen. After going out together to dinner and a film, Hannah went to his room, where the two had sex without uttering a single word. Suddenly Hannah realized that she did not even know his name and, panic-stricken, quickly made up an excuse that she had to go to the toilet, dressed hurriedly, grabbed her handbag, and fled the room. Two hours later she was on a plane to Israel.
>
> Upon arriving home, Hannah phoned the hotel where she had stayed to inform them that she had left a pair of shoes there, and

gave her address so that the shoes could be forwarded to her. Immediately afterward she came looking for me in desperation, convinced that the "Arab spy" would pursue her.

Hannah connected this episode to the film *The Night Porter*, which she had seen many years before. She related that the story in the film took place some time after the Nazi concentration camps had been liberated, and it portrayed an encounter between a Jewish woman who had been imprisoned in a concentration camp as an adolescent and the Nazi officer who had been her tormentor there. In this encounter, said Hannah, the past prevailed over the present, and the protagonists, propelled by a force greater than themselves, resumed their concentration camp roles of victim and persecutor. The man sexually abused the woman, and then—unable to return to reality—killed her.

Attempting in the transference to understand Hannah's need to enact her unconscious wishes and fantasies with regard to her father's first wife, I pointed out that she was assigning to me the role of being her saviour while attempting to bring this woman back to life by becoming her. But, I added, she was trying to kill her father's first wife by placing herself in danger of being killed by the Arab/Nazi.

During this phase of treatment Hannah achieved some "affective understanding" (Freud, 1915e) of her enactments by making the unconscious conscious and linking to it her feelings of pain and mourning for the losses incurred by her father. Without describing this phase in detail here, suffice it to say that, following the above-mentioned episode, and supported by her analyst, Hannah summoned the courage to question her father about his traumatic past. Their discussions produced an unexpected result. Her father, concerned that he was nearing the end of his life, decided to write an autobiography and asked Hannah to be his editor.

In analysis, we understood that her willingness to edit this work demonstrated Hannah's readiness to become acquainted with negated details of her father's trauma and, furthermore, to place it in a past that was not her own. Only after filling the "psychic hole" with knowledge could we work through feelings of mourning and guilt that belonged to her father, which had been transmitted to her in nonverbal forms of communication. This long process of working through eventually led Hannah to a better differentiation between herself and her father, between past and present, between reality and fantasy.

Kay

Kay was the stepdaughter of a Holocaust survivor who had been castrated by Mengele's doctors.[8] Kay communicated with me (in the first phase of treatment) through infantile drawings. One of her pictures, bearing the title "Electricity", depicted a man with a wiry flower emerging from his head. Only at a later stage in analysis, when Kay was able to communicate with me verbally, were we able to understand her unconscious fantasy: the flower of death symbolized her stepfather's traumatic experience of having to avoid death by spending an entire night standing naked in the cold between the two rows of electric wires of the concentration camp.

Kay was referred to treatment after attempting to jump from the eighth floor of a building. In analysis, we were able to understand her desire to jump to her death from high places as an attempt to enact the torment associated with her stepfather's survival and close encounters with death. For her stepfather, falling would have meant touching the wires, electrocution, and a horrible death. When Kay ascended to the eighth floor, intending to jump out of the window, she was convinced that she would survive. Her delusional, paranoid fantasies of magically and omnipotently conquering death were endangering her life.

In analysis, Kay demonstrated a constant preoccupation with her body—physical fitness, weight, and muscle tone—as part of her survival complex. This preoccupation was based on her unconscious fantasy that "I feel my body, therefore I exist". I will go into detail on this matter later on.

The following episode illustrates Kay's compelling need to enact the reparation of her stepfather's castration upon her own body:

After my summer holiday, she informed me that she had undergone breast surgery during my absence. She stressed that she had chosen to undergo the surgery while I was away because she did not want to cancel her sessions after I returned home. Elaborating, she explained that the operation was the fulfilment of a wish she had had since she was young—to enlarge her breasts with silicone implants.

Kay went to a doctor who examined her breasts and described them as "empty" rather than small. He stated that an operation was possible but was not without risks, warning her that her body might reject the silicone, a condition accompanied by tissue inflammation, fever, and pain, and the necessity for further operations. She was informed that she might never be able to breastfeed a child. Despite being terrified of these prospects, Kay nevertheless decided to go ahead with the operation. She was referred to a shop where she was measured for implants and selected them from a catalogue, choosing a medium size, which she felt would make her look much more like a "whole" woman.

Kay came to analysis on the appointed date, two weeks after her operation. She entered the room walking upright and, pulling her blouse against her breasts, asked if I could see any change. Only afterwards, when lying on the couch, did she tell me the entire story. She was overjoyed and emphasized her satisfaction at being able to conquer her fears.

In my countertransference feelings I felt a heavy weight lying on my heart. This feeling made me aware that Kay was not in touch with her sadness, which was conveyed to me by massive projective identification. Attempting to understand what had compelled her do this deed during my absence, I pointed out to Kay that she had begun feeling that her breasts were "empty" only when I was not around, when she was not getting the feeding and support from our regular sessions. Kay laughed a short laugh and then confirmed my hypothesis in an angry voice: "I don't need you; I don't need anybody. I want to depend only on myself."

I pointed out Kay that her need to "fill" her breasts stemmed from her anger and frustration at feeling abandoned by me. Over the course of that session she became aware of these feelings and accepted them. Working through these feelings in the transference led her to reveal her fantasies of flirting with death on the operating table. She had undergone the operation in order to repair her femininity, but she was aware that she might die as a result. Of course, she now felt that she had once again overcome a terrible danger.

Kay associated her victory over possible death on the operating table with a story from her stepfather's life. After the war, he met one of the few other men who had survived castration in Mengele's experiments. The man told Kay's stepfather about a Jewish doctor in Paris who performed restorative surgery (implantation of testicles) on these victims free of charge. Her stepfather decided to go to Paris and have the operation. It was successful, and he was able to resume sexual relations with women, though he remained infertile.

Kay and I then began to elaborate upon the unconscious fantasies that compelled Kay to enact her stepfather's life story on her own body. I pointed out to Kay that she may have been trying to implant her femininity into her breasts in the same way in which her stepfather had had his manhood implanted into his empty testicle sacs.

A pregnant silence filled the room as Kay absorbed my words. Then, understanding the meaning behind her decision to undergo surgery, she was overwhelmed by a powerful surge of emotion. It took us many months to work through the feelings of fear, depression, and pain that replaced her euphoria. We also tried to elaborate on the complex needs she had expressed through her surgery. Consciously, she was trying to attain a better, repaired sexuality. Unconsciously, she was attempting to endanger herself in a concrete way, to come as close as possible to an imagined death, in order to overcome it.

Kay knew few details of her stepfather's experiences during the Holocaust, as he kept them mostly to himself. The atmosphere of silence at home masked a past full of terror and violence, which Kay absorbed. For the last 20 years her stepfather had been writing his Holocaust memoirs, but Kay had never had the courage to ask to see them. In analysis, after working through her fear of discovering what had really happened to him and encouraged by my supportive attitude, she decided that the time had come to do so. To her great surprise and excitement, her stepfather sent her his complete autobiography, which he had dedicated to his adopted children. Kay read it avidly and brought it to me so that I, too, could read it. I read it, feeling that I had to participate in this act; thus I "actualized" (Sandler & Sandler, 1978) her wish to make me her partner in "the search for the self through family secrets" (Gampel, 1982).

The elaboration of Kay's enactment enabled us to begin an exploration of the way she had communicated with me during the first part of treatment, and the way she had lived her life until then, using her body to express unconscious fantasies pertaining to physical occurrences, anxieties, and emotions that were experienced by her stepfather during the Holocaust.

All through her treatment, Kay had complained at length about her defective sense of smell. Only now could we connect this impairment to her stepfather's story of the awful stench emanating from people dying in their excrement and vomit, unable to reach the public latrine. Impairment of the olfactory sense thus became a survival mechanism for him. Kay's constant state of hunger, as well as her suffering from cold and her inability to find suitably warm clothing, were also primary aspects of her stepfather's wartime experiences.

Kay had a fear of incontinence—which she expressed by running repeatedly to the toilet during sessions. In this regard, she related a story of woe and humiliation from her stepfather's memoirs: "Father stood for hours at roll call, peeing in his pants, knowing that any movement could incur a death punishment." Urine was the substance used by her stepfather to treat a wound on his leg caused by a brutal kick from a German soldier.

During this phase of analysis, in which she recounted these stories, Kay was treating the wounds in her soul by uncovering negated bits of information from her repressed consciousness—information that she had known but had forgotten over the years.

Discussion

As I have shown in various case illustrations that I have published over the years, history is never truly past—that is, the past is never dead; it lives in the mind, never to perish. Turner (1938) eloquently described the intermeshed nature of past and present by viewing the present as an undeveloped past and the past as an undeveloped present.

This connection between past and present derives from the difference between the "facts" of history and the meaning and significance we attribute to these facts. The initial fact has many ramifications and is not a thing unto itself with sharp, clear outlines. Becker (1955) posed three simple questions about historical fact: what, where, and when. Regarding the "what", Becker states that historical fact is not the past event but a symbol that enables us to recreate it imaginatively. As to the "where", Becker places it in someone's mind and insists that a historical fact *is*—not *was*. While the actual past event is gone forever, it is remembered; it is the persistence of records and memories, rather than the ephemeral event, that makes a difference to us now. Becker then addresses himself to the "when" of a historical fact, claiming that if the historical fact is present, imaginatively, in someone's mind, then it is now part of the present.

The transformation process

In the case of Holocaust survivors' offspring, the historical past is always present, and unconscious fantasies about this past fill the "psychic hole", generating enactments. I believe that the most effective way to transform these unconscious fantasies into conscious psychic representations is by making patients aware of the connection between their enactments and their parent's traumatic past. This awareness, making the unconscious conscious, which was stressed by Freud in many of his works, can transform the enactments into a cognitive mode and uncover what has been negated. The transformation may be achieved by helping these individuals to find the meaning of the trauma in their parents' lives and to bind[9] it in a meaningful context, thus consigning it to the past of their parents rather than to their own.

During the first phase of analysis, the analyst deals with cognition and emotions that were severed in the offspring by the parents' negation of the trauma, leaving in the child traces of what has been negated. Finding the parents' "unknown" story, which facilitates the removal of negation, followed by a process of working through, which links thoughts and feelings, transforms the enactment of negated contents into an "affective understanding" (Freud, 1915e). The resulting integration of cognition and emotions greatly diminishes the offspring's need to externalize the "negative" by repeatedly re-enacting the parents' stories in their current life.[10]

The quest for information—the purpose of which is to enable the patient to fill the "hole" with psychic representations and give up enactments—is a difficult experience for the survivor's offspring. It is my view that in the initial stages of analysis, only a supportive, nurturing environment, which includes a "holding relationship" (one that decreases the patient's tremendous anxiety) and "holding interpretations" (those that help the patient to mobilize his/her forces to find the meaning of the trauma in the parents' lives) can strengthen the patient's mental organization to the point that negation is removed and psychic representations of the Holocaust past replace fragmenting, potentially life-threatening enactments (Kogan, 1995, 1996, 1998, 2002, 2003, 2007a, 2007b).

The information resulting from the offspring's quest for knowledge facilitates differentiation and the creation of a new and separate self. This quest for information might, however, be accompanied by torment and anxiety. Consciously, the child is afraid that questions about the past will force the parent to uncover what has been negated and relive painful, traumatic memories that may threaten the parent's psychic survival. Unconsciously, the child experiences the wish to know his parent's history as a step towards differentiation and a relief from the burden of the parent's past, while at the same time realizing that this differentiation and separation may be potentially destructive for the parent. The quest for information is usually facilitated by the holding atmosphere in analysis and by the patient adopting the analyst as an ally in his quest.

It is only after this initial phase of holding, in which the patient's self is strengthened, that interpretations of his or her unconscious life become not only acceptable but also necessary. During these later phases, it is possible to work through the negated—and thus missing—piece of the parent's history that is often connected with the offspring's feelings of shame and guilt and which created a myriad unconscious fantasies that filled the "hole".

In some cases, the parent's story does not emerge easily, but has to be actively sought. The therapist's supportive attitude facilitates the patient's discovery of that part of the parent's history that has been negated and that will fill the "hole" with psychic representations. This process is realized through the acquisition of concrete details from the parent's past. Examples from the cases cited are Kay's request to read her stepfather's memoirs in order to learn, among other things, about his castration by the Nazi doctors, and Hannah agreeing to edit her father's autobiography of his Holocaust past.

The construction of an unbroken narrative—one that fills the gaps in the offspring's knowledge, that makes it permissible to mention the unmentionable, that interweaves awareness of the realities and horrors of the Holocaust with the present—enables the offspring of survivors to uncover what has been negated and gradually gain some comfort from the split-off knowledge that has been accompanied by unacknowledged affects and fears. The events and narratives that formed the starting point of the child's traumatic wound can be reconstructed, so that the split-off and diffusely enacted memory fragments from a persecutory world are elucidated. Thus, the interpretation of the "negative", which is often expressed through fragmentary, defensive enactments, leads the patient to an awareness of the reality of the trauma and fills the "psychic hole" with psychic representations. The work of mourning that continues during the latter phases of analysis eventually frees him from the burden of the past and enables him to achieve a stronger, better integrated self.

Notes

1. The offspring of other war-affected people (e.g., Vietnamese refugees) and genocide survivors (e.g., Rwanda) may suffer from "psychic holes" as well. As I have described elsewhere (Kogan, 1995), while the modes of transmission of trauma are universal, in cases of Holocaust survivors the modes of transmission bear the unique quality that the Holocaust trauma imparted to them. This is often expressed in analysis through specific imagery connected to the Holocaust experience.
2. The "work of the negative" is André Green's (1993) collective designation for mental functions that are designed to reject objects, disinvest perception, and impoverish the ego. Under the broad rubric "the work of the negative" he includes the "negative therapeutic reaction" (Freud, 1923b) as well as the mechanisms of repression, negation, splitting, and disavowal. He adds five additional notions of his own: "negative hallucination", "negative hallucination of thought", "subjective disengagement by the ego", "negative narcissism", and the "ego's sense of self-disappearance". Fuelled by destructive drives, these processes impel the individual to accept or reject something: an object, a perception, a thought, or even one's own subjective existence (Akhtar, 2009a).
3. According to Danielle Quinodoz, the "hole-object" is created by the patient to defend against psychic suffering and aggressive drives towards the object. Quinodoz makes a careful distinction between the "hole-object", which is defined in terms of its nonexistence, and the "absent object", the "melancholic object" and the "bad-breast feeling", all of which exist or have existed at some time.
4. Parents who did not deny (negate) their traumatic past and who succeeded in working through the feelings of mourning and guilt connected to it may have conveyed their history to their children in a healthier manner. In these cases, the children are much less likely to experience a "psychic hole" in their psychic reality.
5. See Klein & Kogan (1986, 1995) for additional descriptions of this case.
6. As a result of their traumatization, Holocaust survivors often create personal myths and fantasies—their "mythos of survival" (Klein, 1981; Kogan, 1995)—which differ from other types of neuroses. The mythos contains memories from the past, and its function is to maintain a traumatic screen (Kris, 1956) that hides huge amounts of ambivalence and hostility which can be unleashed by brutality, anxiety, or emotional pathology. This longitudinal process, which began in the Holocaust, continues to influence the survivor at different stages of his life cycle. It affects his perception of his body image, his object relations, his political views, and the way he relates to issues of life and death. The "mythos of survival" is the realization of conflicting emotions and unconscious wishes regarding living and dying; it often permeates boundaries between generations and is unconsciously transmitted to the next generation by processes of projec-

tion–introjection (Kogan, 2007b). As a result, the death wish, as well as the struggle against it, that existed in the lives of the parents may become a compelling need in the lives of the offspring.

7. See Kogan (1993, 1995) for a more detailed description of this case.

8. See Kogan (1987, 1995) for a more detailed description of this case.

9. The concept of "binding" was first described in Freud's (1920g) theory of why certain events have a traumatic effect upon the mind, and how personality takes account of and adapts to the resulting changed internal conditions. "Binding" appears in connection with Freud's famous meta-psychological explanation (1920g, p. 31) of trauma as an "extensive breach made in the protective shield against stimuli", which occurs only when the mental apparatus is not prepared for anxiety—that is, when the parts of the system that are to receive the excessive stimulation are not properly hypercathected and therefore "the inflowing amount of excitation could not be *bound*". It is hard to be sure what precisely Freud meant by "binding", since he used the term at different stages of his work in different ways (Laplanche & Pontalis, 1973). However, by 1920 it had taken on the general meaning of a defensive operation that restricts free-flowing "excitation". Once the catastrophic breach in the protective shield has taken place and mental functioning is in turmoil and disarray, the problem is one of "mastering the amounts of stimulus which have broken in and of binding them in the psychical sense, so that they can then be disposed of". In the recent literature (Garland, 1991, 2002), "binding" is described as a process by which the ego creates links between the free-flowing excitation and functions of the mind. In this way the ego attempts to recreate structures of some permanence in which ego functioning is possible.

10. Wilson (1985) writes that offspring of survivors can acquire greater affect tolerance through the joint construction, with the analyst, of the historical narrative of the parents, which includes their Holocaust experience. This then lessens their need to enact the traumatic past of their parents.

9

Negation, negative capability, and the work of creativity

Antonino Ferro

Freud (1925h) argues that negation entails an intellectual acknowledgement of what has been repressed even when the essential part of repression—or in other words, its emotional counterpart—remains. Of course, even stronger defence mechanisms than negation also exist, such as the Jekyll-and-Hyde sort of splitting or "hyperbole" (Bion, 1965) whereby affect is violently expelled and lost "in space". It goes without saying that the other side to negation is affirmation, whether this comes from the analyst's interpretive activity or from the patient himself.

In this chapter I consider these defence mechanisms as gradations of the same phenomenon. This is not because I think there is no point in looking at the differences, the specific characteristics, and even their various degrees of seriousness, but because I think it is more useful to offer some reflections on a common antidote to these defence mechanisms: the negative capability of the analyst in Bion's (1970) understanding of the term taken from Keats's letter (1817) to his brothers, George and Thomas. The key point of this capability is knowing how to be in a state of doubt without having to saturate it immediately with answers—in Keats's words, "being in uncertainties, mysteries, doubts, without any irritable reaching after fact and reason". Or, in Bion's terminology, being for a long time in the paranoid-schizoid position but free from persecution.

It is true that by doing so I am assigning fixed roles, but I do so for the sake of convenience: if we hold that a field is established between analyst and patient, as we are taught by the Barangers (Baranger & Baranger, 1961–62, 2009; Ferro & Basile, 2009), it is not uncommon to find the opposite situation—one in which it is the analyst who, in order to escape from excessive anxiety, puts up defences against listening authentically to the patient by offering the kind of interpretation that Bion (1963) placed in Column 2 of the Grid (where we find Lies). It is the patient who persists in iterating an emotional truth. From the intrapsychic point of view, I would see negation as a "dam" that prevents flooding downstream: what cannot be metabolized and transformed and whose irruption on the scene would be disastrous for the psychic apparatus is "negated". There is a literary example I would like to mention (only briefly, however, because it is too well known): Melville's (1983) story of Bartleby, the Scrivener, who is asked in every possible way to leave his workplace and always replies firmly but politely: "I would prefer not to", thus escaping the catastrophic experiences that leaving would cause.

The relational dimension of negation

There has been a great deal of discussion about how we can work with patients who elude interpretation though negation. I think we should remember that Freud was not always very sensitive to replies given to his interpretations: there is an amusing episode in "Notes Upon a Case of Obsessional Neurosis" (1909d) in which he almost forces the patient (the Rat Man) to accept a reconstruction of his childhood without understanding that the patient's associative response was in actual fact a negation of the analyst's intervention. Immediately after Freud's imperious reconstruction, the patient speaks about a law professor who posed the question about a rent bill, which, if it was not paid, was taken to the debtor's domicile to make it impossible for him to avoid paying. This problem arises especially with narcissistic patients, and in this context I would like to recall the famous story of a boy who was the youngest child in a poor family and who was the first whom, with the help of his elder brothers, his parents could afford to send to school. Everyone was convinced he would enjoy a brilliant future, which would repay the family's sacrifice. Then, on his third day at school, the boy says, "I don't want to go to school any more", thus plunging the family into despair. Realizing that their threats and promises are in vain, the parents give up trying to change his mind. However, they do ask him at least to tell them why he doesn't want to go to school. His answer is: "Because they teach me things I don't know."

Of course, the landscape has changed since the Barangers (1961–62) introduced their field theories and gave a non-Kleinian reading of Bion—the Bion (1994) who says, for example, that an interpretation can be given "six sessions later, six months later, six years later" (p. 85) and that "you can't launch out into a great explanation of the biology of the alimentary canal to a baby" (p. 17). Pointing in the same direction are Widlöcher's conceptualization of co-thought (1996) and what, in Italy, are known as "weak interpretations", "unsaturated interpretations", or "narrative interpretations" (Ferro, 2002b, 2004). I have taken this long path to emphasize how, very often, the more assertive an interpretation is, the more it activates negation and at times encourages or reinforces splitting. One is then more likely to get stuck in impasse situations and to run up against negative therapeutic reactions.

Antidotes to negation

I think the best antidote to negation is the creation of affective–climatic coordinates or, in my parlance, a field in which there is a kind of extraterritoriality. Here the level of what is true/false is not measured against the elevated plane occupied by a holder of truth, and at the same time we have a sort of duty-free zone where it is possible to generate shared narratives that gradually make the unthinkable thinkable. Besides, the movement towards "O" (absolute truth and ultimate reality) can only be gradual and must always take into account the degree of emotional truth that patient and analyst can bear. Incidentally, it is interesting to point out that Grotstein

(2007) also considers dreams as mediators between the truth and the need for masking the unknowable absolute truth. Basically this is the same as Winnicott's view (1971) of analysis as a transitional space, an area for what I would describe as unsaturated interpretations, which are very different from those that engulf and become sources of persecution (Tuckett et al., 2008).

The following clinical examples demonstrate the fact that although this kind of operation sometimes fails and sometimes succeeds, what matters is that there is an oscillating movement between these two dimensions: on the one hand, the more open, unsaturated dimension, and one in which an attempt is made—sometimes successfully, sometimes unsuccessfully—to give an exhaustive interpretation. In Italy the idea of considering what a patient says after an interpretation as a response to the interpretation is a notion we owe above all to Nissim Momigliano and Robutti (2001), although important contributions have also been made by Faimberg (1996) and even earlier by Ferenczi, who became aware of this aspect of the patient's communication and described it in his remarkable paper on "Transitory Symptom-Constructions during the Analysis" (1912). To come back to "negative capability": this is what gives us the particular kind of unsaturated receptivity that enables anxieties, sensoriality and projective identifications to find a sort of "vacuum" where it is possible for there to be both the complete reception and the collapse of "truths" that thought cannot bear. In this sense I would say that negative capability is the forerunner of reverie. Technically, it entails tolerating the deferral of meaning that can often occur due to the unsaturated nature of interpretive interventions.

I believe that much can be gained by substituting a comprehensive interpretation with a commitment to narrative transformations that can be activated by the enzymatic action of the analyst. What also becomes central is the way we use the patient as our satellite navigation system (GPS). We can take the patient's responses as pointers to go deeper and deeper. Bion (2005) often talks about the patient as the analyst's "best colleague", and in this context my mind always turns to Conrad's (1909) remarkable story, "The Secret Sharer", about a stowaway whom the captain keeps on board ship and who then throws himself off the ship close to the shoreline. He realizes that the ship is about to crash into rocks, and so he puts his hat on the surface of the water to mark the spot, thus enabling the captain to avoid going aground. This for me is the essential function of the patient: at any given moment he throws his hat to inform us how we are getting along. This is basically the only way we have to be in contact with the patient—and I insist on the concept of unison—rather than in touch with our theories, because otherwise we end up in a kind of primal scene with our theories that exclude the patient.

So we see an emotional field in which there is an oscillation between denial, negation, and negative capability that ultimately modulates and regulates the emotional forces that enter the field and are metabolized. On this point it is interesting to look again at Bion's suggestion that even dreams and waking dreams (alpha function) are to be considered barriers and cavities with respect to a reality (O) that is unobtainable. I believe that a dialectic between defences and O (the oscillation K—knowledge ↔ O—ultimate reality) remains the only method our species has at its disposal to enable it to come close to the truth without getting burned. After going through "negation" and "negative capability" [we should always remember that negation can come from the analyst who may be a victim of his own countertransferential blind spots. Under such circumstances, he makes interpretations that can be placed in second column of the Grid (the row that contains Lies), preventing the activation of emotions and affects that arouse fear; or, to use my parlance (Ferro, 2009), giving more space to grasping than to casting], we reach the third point: the work of creativity.

However, before giving some clinical examples, which I use to convey the sometimes complex theory of what I would call the "post-Bionian field", some theoretical explanations are in order.

I shall be speaking in terms of the analyst–patient dyad, although everything should really be rethought in terms of the field (Ferro & Basile, 2009), or in Ogden's terminology (1994) the "analytic third", or a new, third structure that is formed from the meeting of minds that takes place between analyst and patient. However, I leave this highly complex task to the reader who wishes to rethink what I say in terms of the field. There are many "places" where creative processes are carried out. The most significant is the work that leads to the transformation from sensoriality (Bion's beta elements) to waking dream thought, in other words to a sequence of pictograms (consisting of Bion's alpha elements) that make up the film of thought that gives rise to the contact-barrier (Bion, 1962) and to what Bion (2002) called "alpha dreams"—images not directly knowable except in reverie, in visual flashes, and in night dreams which are a re-dreaming (or at least some sort of montage) of all the alpha elements (pictograms) constructed while awake. The sequence of images thus formed soothes and pacifies the mind somewhat every time this transformation is successful.

In themselves these pictograms (Rocha Burros, 2000) are normally unknowable. For example, if we have a sequence of strong indistinct sensory inputs that could be organized by the alpha function into the not very well defined states of anger–relief–nostalgia, then the sequence of signs could be: "Storm–Sun peeping through the clouds–autumn sunset".

Of course, the choice and construction of the "pictogram" and its sequences are highly subjective. It is as if a "motif" were painted by Degas, and then again at different times by Caravaggio, Monet, Chagall, or Picasso. So this is the first "locus" of the creativity of the mind. In Bionspeak this would be the transformation from beta to alpha—via alpha function. At this point we come to the second place where we find the creativity of the mind or, rather, the very subjective way in which the sequence of pictograms (waking dream thought) are "told" or put into words, through a multitude of literary genres: here we have the narrative derivatives of pictograms (or alpha elements) (Ferro, 2002a, 2005a, 2006a). The proposed sequence could become a series of stories with anger–relief–nostalgia as a constant. They range from a "memory" of childhood to a diary-like story, from a true story taken from a newspaper to a fantasy, and so on. It is also true that we can get in touch with a pictogram of the sequence that forms in our mind in the session through the phenomenon called reverie. This helps us to come into contact with or to "see" in our mind's eye, for example, the pictogram for "storm": it is up to us to find a use for it in the session.

A brief example: reveries are always dream fragments of situations imbued with projective identification, or, if we prefer, with beta elements. Giovanna and I are at an impasse, with no apparent way out. Then I get in touch with, or I see, "a sailing ship inside a bottle", which gives me a visual description of what is happening in the analytic field: the analytic sailing ship is bottled up. Hence the interpretation: it seems to me that we have reached deadlock and are like a sailing ship inside a bottle, a boat, like the analysis, that is designed to sail.

This would be a metaphor and not a reverie, however, if I were to use my encyclopaedia—in other words, my set of knowledge about this subject—and were to take an example from Conrad of one of those situations of "dead calm" in which sailing ships will sometimes find themselves; this would help me to describe more clearly a situation I am already aware of, whereas the image of a "sailboat in a bottle" is active, it makes a suggestion. It acts as a starter and inspiration for the interpretation. I think there is a big difference between "free associations" and reveries: the latter involve direct contact with an image (which will, of course, not be communicable—unless in exceptional circumstances to the patient, in which case it would fall into the category of self-disclosure). Free associations concern what I have called "narrative derivatives", whereas reveries have to do, as I said, with taking up direct contact with the pictograms that make up waking dream thought. Another situation in which we see a pictogram of the sequence of this waking dream thought is when the patient projects in a non-violent way outside one of these images, without it being a true hallucination, because this image can easily be understood in the meaning it conveys. By way of an example, I recall once proposing a fee increase to a patient whose reaction was to say: "My God, I can see a chicken being plucked on that wall over there."

To get back to explaining the model of the mind I refer to: during the day we store huge amounts of pictograms (alpha elements), and then it is up to an "alpha superfunction" (Ferro, 2006a; Grotstein, 2007) to perform a kind of second pressing or weaving of these stocks up to the point of creating dream images—that is, the most highly digested products of our apparatus for thinking.

Significantly, Ogden (2009) argues that the goal of psychoanalysis and the work of the psychoanalyst consist in having those dreams, in carrying out those transformations from storms of sensoriality into images that the patient has not been able to do alone. It also follows that the purpose of analysis is the development of the ability to "generate images", to create dreams where there were once symptoms—in other words, concrete embodiments of sensoriality. The great success of creativity in psychoanalysis is a question not so much of content but, rather, of the ability to develop these tools (alpha function and ♀ ♂ container/contained) that enhance the capacity to dream, think, feel—in other words, the operation described by Grotstein as the ability to subjectify "O" and which I have called the "transformation into dream" that allows each communication by the patient to be deconcretized, deconstructed, and re-dreamed. Again, this requires reformulation in terms of the functions of the analytic field.

Five clinical vignettes

The line of interpretation

It occurs quite frequently that we are taken over by a line of interpretation that comes to organize all our listening (or lack of listening). Since I was thinking that the right thing for Filippo would be for him to integrate violent split-off aspects of his personality, I had automatically tuned into this frequency. I even saw the "big bolts" [*bulloni*] on the wheels he talked about as "big bullies" [*bulli*]. Then one day Filippo started talking to me about his dentist, who keeps on making an x-ray of the same tooth without even bothering to ask whether the sharp pain he feels might actually be in another tooth. At this point I cannot help noticing how insisting on my line of interpretation had led me completely astray.

The line of interpretation implies failing to listen to what is new about what the patient tells us every day. As Bion (1987) tells us, the patient who finishes a sentence is not the same as the one who started it. This is part of what it means to listen without memory or desire: not to be cluttered with preconceptions about the patient or about the line of interpretation because these preconceptions obstruct original and creative developments of the field.

Isotta and her boyfriend

Isotta is in her first year of analysis. One Monday she comes to the session and describes the following picture. A patient has escaped from the community where she is obliged to live; then her brother has had several outbursts of anger, even going as far as kicking in the door; her mother had burst out crying because of her son's unrestrained behaviour, and when her husband arrived, she once again reproached him for being absent while they were bringing up the children, and also digging up other old grievances. Here the question arises of how to cook these various ingredients. It would be easy to do so in a decoding way. At the weekend the analyst had made a move, he had gone away; uncontrollable anger makes her kick down the closed door, and then the recriminations about being abandoned are set off.

This interpretation has two drawbacks: first, it is the product of a single mind, and, second, it comes across as saturated and automatic. There is only one meaning—namely, the one given by the analyst–magician who knows and understands everything. The other alternative would be to work with the characters and their interrelationships and to highlight the emotions that pass between them.

This can, however, be too generic. The method is, then, to start from the second modality—in other words, to taste the patient's replies so as to be guided by them as the session proceeds, looking at what can be "hinted at" and what can be said "clearly and explicitly". The same problem had arisen when Isotta had spoken of her boyfriend—a "bear" who always turned down invitations to dinner with friends. During one session I work on the difficulties she has in dealing with "her bear–boyfriend", the disappointments that arise, the frustrations, but also the difficulty of seeing his point of view, of being with other people. At the end of the session I am dissatisfied, I feel that I have neither grasped nor passed on the "gist of emotional meaning". At the next session Isotta begins by saying: "yesterday the light bulb in my room blew, and I was left in the dark." This announcement—that the session had shed no light—authorizes me, albeit gently and via a series of moves, to show Isotta how being a bear can also be an aspect of herself she knows little about because it is kept in the shadows by her more easy-going way of functioning, and perhaps all her talk serves as a barrier to protect the bear. When Isotta talks with great interest about a fantastic film she has seen, I am able to add a further meaning: coming to analysis is something that, on the one hand, she likes to do and is willing to do, but, on the other hand, she also has difficulties in coming and showing herself. She remembers at this point that as a child she used to liked to dance but was always ashamed if her parents saw her doing it. What I am trying to say is that there is no right or wrong way of interpreting, but that it must be continually adjusted according to the invaluable indications given by the patient.

The embryo and its development

In a previous session Filippo had brought with him a pregnancy test he had bought at the chemist's. During the session he tells me that the necessary number of days for implanting the embryo after the in vitro fertilization have passed (Ferro, 2010). The next day he starts off the session by describing the disappointment he and his wife had felt when they discovered that the embryo implantation had failed. He goes on to talk about a dinner party due to take place at his parents' house at which his brother and pregnant sister-in-law will also be present. When he heard the news that his sister-in-law was expecting, he was happy—perhaps excessively so; he even jumped for joy. He then talks about the arrest of Roman Polanski, but he again goes back to the point that his joy doesn't convince him completely. Did he secretly feel disappointment, anger? He then returns to the first subject, explaining that the embryo had formed, the spermatozoon and the egg-cell had fused, but the embryo itself had not developed. He comes back to the subject of Polanski; he talks about the director's difficult life, the rape charge he faced, and various other painful experiences.

At this point, after showing sympathy for his disappointment at the failure of the fertility test, I say: "What about trying to look at things from our point of view? Perhaps we are at the point where we can form the embryo of a thought but we are not ready to develop it. We have, so to speak, a trailer, but we don't yet have the film." Interested, he replies: "What could this film be that hasn't developed yet? What are we missing?" "Perhaps we're missing a character", I reply, responding to a reverie of mine in which I "dreamt" of the hidden violence that the patient was not able to dream. "Manson and his sect, who butchered to death Sharon Tate, Polanski's wife, who was expecting a baby". He replies: "Are you saying that I jumped for joy to mask the fact that I wanted to butcher my sister-in-law and perhaps even bugger her, just like Polanski apparently did with that young girl all that time ago?" I reply, in turn: "Well, that could be the film. Manson cannot stand the idea of something new being implanted permanently; precisely your creative and inventive ability is blocked by complying with what one ought to think. The crime story comes to life at the moment when the analyst's function of casting-reverie "captures" a missing character—in this case Manson—thus making it possible for the film to move forward. (I would like to remind readers that Sharon Tate, the wife of the film director Polanski, was killed in 1969 while pregnant. The killer's name was Manson.)

Some months later, after he has acquired the ability to think original thoughts, Filippo has a dream that affords him some relief even though he doesn't understand why. "Manson lost something, and there was a strange atmosphere of legality." In turn, I say: "It's enough to simply lose the 'n' and Manson is transformed into Mason—in other words, into Perry Mason and his law firm. Now your creativity appears to have become legitimate." (Recently Polanski has been found guilty of rape in Europe. Perry Mason is the main character of Erle Stanley Gardner's books, a lawyer who defends people who have been unjustly charged.) One of the analyst's functions thus seems to be to dream the missing pieces so that the patient's dream can develop. It doesn't matter then what the dream is, as long as it develops.

Laura's dream

Laura dreams of *climbing down a skyscraper and then of being in a princely palace full of scarves and Swarovski glassware*. Her dream also features *a housekeeper doing the hoovering, a girl putting on a beauty mask made up of rather unromantic cucumber slices covering her eyes, an iron bookcase where she can keep large numbers of thrown-away Barbie accessories*. The descent from idealization is long, removing the cucumber slices from one's eyes to see the reality of life is not easy, but there is a housekeeper who does the cleaning and an iron structure where you can place the fairytale world of childhood.

Finally, a drawing

A young patient makes a stylized drawing of a child, then draws the same child behind vertical lines, rigid, not speaking: here we have phimosis, "the gorilla is imprisoned behind bars". Some time later, in an outburst of violence and screaming, he smashes everything. Then he makes a drawing with vertical lines and a frame: the small gorilla has quite simply escaped from his cage, and the incontinence exploded. When presenting the case, the analyst had spoken of a cold mother and also of the child as having chickenpox and a 41° temperature. His father was a computer expert who broke out in sobs during one session.

Here are a further two ways to narrate the double function. The cold mother and the scorching 41° heat. The father who "computerizes" and miniaturizes all emotion and then the tears of incontinence.

Back to theory

This example helps us reflect on the way in which each and every communication, even those that are apparently more realistic, can be seen as conveying emotional reality, and how each communication made by the patient may be seen and heard as a "secondary narrative of his waking dream thought", as long as we dare to listen from the vertex of transformations into dream. This makes for a completely different kind of listening. The task becomes all the more difficult, the more situations that apparently belong to external reality occlude the receptive-dreaming faculty of the analyst, who might get lost in the labyrinth of the type of listening typical of the social worker, family counsellor, or support psychotherapist if he gives up the analytic vertex. Likewise there is also the opposite risk of an interpretive simultaneous translation that strips a story of its intense emotions and turns it into an act of non-affective deciphering intellectualization. It then becomes necessary to interpret and understand until the myth of passion can be extended into the field of meaning (Bion, 1963). In other words, interpretation should relate to something the patient can see at least the tip of (the patient needs to see the tips of the rabbit's ears in order to be able to pull it out of the hat). The narrative has to be warm and made there and then; equally, there should be shared visibility on the narrative–visual–mythical axis.

I postulate as therapeutic factors the quality of the analyst's mental functioning in the session and, in particular, his faculties of receptivity, flexibility, transformative capacity, tolerance, and patience. These skills enter the field and carry out previously inconceivable transformations. Beta elements, emotional or sensory protomental content previously not transformed into pictograms (alpha elements) or not containable, can no longer be "disguised", "stored", split off, projected, or evacuated, but may become thinkable. In the cases described, I have tried to show how the quality of the analyst's mental functioning during the session is a variable in the analytic field and helps to co-determine the field, just as interpretive choices in the broadest sense co-determine the opening up or closing down of all possible worlds.

I believe that our knowledge is, as I said above, more similar to a Swiss cheese full of holes. But as we are ashamed and afraid to show how many holes we have, we spend much of our time creating *trompe l'oeils* to fill—or pretend or convince (ourselves) that we are filling—these holes. Religions, ideologies, fanaticism are some of the main "hole-fillers" that we use. The same goes for the use of theories in the analytic session. We delude ourselves into thinking that we come across as solid chunks of Parmesan rather than as perforated pieces of Emmental. In *Attention and Interpretation* Bion (1970) writes about the necessity for lies, pointing out that we should be modest and tolerant with ourselves and with others, how we should stop being "defenders" of the truth and take pleasure in being craftsmen, fashioning the degree of mental development that we and our patients are able to tolerate. Bion wrote a paradoxical eulogy of lies, not only because the lie pre-supposes a thinker but, above all, because what counts is a truth that is acceptable to our thinking. This applies to the patient's defences, but equally to the defences the analyst brings into play so as not to succumb to anxiety.

Conclusion

Perhaps an effective antidote to too many lies is the transformations into dreams I have described (Ferro, 2009)—transformations that open up the path to play, to narration, to creativity. If in presenting a case the analyst focuses both on the "hernia" operation and the phimosis operation a child has undergone, and if the symptom is mutism, it is not difficult to "dream" the communication as the child's alternating issues of incontinence (hernia) with issues of hypercontinence (phimosis)—and the silence can only stand for shouting.

Deconstructing the narrative and the dream here and now is the specific quality of the analyst—an analyst who is not too frightened. Generally, however, he is, and he clings to theory like a lost child to its mother. Among the many diseases of man the animal (symptomatic of his anguish) is his compulsion to give meaning, to find—often to attribute—a meaning to things that have no meaning. But this meaning- and sense-creating machine can be useful as long as we can control it and are aware of it. Hume warned us that *post hoc* is not necessarily *propter hoc*, the consequence being that we are left with no certainties of any kind, and we are always forced to improvise. We know very little about autism, either as a full-blown disease or in the form of the functions we all have, yet we saturate what we cannot tolerate not knowing with stoppers that plug the gaps in our knowledge. It is as if we can only stay afloat by clinging to meaning and significance—as if we were unable to float in non-meaning or to wait for meaning, like certain figures in Chagall.

The problem is how to find a median between a container that explodes and a claustrum that holds, or how to find a flexible container capable of doing just that. Extending the concept of reverie to the whole manner in which we listen to the session—that is, as if it were a dream—leads us to the concept of transformation into dreams. What the patient narrates is deconstructed *vis-à-vis* any aspect of external and factual reality and is regarded as a further explanation of his dream-thought or narrative derivative. This derivative will be restored to its dream matrix.

When a patient talks about his violent brother, his fragile sister, his incontinent grandmother, his biting dog—all these characters should be understood as functions of the field. The analyst should be able to make a dreamlike transformation of what is being communicated to him. In other words, the creativity of the field is also a function of our degree of freedom and courage.

Epilogue

Mary Kay O'Neil

> A "NO" uttered from the deepest conviction is better than a "YES" merely uttered to please, or worse, to avoid trouble.
>
> Mahatma Gandhi

> Catherine: I am Heathcliff—he's always in my mind—not as a pleasure any more than I am a pleasure to myself—but as my own being—don't talk of our separation.
> Heathcliff: I cannot live without my life! I cannot live without my soul! Be with me always—take any form! Do not leave me in this abyss, where I cannot find you!
>
> Emily Brontë, *Wuthering Heights*

Freud's "Negation" (1925h) is a small paper and yet it is large. Brief though it is, much depth is contained in it. Freud not only conveys ideas that are clinically useful but also deepens understanding of minds replete with paradoxical opposites. Here is one paradox: "the content of a repressed image or idea [*a truth*] can make its way into consciousness, on condition that it is *negated*" (1925h, p. 235). And here is another: "A negative judgement is the intellectual substitute for repression" (1925h, p. 236). Yet intellectual awareness of repressed thought does not guarantee emotional acceptance. Whether a thought is positive or negative, free or repressed, conscious or unconscious, it is a function of judgement to accept or reject, to affirm or disaffirm, to assert or dispute, to take in or spit out. Such judgement Freud relates to the pleasure-ego, which "wants to introject into itself everything that is good and to eject from itself everything that is bad" (1925h, p. 237). Judgement also involves reality-testing. Based on perception, it is an ego function to decide whether something does or does not exist in reality. In turn, this function allows the re-finding of a perceived object. Judgement, an intellectual function, also allows the "choice of motor action" (1925h, p. 238). For Freud, "The polarity of judgement appears to correspond to the opposition of the two groups of instincts which we have supposed to exist. Affirmation—as a substitute for uniting—belongs to Eros; negation—the successor to expulsion—belongs to the instinct of destruction" (1925h, p. 239). In this short paper, Freud does more than succinctly introduce the importance of recognizing truth in an opposite thought and does more than build his "model of the mind". With tiny examples of patients' words (e.g., it is *not* my mother), Freud opens the door for broad discussion of the concept and the technical handling of "negation". Although he does not discuss the certainty that the capacity to say "yes" or "no" is essential to human development and that negation in its most extreme form denies reality, his views leave room for deeper expansion by others. Great leaders and writers have intuited both these normal and extreme aspects of "negation".

Gandhi's words highlight the vital importance of developing the capacity to say "no" in an informed, convincing and meaningful way. This "no" is not "negation" in the clinical sense of avoiding the painful repressed opposite; it is a "no" said with conscious understanding and deep feeling, something that must be said in one's best judgement and most often to another person or about an action or an idea. For Gandhi, a too ready "yes" may hide the opposite and avoid the pain of asserting an affirming "no". In psychoanalytic terms, this is saying that reaction formation is a twin of negation.

Emily Brontë's unforgettable Catherine and Heathcliff epitomize the depth of paradox—of opposites—of love and hate. In their wild love yearning for the other, both deny the reality of separateness—of two minds, of individuality, of final separation

Epilogue

through death, and of having brought about their own separation with their respective destructive actions. Both expressed rejection and hate in their actions, yet maintained love by denying separation and internalizing the other. Brontë knew the psychic extremes of "negation".

While Gandhi appreciated the importance of the capacity to say "no" and Brontë illustrated the extreme forms of "no" through denial of separateness, Freud showed the clinical relevance of recognizing negation as a defence mechanism. Analysts know well that the negative is frequently used defensively to prevent a painful and unacceptable thought from entering consciousness. This is the first nugget of Freud's understanding of the human tendency to use "negation" in place of unthinkable thoughts and intolerable feelings. Many valuable nuggets follow: for example, ideas about judgement, perception, reality-ego, subject and object relationship. Freud ends with encouragement for the analytic endeavour when he notes that analysands give evidence of therapeutic accuracy with words such as "I didn't ever think that." The contributors to this volume explore and expand, within a contemporary context, understanding of this defence of negation, which, seemingly paradoxically, we all use to both protect ourselves and allow awareness.

Bonnie Litowitz provides our first chapter. Coming from a background in developmental psycholinguistics, she is "aware that children are not born with the capacity to negate as Freud described it". Children must develop the capacity to say "yes" and "no". Parents are well aware that children learning to speak go through stages of saying yes and then no to everything, indiscriminately. They then develop the ability to distinguish between the two, to judge whether yes or no fits their thoughts and feelings. As language develops, children learn to make more challenging and needed distinctions: desirable versus dangerous; internal versus external; self versus other; their own thoughts versus others' thoughts. My own 3-year-old son once demonstrated how a child learns to distinguish external from internal perceptions: when asked, "how did you know that?" he responded, "I found it in my feelings."

Litowitz's careful delineation of this linguistic developmental sequence utilizes not only Freud's original insights into "rejection, refusal, and denial" as aspects of negation but also extends her own earlier exploration (Litowitz, 1998), to incorporate today's psychoanalytic theorists who focus their developmental data on the pre-oedipal period. After a thorough explication of "Freud on Negation" and the difficulties of accurate translation, she teaches the reader—most analysts are neophytes in the area of developmental psycholinguistics—to distinguish between the primitive and more mature forms of negation. Current research and clinical examples are used to demonstrate that this human capacity is expressed through language. She is aware that as the capacity for negation develops, so too do reciprocal object relations. Like Gandhi, she also understands that a firm "no" rather than a compliant "yes" can be a developmental step forward. Recognizing that Freud's classic paper reveals more than one type of negation, with developmental implications, Litowitz explains types such as verbal, performative, refusal, and rejection, which can include the nature of engagement with others (including the therapeutic relationship) and judgements about truth and falsity. Her ending harkens back to Freud while moving our understanding of negation forward: "While for Freud the patient's struggle is intrapsychic—forces pushing for expression or held in check, mental agencies split or in opposition, . . . the developmental view presented here adds an interpsychic or intersubjective perspective consistent with post-Freudian theoretical approaches." While increasing understanding of the mature "no" as a necessary human capacity, Litowitz also helps "clinicians to determine what the patient is defending against and at what level of development his current internal struggle is being waged".

Jorge Canestri focuses on "negation as a psychoanalytic notion . . . a specific defensive mechanism. Canestri, coming from an Italian psychoanalytic viewpoint, utilizes his knowledge of the history of the concept and his rich familiarity with world literature (e.g., Italian, German, Chinese) to view Freud's 1925 idea of negation. He questions whether subsequent elaborations have changed the original intent of the concept. With reference to two early papers (Ferenczi, 1913; Laforgue, 1926) that examine this defence mechanism, he gives precision to Freud's idea of negation. His reading suggests that negation is subsequent to repression; he views it as a mechanism that enriches thought with contents that are otherwise inaccessible; this occurs through the use of the symbol of negation; and repression remains: it is not eliminated, only revoked. Disagreeing with Klein (1928, 1935) who suggested that negation is prior to repression, he considers additional issues that contribute to Freud's model of the mind.

The classic distinction between "attributive judgement and judgement of existence" is taken up by Canestri to discuss Freud's hypothetical model, which tallies with the drive model and includes his views on inside/outside, on subject/object, on reality-testing in normal/pathological. Canestri's analogies ("though clay may be moulded into a vase, the utility of the vase lies in what is not there") clarify two essential terms: object and representation. That is, we establish a relationship with reality: "how what is not there—the object—is used by taking advantage of what is there—the representation". Canestri's subtle reflections on the details of language both in the translation of Freud and in tiny clinical moments are used to demonstrate how the analyst can assist patients through careful consideration of their defences of negation (what is there, be it denial, disavowal, repudiation, foreclosure) to understand what they have repressed (what is not there). He maintains that the "attentive analyst" can, through ongoing reflection on Freud's paper, better comprehend both neurotic and non-neurotic pathologies and will be better able to work with patients suffering from various levels of difficulties.

Brian Robertson also recognizes the paradox in Freud's concept of the negative as a defence against and acknowledgement of what is repressed. His chapter on the "negative therapeutic reaction" (NTR) traces the Freudian concept, its subsequent development, and contemporary understanding. As analysts understand, NTR is most evident when patients, seeming to have made recognized progress, suddenly seem to become clinically worse or attempt to leave treatment. Although Freud's description of the negative therapeutic reaction appeared in *The Ego and the Id* (1923b), his views on intellectual and emotional acceptance or rejection in "Negation" (1925h) provided further understanding of the NTR concept. Robertson's tracking of Freud's concept, from its foreshadowing in earlier 1914 and 1918 papers, its description in 1923 and reconsideration in 1924, 1925, 1926 and in subsequent papers in 1937 provides a guide for comprehending the development of Freud's concept (1937d).

Robertson's offering does not stop there but goes on to explain Abraham's 1919 foreshadowing of the writings of later analysts, such as Riviere, Olinick, Rosenfeld, and Spillius. His review of other later contributors' clarifications, extensions, and technical management of NTR brings the reader up to date on this concept. He recognizes that Freud's specific definition has not only been extended to encompass a patient's characterologically based negativism, but it is also employed to designate any particularly deep-rooted resistance emerging during an analysis. Additionally, Robertson discusses where Freud's view of NTR fits within the tripartite model of the mind and the relationship of this to other concepts, such as the death instinct, masochistic ego, erotic and sadistic object cathexes, borrowed guilt, and unconscious guilt. The presentation of pessimistic and optimistic views of recognizing and interpreting a patient's unconscious negative reaction provides technical options for analytic work. Robertson's update incorporates suggestions for a contemporary teaching of NTR.

Case vignettes bring Robertson's chapter alive and give it clinical relevance. Hope is provided by a summary of Levy's (1982) case, which illustrates that if a former object cathexis can be unmasked, then the therapeutic success can be "brilliant". By describing in useful detail his attempts to understand and manage negativity in his own patient, Robertson offers further encouragement to therapists faced with patients who are not able to allow their treatment to succeed. He demonstrates how both Freud's views and contemporary ones, including Green's "negative hallucination", assist his understanding of his patient. In his final statement, Robertson brings the reader back to the analytic relationship, remarking that intense self-destructive impulses and wishes to destroy the object could be a manifestation of the controversial "death instinct" but that "not all instances of the negative therapeutic reaction represent impasse and a failed analysis". Since "we do not fully understand why some patients can change and others cannot", Robertson challenges us to "study in detail specific instances of analytic interventions with particular patients that led to negative therapeutic reactions".

Any discussion of "Negation" without André Green's "The Work of the Negative and Hallucinatory Activity (Negative Hallucination)" would be severely wanting. It is a privilege to have been permitted to include this chapter of his book in its near-50-page entirety. This is a rich and dense paper that cannot easily be summarized or taken in but requires close, reflective reading over time.

It is a pivotal paper and a seminal extension of Freud's view of negation as a defence mechanism as well as of Ferenczi's speculations on the difficulty in accepting unpleasant ideas (Ferenczi, 1926). To assist the reader, Otto Kernberg (1993), in his introduction to Green's *The Work of the Negative*, explained that the "negative" as formulated by Green

> refers to two closely related aspects of human psychology; the first one includes the consistent rejection of whatever is intolerable to the ego, exemplified by the mechanism of repression, the ongoing and unavoidable shadow of the need to control the drives that challenge all ego activities. The second aspect refers to the profound and pervasive destructiveness of the death drive that operates as a radical refusal of satisfaction and pleasure, and becomes so dominant in some personalities that it effectively leads to a global destruction of object relations. [Kernberg, 1993, p. xiv]

Green is pivotal in that the attention to negation as an ego function defence also becomes a more primitive pre-oedipal defence in forms such as denial, disavowal, and object-destructive envy.

Salman Akhtar (2009a, p. 309) has noted that after incorporating Freud's notions of neurosis as the inverse of perversion, the concept of negative therapeutic reaction, and the defence mechanisms of repression, negation, splitting and disavowal, Green adds five original ideas:

1. negative hallucination: a non-perception of an external object or internal perception;
2. negative hallucination of thought: the mind suddenly goes blank;
3. subjective disengagement by the ego: indifference even to the negative effect of indifference on internal and external life;
4. negative narcissism: the individual idealizes destructiveness and desires contempt; and
5. the ego's sense of self-disappearance: traumatic abandonment by mother or "dead" mother defended by wishes to invade her; fuelled by destructive drives (the death instinct) a person decides to accept or reject an object, a perception, a thought or one's subjective existence.

Close reading of Green's reprinted chapter is well worth the effort and will set the stage for understanding not only Green's work but extensions proposed by contributors in subsequent chapters.

Sara and Caesar Botella's clinical illustration and conclusion illuminate their distinctive contribution to the understanding of the Oedipus complex. All analysts are familiar with the oedipal notion of wishing to replace the parent of the same sex as the love object of the parent of the opposite sex—the Oedipus of the *Ucs.*—whereas most are less familiar with the Oedipus of the *id*. The Botellas, with their Freudian model of the mind, propose paradoxical sides of the Oedipus based on whether or not the "parricide" is already accomplished, though without memory traces (id) or whether there is an unconscious wish to murder the father (*Ucs.*). Their proposal—a difficult one for those not familiar with the South American psychoanalytic ideas—becomes clearer when using Green's concepts of "negative hallucinations" and negation of perception of the analyst: "I am looking for you in image, and I can't find you any more." With the analyst waiting patiently and silently, the authors demonstrate how the "unrepresentable negative" is transformed and made representable through the analytic process—that is, the patient is helped through analytic intervention (derived from the "figurability" or representation that emerges in the analyst's mind) to liberate a repression that is more primitive and disturbing (Oedipus of the id), which had been defended against by allusions to the negative Oedipus of the *Ucs.* (homosexuality). The Botellas' hypothesis of the Oedipus of the id and their idea of a transformational path contributes to a further broadening of the analytic theory of Freud's "negation".

Joachim Danckwardt's "The Negative in Dreams" moves beyond Freud's views of negation in the analytic situation. While nodding to the value of Freud's negation as a way of becoming aware of what is repressed and implying a specific way of perceiving, he discusses what Freud does not explicitly deal with—"negation in dreams". Indirectly, however, Freud recognized that "the dream-work effects the 'no' by means of inhibition of affect which is achieved by the censorship of the dream". Freud's dream of the open-air closet is used effectively as an example of affect in dreams. Danckwardt's deep reflection on "Negation" leads him to conclude that negation in dreams is clinically relevant. He summarizes that

Negation denotes a mental process that, like denial or disavowal, belongs to the wide range of defence mechanisms the human psyche develops in its attempt to ward off internal dangers linked to ideational representatives and mnemic images threatening the subject from within. Thus negation can be said to be directed at an ideational content with the intent to avoid the disagreeable implications that go along with the mental recognition of reality. Negation, therefore, must be ascribed a somewhat intermediate or transitional position between denial and disavowal, which have to be conceived as more primitive and rudimentary forms of psychic operation. Repression represents a more highly developed and complex mental process.

The clinical sequence that follows links with Freud's almost throwaway statement: "Judging is the intellectual action which decides the choice of motor action, which puts an end to the postponement due to thought and which leads over from thinking to acting (1925h, p. 238)." Danckwardt offers a fitting example of the nonverbal "no" expressed in barely perceptible action ("a quick glance towards the *analyst* in a condescending manner) and connects this act with dreams that take place between sessions. Dreams are brought into the session and here were used to "de-objectilize" the analyst; that is, to express negative feelings about the analyst that could not be expressed verbally. The dream's negative allows the dreamer, through the antithetical idea, to reveal the reality of intolerable thoughts and feelings. Certainly, Danckwardt's exquisite attention to his patient's non-verbal action and to the meaning of his patient's dream is akin to Freud's understanding of the meaning of a semantic "no"—"Now you'll think I mean to say something insulting, but really I've no such intention"—expressed through action. In this way, Danckwardt gives distinct form to Freud's view of "no" in action and extends Freud to give credence to the negative in dreams.

Jorge Maldonado moves even closer to the analyst–analysand relationship when he considers the effects of negation and the paradoxes of narcissism. Harkening back to Akhtar's Introduction and his questions (Whom is Freud calling "we" here? And, what does "it" stand for . . .?) about Freud's statement "There is no stronger evidence that *we* have been successful in our effort to uncover the unconscious than when the patient reacts to *it* with the words . . ."

(1925h, p. 239, italics added). There is no doubt that for Maldonado *we* stands for the analyst–analysand couple and *it* refers to the unconscious content brought forward by "our effort". Maldonado brings the reader clearly into the analytic relationship by linking with Green's "work of the negative". While Freud's states "we never discover a 'no' in the unconscious", Green maintains that this does not imply an absence of negativity in the unconscious. Acknowledging Freud's 1925 exploration of three important areas—the linguistic "no"; the double function of judgement as attribution and as existence; and the relationship between the subject and reality—Maldonado underlines the subsequent expansion of Freud's thinking. In "Constructions in Analysis" (1937d), Freud broadened the spectrum of meanings that the patient's negation could have. That is, the validity of the response to an interpretation, whether this be "yes" or "no", must be found in "indirect forms of confirmation"—for example, in memories or "corroborative dreams"—as Danckwardt proposed. These indirect confirmations may have greater value than the patient's "yes". Through a detailed case study of a woman who used schizoid defences, the author sheds light on the two types of judgement. The negative judgement of attribution can remove vitality from the analyst, rendering him an inanimate object, thereby negating the analyst–analysand relationship. The existence of the other is the source of conflict for those suffering from narcissistic pathology expressed through indifference. A "judgement of existence" is then used to negate the existence of someone who arouses both love and hate. Transference can be expressed through the latter type and countertransference through the former type of judgement. Innovatively, Maldonado offers thoughts about the "negative" as a possible sign of progress rather than a sign of resistance or negative therapeutic reaction. He states, in conclusion,

> The striking contrast between the constant negation of interpretations, on the one hand, and the improvement and progress in the patient's symptomatology, on the other, show that negation and the consequent negativity evident in the clinical material are a visible aspect of a state of transition that culminates in the resolution of the patient's conflicts. Underlying this manifest negativity, the unconscious process of working through and the transformation of conflicts are taking place.

Epilogue

Replete with case examples at different levels of ego integration, Ilany Kogan, like Maldonado, is optimistic that the "events and narratives that formed the starting point of the child's traumatic wound can be reconstructed, so that the split-off and diffusely enacted memory fragments from a persecutory world are elucidated". She begins with a novel idea that the "Voids" central to the architecture of the Berlin Holocaust Museum are symbolic of the "empty circle" and "psychic hole" unconsciously present in the second-generation offspring of Holocaust survivors who are consciously unaware of any details of the parental or grandparental trauma. The terms "empty circle" and "psychic hole" are expressions of Freud's "negation", as they represent death and destruction. Both result from the negation of traumatic experiences that are too painful to be integrated into the victim's cognitive and affective framework. That is, what is *not* there—emptiness—represents what *is* there. A central aspect of Kogan's chapter is her explanation of the problematic (pathological) implications of the cognitive and emotional denial of an unbearable trauma. The psychic representation of this "psychic hole" is transmitted through unconscious fantasy and revealed through enactments. Her definition of enactment involves the compulsion of some Holocaust survivors' offspring to recreate their parents' or grandparents' experiences in their own lives through concrete acts. She emphasizes the importance of separating the externalization of traumatic themes from the past from what occurs in the relationship between the patient and the analyst. The work of analysis is to transform the fantasies in the "psychic hole" into "psychic representations". The interpretation of the "negative", which is often expressed through fragmentary, defensive enactments, leads the patient to an awareness of the reality of the trauma and fills the "psychic hole" with psychic representations. In keeping with Freud, she affirms that intellectual awareness of what is repressed does not by itself undo the repression. When knowing is linked with feelings, change occurs. Because these feelings often include torment and anxiety, she proposes that a modification of technique could be required. Frequently, seeking knowledge about such trauma can be facilitated by an analytic holding environment and by the analyst being an ally in the patient's quest. Kogan recognizes the remarkable healing value of knowing what was previously unknown and how this facilitates a new and separate self.

Antonino Ferro's chapter, "Negation, negative capability and the work of creativity", was saved until last because not only is he positive about what can be done analytically but he provides the analyst with thoughts on how change can be brought about. Such creativity is not easy but results from open, honest reflection on the part that the analyst plays in succeeding or not with patients who need to use negation defensively. He makes his points in an open, at times playful way: "interpretation should relate to something the patient can see at least the tip of (the patient needs to see the tips of the rabbit's ears in order to be able to pull it out of the hat)." Unlike Akhtar's alternative interpretation of Freud's *we* and *it*, where "we" stands for "we analysts" and "it" stands for the analyst's authoritarian and one-sided intervention, Ferro postulates "as therapeutic factors the quality of the analyst's mental functioning in the session and, in particular, his faculties of receptivity, flexibility, transformative capacity, tolerance, and patience. These skills enter the field and carry out previously inconceivable transformations." Ferro's method promotes the reverie or receptive-dreaming faculty of the analyst, avoids non-affective intellectualization, and encourages thinkable feeling in both analyst and analysand. His method (illustrated with clinical examples) does not cling to theory but, like Bion, encourages the analyst to be "modest and tolerant with ourselves and with others, how we should stop being 'defenders' of the truth and take pleasure in being craftsmen, fashioning the degree of mental development that we and our patients are able to tolerate". Ferro's method also concurs with Akhtar's caution that "to refute something in response to the analyst's suggestion is not negation". Nor is disagreement always resistance.

Freud's brief but complex and highly nuanced paper "Negation" has been turned this way and that by the contributors to this volume. They all refer to Freud's main points, and this could have become repetitious rather than new and creative. Their contributions, however, are unique developments and extensions of the original psychoanalytic view. American, Canadian, French, German, Israeli, Italian, and South American analysts reveal both their surprising similarity and their refreshing differences. While each author writes from his or her own psychoanalytic thinking and experience, they intuitively connect with each other: for example, both Canestri and Kogan think of negation as symbolized by "what is not there". Beyond Freud, Green's work on the negative is indeed pivotal as he is included in the thinking and references of most contributors—for example, Robertson's reference to "negative hallucination", Maldonado's and Danckwardt's thoughts about "the work of the negative", and Green's and Kogan's elucidation of Freud's "death instinct". The nine authors here contribute considerably to psychoanalytic theory and technique, but is their work art? Their clinically relevant thoughts about negation as a psychic defence fall between Gandhi's insight into the capacity to say a meaningful "no" or a firm "yes" and Brontë's intuitive grasp of the deepest psychic need for negation. Great leaders and writers are creative artists, and so, too, beginning with Freud, are these author/analysts. No wonder Joyce Cary's words on "art and reality" come to mind in this context:

> . . . art is the only means by which we can achieve it (*real truth*). It is only in great art and the logic of the subconscious where judgment has become part of the individual emotional character that we move freely in a world which is at once concept and feeling, rational order and common emotion, in a dream that is truer than actual life and a reality which is only there made actual, complete and purposeful to our experience. [Cary, 1958, pp. 174–175]

REFERENCES

Abraham, K. (1919). A particular form of neurotic resistance against the psychoanalytic method. In: *Selected Papers on Psychoanalysis*. London: Hogarth Press, 1968.
Akhtar, S. (2009a). *Comprehensive Dictionary of Psychoanalysis*. London: Karnac.
Akhtar, S. (2009b). Keyword: Arrogance, curiosity, and pseudo-stupidity. In: *Comprehensive Dictionary of Psychoanalysis* (pp. 26–27). London: Karnac.
Angelergues, S. (1969). Memory disorders in neurological disease. In: P. J. Vinken & P. W. Bruyen (Eds.), *Handbook of Clinical Neurology: Disorders of the Higher Nervous Activity, Vol. 3* (pp. 268–292). Amsterdam: North Holland.
Anzieu, D. (1986). *Freud's Self-Analysis*, trans. P. Graham. London: Hogarth Press.
Asch, S. S. (1976). Varieties of negative therapeutic reaction and problems of technique. *Journal of the American Psychoanalytic Association*, 24: 383–407.
Atlan, H. (1983). L'emergence du nouveau et du sens. In: P. Dumonchel & J. P. Dupuy (Eds.), *L'auto-organization*. Paris: Le Seuil.
Auerhahn, N. C., & Laub, D. (1998). Intergenerational memory of the

Holocaust. In: Y. Danieli (Ed.), *International Handbook of Multigenerational Legacies of Trauma*. New York: Plenum Press.

Auerhahn, N. C., & Prelinger, E. (1983). Repetition in the concentration camp survivor and her child. *International Review of Psychoanalysis, 10*: 31–46.

Austin, J. L. (1962). *How to Do Things with Words*. Oxford: Oxford University Press.

Axelrod, S., Schnipper, O. L., & Rau, J. H. (1978). *Hospitalized Offspring of Holocaust Survivors: Problems and Dynamics*. Paper presented at the Annual Meeting of the American Psychiatric Association, May.

Baranger, M., & Baranger, W. (1961–62). La situacion analitica como campo dinamico. *Revista Uruguaya de Psicoanalisis, 4*: 3–54. [The analytic situation as a dynamic field. *International Journal of Psychoanalysis, 89* (2008): 795–826.]

Baranger, M., & Baranger, W. (2009). *The Work of Confluence: Listening and Interpreting in the Psychoanalytic Field*, ed. L. Glocer Fiorini. London: Karnac.

Baranger, M., Baranger, W., & Mom, J. (1988). The infantile psychic trauma from us to Freud: Pure trauma, retroactivity and reconstruction. *International Journal of Psychoanalysis, 69*: 113–128.

Barocas, H., & Barocas, H. (1973). Manifestations of concentration camp effects on the second generation. *American Journal of Psychiatry, 130*: 820–821.

Barton, R., & Whitehead, J. (1969). The gaslighting phenomenon. *Lancet, 1*: 1258–1260.

Basch, M. (1981). Psychoanalytic interpretation and cognitive transformation. *International Journal of Psychoanalysis, 62*: 151–175.

Basch, M. (1983). The perception of reality and the disavowal of meaning. *Annual of Psychoanalysis, 11*: 125–153.

Bates, E. (1976). *Language in Context: The Acquisition of Pragmatics*. New York: Academic Press.

Becker, C. L. (1955). What are historical facts? *Western Political Quarterly, 8* (3).

Beland, H. (2008). Erklärungs- und Arbeitswert der Todestriebhypothese. Diskussion anhand klinischer und theoretischer Beispiele. *Jahrbuch de Psychoanalyse, 56*: 23–47.

Benveniste, E. (1971). *Problems in General Linguistics*. Coral Gables, FL: University of Miami Press.

Bergmann, M. V. (1982). Thoughts on super-ego pathology of survivors

References

and their children. In: M. S. Bergmann & M. E. Jucovy (Eds.), *Generations of the Holocaust* (pp. 287–311). New York: Basic Books.
Bion, W. R. (1957). Differentiation of the psychotic from the nonpsychotic personalities. *International Journal of Psychoanalysis, 38*: 266–275.
Bion, W. R. (1958): On arrogance. *International Journal of Psychoanalysis, 39*: 144–146.
Bion, W. R. (1962). *Learning from Experience.* London: Karnac, 1984.
Bion, W. R. (1963). *Elements of Psycho-Analysis.* London: Karnac, 1984
Bion, W. R. (1965). *Transformations.* London: Karnac, 1991.
Bion, W. R. (1967). *Second Thoughts.* New York: Aronson.
Bion, W. R. (1970). *Attention and Interpretation.* London: Karnac, 1984.
Bion, W. R. (1994). *Clinical Seminars and Other Works.* London: Karnac.
Bion, W. R. (2005). *The Italian Seminars,* ed. F. Bion. London: Karnac.
Bleger, J. (1967). *Simbiosis y ambigüedad.* Buenos Aires: Paidós.
Bloom, L. (1970). *Language Development: Form and Function in Emerging Grammars.* Cambridge, MA: MIT Press.
Bollas, C. (1987). *The Shadow of the Object.* New York: Columbia University Press. [*La Sombra del Objeto.* Buenos Aires: Amorrortu, 1991.]
Botella, C., & Botella, S. (1992). Névrose traumatique et cohérence psychique. *Revue Française Psychosomatique, 2*: 25–36.
Botella, C., & Botella, S. (1995). Sur le processus analytique. Du perceptif aux causalités psychiques. *Revue Française Psychosomatique, 2.*
Botella, C., & Botella, S. (1996). La tendance convergente de la régression narcissique. *Revue Française Psychosomatique, 9*: 109–125.
Botella, C., & Botella, S. (2004). *The Work of Psychic Figurability: Mental States without Representation,* trans. A. Weller. London: Brunner-Routledge.
Botella, S., & Botella, C. (1990). La problématique de la regression formelle de la pensée et de l'hallucinatoire. In: *La psychanalyse. Questions pour demain.* Paris: Presses Universitaires de France.
Botella, S., & Botella, C. (1992). Le status métapsychologique de la perception et l'irreprésentabilité. *Revue Française de Psychanalyse, 56*: 23–42.
Bowerman, M. (1973). *Early Syntactic Development: A Cross-Linguistic Study with Special Reference to Finnish.* London: Cambridge University Press.
Brenner, C. (2006). *Psychoanalysis or Mind and Meaning.* New York: Psychoanalytic Quarterly.

Brenner, I. (2002). Foreword. In: V. D. Volkan, G. Ast, & W. F. Greer, Jr. (Eds.), *The Third Reich in the Unconscious: Transgenerational Transmission and Its Consequences* (pp. xi–xvii). London: Brunner-Routledge.
Brown, R. (1973). *A First Language*. Cambridge, MA: Harvard University Press.
Bruner, J. (1975a). From communication to language. *Cognition, 3*: 255–287.
Bruner, J. (1975b). The ontogenesis of speech acts. *Journal of Child Language, 2*: 1–19.
Bruner, J. (1983). *Child's Talk: Learning to Use Language*. New York: W. W. Norton.
Cary, J. (1958). *Art & Reality*. Cambridge: Cambridge University Press.
Chomsky, N. (1957). *Syntactic Structures*. The Hague: Mouton.
Chused, J. (1991). The evocative power of enactments. *Journal of the American Psychoanalytic Association, 39*: 615–638.
Colli, G. (1977). *La Sapienza Greca, Vol. 1*. Milan: Adelphi.
Conrad, J. (1909). The Secret Sharer. In: *Twixt Land and Sea Tales* (pp. 79–120). Cambridge: Cambridge University Press, 2008.
Couvreur, C. (1992). L'illusion d'absence, hallucination négative and hallucinatoire negative chez Freud. *Revue Française de Psychanalyse, 56*: 85–100.
Danckwardt, J. F. (2011). Die Verleugnung des Todestriebs [The disavowal of the death-drive]. *Jahrbuch der Psychoanalyse, 62*: 137–163.
Danckwardt, J. F., & Wegner, P. (2007). Performance as annihilation or integration? *International Journal of Psychoanalysis, 88*: 1117–1133.
Darwin, C. (1872). *The Expression of the Emotions in Man and Animals*. Chicago, IL: University of Chicago Press, 1965.
Delorme, B. (2009). *Le Christ Grecque*. Paris: Bayard.
Dorey, R. (1985). Die vereinten Aktionen des Todestriebs und die Verneinung im Strukturierungsprozeß des psychischen Apparates. *Bulletin: Psychoanalysis in Europe, 25*: 95–100.
Dorpat, T. (1984). *Denial and Defense in the Therapeutic Situation*. Northvale, NJ: Aronson.
Dreyfus, R. (1967). Préface. In: *Tragiques grecs, Eschyle, Sophocle*. Paris: Collection La Pleiade.
Duparc, F. (1992). Nouveaux développements sur l'hallucination négative et la representation. *Revue Française de Psychanalyse, 56*: 101–121.
Duyvendak, J. J. L. (Tr. & Ed.) (1954). *Tao Te Ching: The Book of the Way and Its Virtue (Wisdom of the East)*. London: John Murray.

References

Eickhoff, F.-W. (1998). Verleugnung. In: J. Ritter & K. Gründer, *Historisches Wörterbuch der Philosophie, Vol. 11* (pp. 719–722). Basel: Schwabe.
Erlich, S. (1978). Adolescent suicide: Maternal longing and cognitive development. *Psychoanalytic Study of the Child, 33*: 261–277.
Eshel, O. (1988). "Black holes", deadness and existing analytically. *International Journal of Psychoanalysis, 79*: 1115–1131.
Etchegoyen, R. H. (1981). Instances and alternatives of the interpretive work. *International Review of Psycho-Analysis, 8*: 401–421.
Etchegoyen, R. H. (1983). Fifty years after the mutative interpretation. *International Journal of Psychoanalysis, 64*: 445–459.
Etchegoyen, R. H. (1991). *The Fundamentals of Psychoanalytic Technique*. London: Karnac.
Ey, H. (1950). *Etudes psychiatriques, Vol. 2: Etude No. 16* (pp. 427–451). Paris: Desclée de Brouwer.
Ey, H. (Ed.) (1966). *L'inconscient. 6e Colloque de Bonneval, 1960*. Paris: Desclée de Brouwer.
Ey, H. (1973). *Traité des Hallucinations*. Paris: Masson.
Faimberg, H. (1996). Listening to listening. *International Journal of Psychoanalysis, 77*: 667–677.
Fenichel, O. (1945). *The Psychoanalytic Theory of Neurosis*. New York: W. W. Norton.
Ferenczi, S. (1912). Transitory symptom-constructions during the analysis. In: *First Contributions to Psycho-Analysis* (pp. 193–212). London: Karnac, 1994.
Ferenczi, S. (1913). Stages in the development of the sense of reality. In: *First Contributions to Psycho-Analysis*. London: Hogarth Press, 1952.
Ferenczi, S. (1926). The problem of acceptance of unpleasant ideas. In: *Further Contributions to the Theory and Technique of Psycho-Analysis* (pp. 366–379). London: Hogarth Press.
Ferguson, C., & Slobin, D. (Eds.) (1973). *Studies in Child Language Development*. New York: Holt, Rinehart & Winston.
Ferro, A. (2002a). *Seeds of Illness, Seeds of Recovery*. New Library of Psychoanalysis. London: Routledge, 2004.
Ferro, A. (2002b). Some implications of Bion's thought: The waking dream and narrative derivatives. *International Journal of Psychoanalysis, 83*: 597–607.
Ferro, A. (2004). Interpretations: Signals from the analytic field and emotional transformations. *International Forum of Psychoanalysis, 13*: 31–38.

Ferro, A. (2005a). Which reality in the psychoanalytic session ? *Psychoanalytic Quarterly, 74*: 421–442.
Ferro, A. (2005b). Commentary [on "Field Theory" by Madeleine Baranger]. In: S. Lewkowicz & S. Flechner (Eds.), *Truth, Reality, and the Psychoanalyst*. London: International Psychoanalytical Association.
Ferro, A. (2006a). Clinical implication of Bion's thought. *International Journal of Psychoanalysis, 87*: 989–1003.
Ferro, A. (2006b). *Mind Works: Technique and Creativity in Psychoanalysis*. New Library of Psychoanalysis. London: Routledge.
Ferro, A. (2009). Transformations in dreaming and characters in the psychoanalytic field. *International Journal of Psychoanalysis, 90*: 2009–2030.
Ferro, A. (2010). Simone's complaisant mutism and the monsters. *Revue Canadienne de Psychanalyse, 18* (2): 216–224.
Ferro, A., & Basile, R. (Eds.) (2009). *The Analytic Field*. London: Karnac.
Fine, B., Joseph, E., & Waldhorn, H. (Eds.) (1969). *The Mechanism of Denial*. New York: International Universities Press.
Fonagy, P., & Target, M. (1998). Mentalization and the changing aims of child psychoanalysis. *Psychoanalytic Dialogues, 8* (1): 87–114.
Fresco, N. O. (1984). Remembering the unknown. *International Review of Psychoanalysis, 11*: 417–427.
Freud, A. (1936). *The Ego and the Mechanisms of Defense*. New York: International Universities Press, 1953.
Freud, S. (1890a). Psychical (or mental) treatment. *Standard Edition*, 7.
Freud, S. (1894a). The neuro-psychoses of defence. *Standard Edition, 3*: 45–61.
Freud, S. (1894/1985). Draft G: Melancholia. In: *The Complete Letters of Sigmund Freud to Wilhelm Fliess, 1887–1904* (pp. 98–105), trans. J. M. Masson. Cambridge, MA: Belknap Press, 1985.
Freud, S. (1895d) (with Breuer, J.). *Studies on Hysteria. Standard Edition, 2*: 1–223.
Freud, S. (1896b). Further remarks on the neuro-psychoses of defence. *Standard Edition, 3*: 159–188.
Freud, S. (1900a). *The Interpretation of Dreams. Standard Edition*, 4–5.
Freud, S. (1905c). *Jokes and Their Relation to the Unconscious. Standard Edition*, 8.
Freud, S. (1905d). *Three Essays on the Theory of Sexuality. Standard Edition*, 7.

References

Freud, S. (1905e [1901]). Fragment of an analysis of a case of hysteria. *Standard Edition*, 7: 3–124.
Freud, S. (1909d). Notes upon a case of obsessional neurosis. *Standard Edition*, 10: 155–318.
Freud, S. (1910a [1909]). Five lectures on psycho-analysis. *Standard Edition*, 11.
Freud, S. (1910c). Leonardo da Vinci and a Memory of His Childhood. *Standard Edition*, 11.
Freud, S. (1910e). The antithetical meaning of primal words. *Standard Edition*, 11: 153–162.
Freud, S. (1911b). Formulations on the two principles of mental functioning. *Standard Edition*, 12.
Freud, S. (1911c [1910]). Psycho-analytic notes on an autobiographical account of a case of paranoia (Dementia paranoides). *Standard Edition*, 12: 9–88.
Freud, S. (1912–13). *Totem and Taboo*. *Standard Edition*, 13.
Freud, S. (1914g). Remembering, repeating and working through (Further recommendations on the technique of psycho-analysis, II). *Standard Edition*, 12: 145–157.
Freud, S. (1915c). Instincts and their vicissitudes. *Standard Edition*, 14: 109–140.
Freud, S. (1915d). Repression. *Standard Edition*, 14: 146–158.
Freud, S. (1915e). The unconscious. *Standard Edition*, 14: 166–215.
Freud, S. (1916–17). *Introductory Lectures on Psycho-Analysis*. *Standard Edition*, 15–16.
Freud, S. (1917d [1915]). A metapsychological supplement to the theory of dreams. *Standard Edition*, 14: 222–235.
Freud, S. (1917e [1915]). Mourning and melancholia. *Standard Edition*, 14: 239–258.
Freud, S. (1918b [1914]). From the history of an infantile neurosis. *Standard Edition*, 17: 1–122.
Freud, S. (1919a [1918]). Lines of advance in psycho-analytic therapy. *Standard Edition*, 17.
Freud, S. (1919d). Introduction to *Psycho-Analysis and the War Neuroses*. *Standard Edition*, 17.
Freud, S. (1920g). *Beyond the Pleasure Principle*. *Standard Edition*, 18: 7–64.
Freud, S. (1923a [1922]). Two encyclopaedia articles. *Standard Edition*, 18.
Freud, S. (1923b). *The Ego and the Id*. *Standard Edition*, 19: 3–68.

Freud, S. (1923c [1922]). Remarks on the theory and practice of dream-interpretations. *Standard Edition*, 19.
Freud, S. (1923e). The infantile genital organization. *Standard Edition*, 19.
Freud, S. (1924c). The economic problem of masochism. *Standard Edition*, 19.
Freud, S. (1924d). The dissolution of the Oedipus complex. *Standard Edition*, 19: 171–188.
Freud, S. (1924e). The loss of reality in neurosis and psychosis. *Standard Edition*, 19: 183–190.
Freud, S. (1925a). A note upon the "Mystic Writing-Pad". *Standard Edition*, 19.
Freud, S. (1925h). Negation. *Standard Edition*, 19: 235–239.
Freud, S. (1926d [1925]). Inhibitions, Symptoms and Anxiety. *Standard Edition*, 20: 77–174.
Freud, S. (1926e). *The Question of Lay Analysis*. *Standard Edition*, 20.
Freud, S. (1927e). Fetishism. *Standard Edition*, 21: 152–157.
Freud, S. (1928b). Dostoevsky and parricide. *Standard Edition*, 21.
Freud, S. (1930a). *Civilization and Its Discontents*. *Standard Edition*, 21
Freud, S. (1933a). *New Introductory Lectures on Psycho-Analysis*. *Standard Edition*, 22.
Freud, S. (1937c). Analysis terminable and interminable. *Standard Edition*, 23: 216–253.
Freud, S. (1937d). Constructions in analysis. *Standard Edition*, 23: 257–269.
Freud, S. (1939a [1937–39]). *Moses and Monotheism*. *Standard Edition*, 23: 7–137.
Freud, S. (1940a [1938]). *An Outline of Psycho-Analysis*. *Standard Edition*, 23: 144–207.
Freud, S. (1940e [1938]). Splitting of the ego in the process of defence. *Standard Edition*, 23: 275–278.
Freud, S. (1950 [1895]). Project for a scientific psychology. *Standard Edition*, 1: 295–343.
Freud, S. (1950a [1887–1902]). The Origins of Psycho-Analysis [Draft K: the neuroses of defence]. *Standard Edition*, 1: 220–229.
Freud, S., & Bullitt, W. C. (1939/1966). *Thomas Woodrow Wilson, Twenty-Eighth President of the United States: A Psychological Study*. New York: Weidenfeld & Nicholson, 1966.
Freyberg, S. (1980). Difficulties in separation-individuation as experi-

enced by offspring of Nazi Holocaust survivors. *American Journal of Orthopsychiatry, 5*: 87–95.

Gampel, Y. (1982). A daughter of silence. In: M. S. Bergmann & M. E. Jucovy (Eds.), *Generations of the Holocaust* (pp. 120–136). New York: Basic Books.

Garland, C. (1991). External disasters and the internal world: An approach to psychotherapeutic understanding of survivors. In: J. Holmes (Ed.), *Textbook of Psychotherapy in Psychiatric Practice*. London: Churchill Livingstone.

Garland, C. (2002). Thinking about trauma. In: J. Holmes (Ed.), *Understanding Trauma: A Psychoanalytic Approach* (pp. 9–31). London: Karnac.

Gast, L. (2008). Die Verneinung. Eine Freud-Lektüre. *Jahrbuch der Psychoanalyse, 56*: 69–83.

Gedo, J., & Goldberg, A. (1973). *Models of the Mind*. Chicago, IL: University of Chicago Press.

Gilbert, M. (1992). *Churchill: A Life*. New York: Henry Holt.

Goldberg, A. (1999). *Being of Two Minds: The Vertical Split in Psychoanalysis and Psychotherapy*. Hillsdale, NJ: Analytic Press.

Green, A. (1965). L'objet *a* de Jacques Lacan, sa logique et la théorie freudienne. *Cahiers pour l'analyse, 3*: 15–37.

Green, A. (1966–67). Le narcissisme primaire. Structure ou état. In: *Narcissisme de vie, narcissisme de mort* (pp. 80–131). Paris: Editions de Minuit, 1983.

Green, A. (1973). *Le discourse vivant*. Paris: Presses Universitaires de France.

Green, A. (1977). L'hallucination négative, note pour un addendum pour un traité des hallucinations. *L'Évolution Psychiatrique, 62*: 645–656.

Green, A. (1982a). La representation de chose entre pulsion et langage. *Psychanalyse à l'Université, 12*: 357–372.

Green, A. (1982b). Travail psychique et travail de la pensée. *Revue Française de Psychanalyse, 46*: 419–430.

Green, A. (1983). *Narcissisme de vie, narcissisme de mort*. Paris: Editions de Minuit.

Green, A. (1984). Le language dans la psychanalyse. In: *Langages*. Paris: Les Belles Lettres.

Green, A. (1986a). The dead mother. In: *On Private Madness* (pp. 142–173). London: Hogarth Press.

Green, A. (1986b). *On Private Madness*. London: Hogarth Press.
Green, A. (1987). La representation de chose entre pulsion et langage. *Psychanalyse à l'Université, 12*: 357–372.
Green, A. (1988). Pulsions, psyché, langage, pensée. *Revue Française de Psychanalyse, 2*: 491–497.
Green, A. (1991). Méconnaissance de l'inconscient. In: R. Dorey (Ed.), *L'inconscient et la science*. Paris: Dunod.
Green, A. (1993). *Le travail du négatif*. Paris: Éditions de Minuit. [*The Work of the Negative*. London: Free Associations Books, 2002.]
Green, A. (1998). The primordial mind and the work of the negative. *International Journal of Psychoanalysis, 79*: 649–665.
Green, A. (1999). *The Fabric of Affects and the Psychoanalytic Discourse*, trans. A. Sheridan. London: Routledge.
Green, A. (2005). *Key Ideas for a Contemporary Psychoanalysis: Misrecognition and Recognition of the Unconscious*. London: Routledge.
Gregory, R. L., & Wallace, J. G. (1963). *Recovery from Early Blindness: A Case Study*. Cambridge: Heffer.
Gribbin, J. (1992). *Unveiling the Edge of Time: Black Holes, White Holes, Worm Holes*. London: Penguin.
Grinberg, L., & Grinberg, R. (1974). The problem of identity and the psychoanalytical process. *International Journal of Psychoanalysis, 1*: 499–507.
Grinstein, A. (1980). *On Sigmund Freud's Dreams*. New York: International Universities Press, 1968.
Grotstein, J. S. (1986). The psychology of powerlessness: Disorders of self-regulation as a newer paradigm for psychopathology. *Psychoanalytic Inquiry, 6*: 93–118.
Grotstein, J. S. (1989). A revised psychoanalytic conception of schizophrenia: An interdisciplinary update. *Psychoanalytic Psychology, 6*: 253–275.
Grotstein, J. S. (1990a). "Black hole" as the basic psychotic experience: Some newer psychoanalytic and neuroscience perspectives on psychosis. *Journal of the American Academy of Psychoanalysis, 18*: 29–46.
Grotstein, J. S. (1990b). Nothingness, meaninglessness, chaos and "black hole". I: The importance of nothingness, meaninglessness and chaos in psychoanalysis. *Contemporary Psychoanalysis, 26*: 257–291.
Grotstein, J. S. (1990c). Nothingness, meaninglessness, chaos and "black hole". II: The black hole. *Contemporary Psychoanalysis, 26*: 377–407.

References

Grotstein, J. S. (1993). Boundary difficulties in borderline patients. In: L. B. Boyer & P. L. Giovacchini (Eds.), *Master Clinicians on Treating the Regressed Patient, Vol. 2* (pp. 107–142). Northvale, NJ: Aronson.

Grotstein, J. S. (2000). Some considerations of "hate" and a reconsideration of the death instinct. *Psychoanalytic Inquiry, 20*: 462–480.

Grotstein, J. S. (2007). *A Beam of Intense Darkness: Wilfred Bion's Legacy in Psychoanalysis.* London: Karnac.

Grubrich-Simitis, I. (1984). From concretism to metaphor. *Psychoanalytic Study of the Child, 39*: 301–319.

Hartmann, H. (1939). *Ego Psychology and the Problem of Adaptation.* New York: International Universities Press.

Hécaen, H., & de Ajuriaguerra, J. (1952). *Méconnaissances et hallucinations corporelles. Intégration et désintégration de la somatognosie.* Paris: Masson.

Hoffmeister, R., & Wilbur, R. (1980). The acquisition of sign language. In: H. Lane & F. Grosjean (Eds.), *Recent Perspectives on American Sign Language* (pp. 61–78). Hillsdale, NJ: Erbaum.

Horney, K. (1936). The problem of the negative therapeutic reaction. *Psychoanalytic Quarterly, 5*: 29–44.

Hyppolite, J. (1956). Commentaire parlée sur la *Verneinung* de Freud. In: J. Lacan, *Écrits* (Appendix 1, pp. 879–887). Paris: Editions du Seuil, 1966. Also in: *The Seminars of Jacques Lacan: Book I* (Appendix, pp. 289–297), ed. J.-A. Miller, trans. J. Forrester. New York: W. W. Norton, 1988.

Jacob, A. (1990). *Les notions philosophiques. Encyclopédie Philosophique Universelle, Vol. 1.* Paris: Presses Universitaires de France.

Jacobs, T. J. (1986). On countertransference enactments. *Journal of the American Psychoanalytic Association, 34*: 289–307.

Jacobs, T. J. (2000). Unbewusste Kommunikation und verdeckte Enactments in analytischen Setting. In: U. Streeck (Ed.), *Errinern, Agieren und Inszenieren* (pp. 97–127). Gottingen: Vanderhoeck & Ruprecht.

Jacobson, E. (1957). Denial and repression. *Journal of the American Psychoanalytic Association, 5*: 61–92.

Janin, C. (1990). L'empiètement psychique. Un probleme de clinique et de technique psychanalytique. In: *La psychanalyse. Questions pour demain* (pp. 151–160). Paris: Presses Universitaires de France.

Jenkins, R. (2002). *Churchill.* London: Plume.

Joseph, B. (1975). The patient who is difficult to reach. In: Peter L. Giovacchini (Ed.), *Tactics and Techniques in Psychoanalytic Therapy.* New York: Aronson.

Joseph, B. (1988). Object relations in clinical practice. *Psychoanalytic Quarterly, 57*: 626–642.
Keats, J. (1817). *Letters* (4th edition), ed. M. B. Forman. London: Oxford University Press..
Keller-Cohen, D., Chalmer, K., & Remler, J. (1979). The development of discourse negation in the non-native child. In: E. Ochs & B. Schieffelin (Eds.), *Developmental Pragmatics* (pp. 305–325). New York: Academic Press.
Kernberg, O. F. (1993). Introduction. In: A. Green, *The Work of the Negative* (pp. xiii–xvii). London: Free Association Books.
Kernberg, O. F. (2009). The concept of the death drive: A clinical perspective. *International Journal of Psychoanalysis, 90*: 1009–1023.
Kestenberg, J. S. (1972). Psychoanalytic contributions to the problem of survivors from Nazi persecution. *Israel Annals of Psychiatry and Related Disciplines, 10*: 311–325.
Kestenberg, J. S. (1980). Psychoanalyses of children of survivors from the Holocaust: Case presentation and assessment. *Journal of the American Psychoanalytic Association, 28* (4): 775–804.
King, P., & Steiner, R. (Eds.) (1991). *The Freud–Klein Controversies 1941–1945*. London: Tavistock/Routledge.
Kinston, W., & Cohen, J. (1986). Primal repression: Clinical and theoretical aspects. *International Journal of Psychoanalysis, 67*: 337–355.
Kirshner, L. (1994). Trauma, the good object, and the symbolic: A theoretical integration. *International Journal of Psychoanalysis, 75*: 235–242.
Klein, H. (1981). Yale Symposium of the Holocaust. *Proceedings*, September 1981.
Klein, H., & Kogan, I. (1986). Identification and denial in the shadow of Nazism. *International Journal of Psychoanalysis, 67*: 45–52.
Klein, M. (1928). Early stages of the Oedipus conflict. In: *The Writings of Melanie Klein, Vol. 1: Love, Guilt and Reparations and Other Works 1921–1945*. London: Karnac, 1992.
Klein, M. (1935). A contribution to the psychogenesis of manic-depressive states. In: *The Writings of Melanie Klein, Vol. 1: Love, Guilt and Reparations and Other Works 1921–1945* (pp. 262–289). London: Karnac, 1992.
Klein, M. (1937). Love, guilt and reparation. In: *The Writings of Melanie Klein, Vol. 1: Love, Guilt and Reparations and Other Works 1921–1945*. London: Karnac, 1992.
Klein, M. (1946). Notes on some schizoid mechanisms. In: *The Writings*

References

of *Melanie Klein, Vol. 3: Envy and Gratitude and Other Works 1946–1963* (pp. 1–24). London: Karnac, 1993. .

Klein, M. (1957). Envy and gratitude. In: *The Writings of Melanie Klein, Vol. 3: Envy and Gratitude and Other Works 1946–1963* (pp. 176–235). London: Karnac, 1992.

Kogan, I. (1987). The second skin. *International Review of Psychoanalysis* 15: 251–261. Also in: *The Cry of Mute Children: A Psychoanalytic Perspective of the Second Generation of the Holocaust* (pp. 46–69). London: Free Association Books, 1995.

Kogan, I. (1993). Curative factors in the psychoanalyses of Holocaust survivors' offspring before and during the Gulf War. *International Journal of Psychoanalysis*, 74: 803–815. Also in: *The Cry of Mute Children: A Psychoanalytic Perspective of the Second Generation of the Holocaust* (pp. 133–148). London: Free Association Books, 1995.

Kogan, I. (1995). *The Cry of Mute Children: A Psychoanalytic Perspective of the Second Generation of the Holocaust*. London: Free Association Books.

Kogan, I. (1996). Die Suche nach Geschichte in den Analysen der Nachkommen von Holocaust Uberlebenden; Rekonstruktion des "seelischen Lochs" [The search for narratives in the analyses of Holocaust survivors' offspring: Reconstruction of the "psychic hole"]. In: H. Weiss & H. Lang (Eds.), *Psychoanalyse Heute und Vor 70 Jahren* (pp. 291–308). Tubingen: edition diskord.

Kogan, I. (1998). The black hole of dread: The psychic reality of children of Holocaust survivors. In: J. H. Berke, S. Pierides, A. Sabbadini, & S. Schneider (Eds.), *Even Paranoids Have Enemies: New Perspectives on Paranoia and Persecution* (pp. 47–59). London: Routledge.

Kogan, I. (2002). "Enactment" in the lives and treatment of Holocaust survivors' offspring. *Psychoanalytic Quarterly*, 71: 251–273.

Kogan, I. (2003). On being a dead, beloved child. *Psychoanalytic Quarterly*, 72 (3): 727–767.

Kogan, I. (2007a). *The Struggle against Mourning*. New York: Jason Aronson.

Kogan, I. (2007b). *Escape from Selfhood*. London: International Psychoanalytical Association.

Krell, R. (1979). Holocaust families: The survivors and their children. *Comprehensive Psychiatry*, 20 (6): 560–567.

Kris, E. (1956). The personal myth: A problem in psychoanalytic technique. *Journal of the American Psychoanalytic Association*, 4: 653–681.

Kristeva, J. (1987). *In the Beginning Was Love: Psychoanalysis and Faith*, trans. A. Goldhammer. New York: Columbia University Press.

Lacan, J. (1936). Au-delà du principe de réalité. In: *Écrits* (pp. 73–92). Paris: Éditions du Seuil, 1966.

Lacan, J. (1949). Le stade du miroir comme formateur de la fonction du je, telle qu'elle nous est révélée dans l'expérience psychanalytique. *Écrits* (pp. 93–100). Paris: Éditions du Seuil, 1966.

Lacan, J. (1953). Fonction et champ de la parole et du langage en psychanalyse. In: *Écrits* Paris: Éditions du Seuil, 1966.

Lacan, J. (1954). Introduction au Commentaire de Jean Hyppolite sur la "Verneinung" de Freud and Réponse au commentaire de Jean Hyppolite sur la "Verneinung" de Freud. In: *Écrits* (pp. 369–399). Paris: Editions du Seuil, 1966. Also in: *The Seminars of Jacques Lacan: Book I* (pp. 52–61), ed. J.-A. Miller, trans. J. Forrester. New York: W. W. Norton, 1988.

Lacan, J. (1957). *Le Seminaire, Livre IV: La relation d'object*, ed. J.-A. Miller. Paris: Editions de Seuil, 1994.

Laforgue, S. (1926). Verdrängung und Skotomisation. *Internationale Zeitschrift für Psychoanalyse*, 12: 54–65.

Laplanche, J. (1996). Der sogenannte Todestrieb—ein sexueller Trieb [The (so called) death drive—a sexual drive]. 9. Sigmund Freud Lecture. *Zeitschrift für Psychoanalytische: Theorie und Praxis*, 11: 10–26.

Laplanche, J., & Pontalis, J. B. (1973). *The Language of Psycho-Analysis*. London: Karnac, 1988.

Laub, D. (1998). The empty circle: Children of survivors and the limits of reconstruction. *Journal of the American Psychoanalytic Association*, 46 (2): 507–529.

Laub, D., & Auerhahn, N. C. (1984). Reverberations of genocide: Its expression in the conscious and unconscious of post-Holocaust generations. In: S. A. Luel & P. Marcus (Eds.), *Psychoanalytic Reflections of the Holocaust: Selected Essays* (pp. 151–167). Denver, CO: Ktav Publishing.

Laub, D., & Auerhahn, N. C. (1993). Knowing and not knowing massive psychic trauma: Forms of traumatic memory. *International Journal of Psychoanalysis*, 74: 287–302.

Laub, D., & Podell, D. (1995). Art and trauma. *International Journal of Psychoanalysis*, 76: 995–1005.

Laufer, M. (1973). The analysis of a child of survivors. In: E. J. Anthony

& C. Koupernik (Eds.), *The Child in His Family, Vol. 2: The Impact of Disease and Death* (pp. 363–373). New York: John Wiley.

Lerner, H. E. (1976). Parental mislabeling of female genitals as a determinant of penis envy and learning inhibitions in women. *Journal of the American Psychoanalytic Association, 24* (Suppl.): 269–283.

Levinson, S. (1983). *Pragmatics.* London: Cambridge University Press.

Levi-Strauss, C. (1958). *Antropologie structurale.* Paris: Plon.

Levy, J. (1982). A particular kind of negative therapeutic reaction based on Freud's "borrowed guilt". *International Journal of Psychoanalysis, 63*: 361–368.

Libeskind, D. (2000). *The Libeskind Building: The Voids.* Retrieved 16 June 2011 from www.jmberlin.de/main/EN/04-About-The-Museum/01-Architecture/01-libeskind-Building.php#h5-3

Lichtenstein, H. (1971). The malignant no: A hypothesis concerning the interdependence of the sense of self and the instinctual drives. In: M. Kanzer (Ed.), *The Unconscious Today: Essays in Honor of Max Schur* (pp. 147–176). New York: International Universities Press.

Lipkowitz, M. H. (1973). The child of two survivors: The report of an unsuccessful therapy. *Israel Annals of Psychiatry and Related Disciplines, 11*: 2.

Litowitz, B. (1998). An expanded developmental line for negation: Rejection, refusal, denial. *Journal of the American Psychoanalytic Association, 46*: 121–148.

Litowitz, B. (2005). The origins of ethics: Deontic modality. *International Journal of Applied Psychoanalytic Studies, 2*: 249–259.

Litowitz, B. (2011). From dyad to dialogue: Language and the early relationship in American psychoanalytic theory. *Journal of the American Psychoanalytic Association* [Advance online publication: doi:10.1177/0003065111406440].

Litowitz, B., & Litowitz, N. (1983). Development of verbal self-expression. In: A. Goldberg (Ed.), *The Future of Psychoanalysis* (pp. 397–427). New York: International Universities Press.

Löchel, E. (2000). Symbolisierung und Verneinung. In: E. Löchel (Ed.), *Aggression, Symbolisierung, Geschlecht* (pp. 85–109). Göttingen: Vandenhoeck & Ruprecht.

Loewald, H. W. (1972). Freud's conception of the negative therapeutic reaction, with comments on instinct theory. *Journal of the American Psychoanalytic Association, 20*: 235–245.

Lyons, J. (1977). *Semantics, Vol. 2.* London: Cambridge University Press.

Maldonado, J. L. (1975). Impasse y mala fe en el análisis de un paciente. *Revista de Psicoanálisis, 32*: 115–141.
Maldonado, J. L. (1984). Analyst involvement in the psychoanalytical impasse. *International Journal of Psychoanalysis, 65*: 263–271.
Maldonado, J. L. (2003). Obstacles facing the psychoanalyst when interpreting narcissistic pathologies: Characteristics of the authoritarian patient. *International Journal of Psychoanalysis, 84*: 347–366.
Maldonado, J. L. (2008). *El narcisismo y el trabajo del analista. Paradojas, obstáculos y transformaciones* [Narcissism and the work of the analyst: Paradoxes, obstacles, and transformations.]. Buenos Aires: Editorial Lumen.
Marty, P., de M'Uzan, M., & David, C. (1963). *L'investigation psychosomatique*. Paris: Presses Universitaires de France.
Matte-Blanco, I. (1975). *The Unconscious as Infinite Sets: An Essay in Bilogic*. London: Duckworth.
McDougall, J. (1986). *Theatres of the Mind*. London: Free Association Books.
McLaughlin, J. (1992). Nonverbal behavior in the analytic situation: The search for meaning in nonverbal cues. In: S. Kramer & S. Akhtar (Eds.), *When the Body Speaks: Psychological Meanings in Kinetic Cues* (pp. 131–161). Northvale, NJ: Aronson.
McNeill, D., & McNeill, N. (1968). What does a child mean when he says "no"? In: E. Zale (Ed.), *Language and Language Behavior* (pp. 51–62). New York: Appleton-Century-Crofts.
Meltzer, D. (1984). *Dream-Life: A Re-Examination of the Psycho-Analytical Theory and Technique*. Strath Tay: Clunie Press.
Melville, H. (1853). Bartleby, the Scrivener: A Story of Wall Street. *Putnam's Magazine*, November and December.
Merleau-Ponty, M. (1945). *La phénoménologie de la perception*. Paris: Gallimard.
Micheels, L. J. (1985). Bearer of the secret. *Psychoanalytic Inquiry, 5*: 21–30.
Money-Kyrle, R. E. (1956). Normal counter-transference and some of its deviations. *International Journal of Psychoanalysis, 37*: 360–366.
Nissim Momigliano, L., & Robutti, A. (Eds.) (1992). *Shared Experience: The Psychoanalytic Dialogue*. London: Karnac.
Novick, K. K. (1990). Access to infancy: Different ways of remembering. *International Journal of Psychoanalysis, 71*: 335–349.
Ogden, T. (1994). The analytic third: Working with intersubjective clinical facts. *International Journal of Psychoanalysis, 75*: 3–20.

Ogden, T. (2009). *Rediscovering Psychoanalysis: Thinking and Dreaming, Learning and Forgetting*. Hove: Routledge.

Olinick, S. L. (1964). The negative therapeutic reaction. *International Journal of Psychoanalysis*, 45: 540–548.

Olinick, S. L. (1970). Negative therapeutic reaction. *Journal of the American Psychoanalytic Association*, 18: 655–672.

Orgel, S. (2007). Commentary on "The Problem of the Negative Therapeutic Reaction," by Karen Horney. *Psychoanalytic Quarterly*, 76: 43–58.

Palombo, J., Bendicsen, H., & Koch, B. (2009). *Guide to Psychoanalytic Developmental Theories*. New York: Springer.

Parsons, M. (1999). Psychic reality, negation, and the analytic setting. In: G. Kohon (Ed.), *The Dead Mother: The Work of André Green*. London: Routledge.

Pea, R. (1980). The development of negation in early child language. In: D. Olson (Ed.), *The Social Foundations of Language and Thought* (pp. 156–186). New York: W. W. Norton.

Phillips, R. (1978). Impact of Nazi Holocaust on children of survivors. *American Journal of Psychotherapy*, 32: 370–377.

Pontalis, J.-B. (1981). Non, deux fois non. *Nouvelle Revue de la Psychanalyse*, 24: 53–73.

Quinodoz, D. (1996). An adopted analysand transference of a "hole-object". *International Journal of Psychoanalysis*, 77: 323–336.

Rakoff, V. (1966). Long-term effects of the concentration camp experience. *Viewpoints*, 1: 17–21.

Rangell, L. (1969). Choice conflict and the decision-making function of the ego. *International Journal of Psychoanalysis*, 50: 599–602.

Reich, W. (1928). Sobre la técnica del análisis del carácter. *Análisis del Carácter* (pp. 61–128). Buenos Aires: Paidós, 1975.

Reiter, B. (1996). Dunkel ist das Leben, ist der Tod—Zu Freuds Todestriebtheorie [Dark is life, is death: On Freud's death drive theory]. *Zeitschrift für Psychoanalytische: Theorie und Praxis*, 11: 27–47.

Renik, O. (1993). Analytic interactions: Conceptualizing technique in light of the analyst's irreducible subjectivity. *Psychoanalytic Quarterly*, 562: 553–571.

Ricoeur, P. (1970). *Freud and Philosophy: An Essay on Interpretation*, trans. D. Savage. New Haven, CT: Yale University Press.

Riviere, J. (1936). A contribution to the analysis of the negative therapeutic reaction. *International Journal of Psychoanalysis*, 17: 304–320.

Rizzuto, A.-M. (1988). Transference, language and affect in the treatment of bulimarexia. *International Journal of Psychoanalysis, 69*: 369–387.
Rocha Barros, E. M. (2000). Affect and pictographic image: The construction of meaning in mental life. *International Journal of Psychoanalysis, 81*: 1087–1099.
Rodari, G. (1978). *C'era due volte il barone Lamberto—ovvero—I misteri dell'isola di San Giulio* [Twice upon a time there was a baron called Lamberto]. Turin: Einaudi.
Rosenfeld, H. (1964). On the psychopathology of narcissism: A clinical approach. *International Journal of Psychoanalysis, 45*: 332–337.
Rosenfeld, H. (1971). A clinical approach to the psychoanalytic theory of the life and death instincts: An investigation into the aggressive aspects of narcissism. *International Journal of Psychoanalysis, 52*: 169–178.
Rosenfeld, H. (1987). Narcissistic patients with negative therapeutic reactions. In: *Impasse and Interpretation: Therapeutic and Anti-Therapeutic Factors in the Psychoanalytic Treatment of Psychotic, Borderline, and Neurotic Patients.* New Library of Psychoanalysis. London: Tavistock.
Sandler, J. (1983). Reflections on some relations between psychoanalytic concepts and psychoanalytic practice. *International Journal of Psychoanalysis, 64*: 35–45.
Sandler, J. (1992). Reflections on developments in the theory of psychoanalytic technique. *International Journal of Psychoanalysis, 73*: 189–198.
Sandler, J., & Sandler, A.-M. (1978). On the development of object relationships and affects. *International Journal of Psychoanalysis, 59*: 285–296.
Sandler, J., Holder, A., & Dare, C. (1970). Basic psychoanalytic concepts: VII. The negative therapeutic reaction. *British Journal of Psychiatry, 117*: 431–435.
Schafer, R. (1982). *Retelling a Life.* New York: Basic Books.
Searle, J. (1969). *Speech Acts.* London: Cambridge University Press.
Segal, H. (1952). A psycho-analytical approach to aesthetics. *International Journal of Psychoanalysis, 33*: 196–207.
Shapiro, T. (1979). *Clinical Psycholinguistics.* New York: Plenum Press.
Shapiro, T., & Kapit, R. (1978). Linguistic negation in autistic and normal children. *Journal of Psycholinguistic Research, 7*: 337–351.
Slobin, D. (1973). Cognitive prerequisites for the development of gram-

mar. In: C. Ferguson & D. Slobin (Eds.), *Studies of Child Language Development* (pp. 175–208). New York: Holt, Rinehart & Winston.
Sonnenberg, S. M. (1974). Children of survivors: Workshop report. *Journal of American Psychoanalytic Association, 22*: 200–204.
Sowa, J. (1984). *Conceptual Structures: Information Processing in Mind and Machine.* Reading, MA: Addison-Wesley.
Spillius, E. (2007). On the influence of Horney's "The Problem of the Negative Therapeutic Reaction". *Psychoanalytic Quarterly, 76*: 59–74.
Spitz, R. (1957). *No and Yes: On the Genesis of Human Communication.* New York: International Universities Press.
Spitz, R. (1965). *The First Year of Life: A Psychoanalytic Study of Normal and Deviant Development of Object Relations.* New York: International Universities Press.
Stein, R. (1994). A new look at the theory of Melanie Klein. *International Journal of Psychoanalysis, 71*: 499–511.
Stern, D. B. (2010). *Partners in Thought: Working with Unformulated Experience, Dissociation, and Enactment.* New York: Routledge.
Stern, D. N. (2004). *The Present Moment in Psychotherapy and Everyday Life.* New York: W. W. Norton.
Stewart, W. (1970). The split in the ego and the mechanism of disavowal. *Psychoanalytic Quarterly, 39*: 1–16.
Taine, H. (1870). *De l'intelligence* (2 vols.). Paris: Hachette.
Tomasello, M. (2003). *Constructing a Language: A Usage-Based Theory of Language Acquisition.* Cambridge, MA: Harvard University Press.
Tomkins, S. (1962–63). *Affect, Imagery, Consciousness* (2 vols.). New York: Springer.
Tuckett, D., Basile, R., Birksted-Breen, D., Bohm, T., Denis, P., Ferro, A., et al. (2008). *Psychoanalysis Comparable and Incomparable: The Evolution of a Method to Describe and Compare Psychoanalytic Approaches.* Hove: Routledge.
Turner, F. J. (1938). The significance of history. In: *The Early Writings of Frederick Jackson Turner.* Madison, WI: University of Wisconsin Press.
Tustin, F. (1972). *Autism and Childhood Psychosis.* London: Hogarth Press.
Tustin, F. (1986). *Autistic Barriers in Neurotic Patients.* London: Tavistock.
Tustin, F. (1990). *The Protective Shell in Children and Adults.* London: Karnac.
Tustin, F. (1992). *Autistic States in Children.* London: Routledge.

Ver Eecke, W. (1984). *Saying, "No."* Pittsburgh, PA: Duquesne University Press.
Volterra, V., & Antinucci, F. (1979). Negation in child language: A pragmatic study. In: E. Ochs & B. Schieffelin (Eds.), *Developmental Pragmatics* (pp. 281–303). New York: Academic Press.
Watzlawick, P., Beavin, J., & Jackson, D. (1967). *The Pragmatics of Human Communication.* New York: W. W. Norton.
Widlöcher, D. (1996). *Les nouvelles cartes de la psychanalyse.* Paris: Odile Jacob.
Wilden, A. (1972). *System and Structure: Essays in Communication and Exchange.* London: Tavistock.
Wilson, A. (1985). On silence and the Holocaust: A contribution to clinical theory. *Psychoanalytic Inquiry*, 5 (1): 51–62.
Winnicott, D. W. (1969). The use of an object and relating through identifications. In: *Playing and Reality.* London: Tavistock, 1971.
Winnicott, D. W. (1971). *Playing and Reality.* London: Routledge.

INDEX

Abel, C., 167
abolition [withdrawal of investment], 80, 115
 of key signifiers, 115
Abraham, K., 57, 187, 241
absence, psychic representation of, 197
absent object, 220
acting in, 177, 205, 206
 see also enactment
acting out [*agieren*], 58, 70, 204, 205, 206
 verbal, 188
Aeschylus, 49
affect, isolation of, 3
 vs. negation, 5
affective understanding, 206, 212, 218
affirmation [*Bejahung*], 7, 37, 43, 45, 116, 143, 169, 222
 and Eros, 17, 170, 238
aggressor, identification with, 37
agieren [acting out], 205
agnosia(s), 93, 109, 121
Akhtar, S., xi, 1–10, 177, 220, 243, 245, 248
alexithymia, 92

alpha:
 dreams, 227
 elements, 227–228, 234
 function, 175, 226, 227, 229
 superfunction, 228
ambivalence, 68, 74, 97, 149, 184, 185, 220
amblyopia, 109
amentia, 45, 77, 87, 89, 113, 115
amnesia, 99, 121
anal eroticism, 96
anal sadistic traits, 57
analysability, 77
analysis:
 representation as reference point of, 128
 therapeutic failure in, 56
 therapeutic success in, 65, 242
 transformational processes of, 145–164
 as transitional space, 225
analyst:
 –analysand relationship, 180–195, 245, 246
 attacks on, 59
 attentive, 51, 241

analyst (*continued*):
  envy of, 73
  hostility of towards patient, 185
  intervention of, negation of, 223
  listening without memory or desire, 229
  mental functioning of, in session, 234, 248
  negative capability of, 222, 225, 226, 248
  patient's dependence on, 194
  projections onto, 60
  receptive-dreaming faculty of, 234, 248
  unconscious envy of, 64
analytic philosophy, 28
analytic practice, theory of, 155–157
  broadening of, 155–157
analytic situation, negation in, 165–166
analytic third, 226
Angelergues, S., 141, 144
animistic regression, 163
anthropology, 27
Antinucci, F., 28, 29, 37
anxiety dreams, 106
  persecutory, 199
Anzieu, D., 168
aphanisis, 105
aphasia, 121
archaeological procedure of analysis, 155
archaic pleasure-ego, 170
Aristotle, 49
Arlow, J., 126
Asch, S. S., 60, 61
astrophysics, 198, 200
Atlan, H., 133
attachment, 31, 101, 103, 105
attacks on linking, 8, 173
attribution (prediction), 23
attributive judgement vs. judgement of existence, 42, 241
auditory hallucinations, 93, 94
Auerhahn, N. C., 199, 202, 203, 210
Aufhebung [sublation], 37, 41
Austin, J. L., 33
autism, 38, 126, 235
  childhood, psychogenic, 200
  autistic shell, 200
auto-eroticism, 104, 131
Axelrod, S., 199

bad-breast feeling, 220
Baranger, M., xiv, 195, 201, 223
Baranger, W., xiv, 201, 223
Barocas, H., 199
Barton, R., 9
Basch, M., 26, 27
Basile, R., 223, 226
Bates, E., 34
Beavin, J., 37
Becker, C. L., 217
Bejahung [affirmation], 43
Beland, H., 175
Bendicsen, H., 30
benevolent neutrality, 78
Benveniste, E., 23
Bernheim, H., 75
beta:
  elements, 227, 228, 234
  -function, 101
biconditional implication, 37
binding, 108, 109, 133, 139, 153–156, 163, 221
Bindung [binding], 163
biological bedrock [*Gewachsener Fels*], 150
Bion, W. R., 2, 35, 120, 162, 177, 190, 222–227, 229, 234, 248
  alpha dreams, 227
  alpha elements, 227
  alpha function, 175, 226
  attacks on linking, 8, 173
  beta elements, 227
  beta function, 101
  black holes, 8, 200, 201
  contact barrier, 227
  containment, 139
  on hallucination, 114
  Kleinian vision of psychosis, 125
  lies, necessity for, 235
  negative capability of analyst, 222
  symbolic thinking, 175
black hole(s), 8, 202
  in astrophysics and psychoanalysis, 200–201
  and psychic hole, 200
blank mourning, 202
blank psychosis, 122, 202
blank thought, 120
Bleger, J., 187
Bloom, L., 37
boasting, 14
bodily narcissism, 115

Index

Bollas, C., 187
borderline pathology, 35, 93, 101, 116, 162, 207
borrowed guilt, 54, 61, 64, 242
Botella, C., xi, 10, 141, 143, 144, 145–164, 244
Botella, S., xi, 10, 141, 143, 144, 145–164, 244
Bowerman, M., 37
Brenner, I., 22, 36, 37, 61, 126, 199
Breuer, J., 76
Brontë, E., 237, 238, 239, 249
Brown, R., 28, 37
Bruner, J., 34
bulimarexia, 30
Bullitt, W. C., 46

"Cäcilie M, Frau", 14
Canestri, J., xii, 10, 39–51, 240, 241, 248
capacity to say "no", 238, 239
Caravaggio, M. M. da, 227
Cary, J., 249
castration, 48, 90, 97, 118, 124, 160, 180, 213, 215, 219
  anxiety, 7, 26
catalytic ferment, 154
cathexis, 16, 147
  erotic, 54, 61, 64
  object, 65, 242
censorship, 92, 121, 167, 244
  in dreams, 84
Chagall, M., 227, 236
Chalmer, K., 37
character-based negativism, 70
Charcot, J.-M., 75
child(ren):
  developing capacities for negation of, 21–37, 239
  observation, 126
childhood, psychotic states in, 124
Chomsky, N., 27
chronic delusion in paranoia, 77
Churchill, W., 1, 2
Chused, J., 206
claustrum, 236
Cohen, J., 37, 198, 202
Colli, G., 49
communication(s):
  as conveying emotional reality, 233
  as secondary narrative of waking dream thought, 233
condensation, 119, 150

conjunction, 37, 88, 97, 132
Conrad, J., 225, 228
conscience, 62
contact:
  -barrier, 227
  -movement, 137
corroborative dreams, 181, 246
Cotard, J., 91
Cotard's syndrome, 91
co-thought, 224
countertransference, 56, 60, 61, 181, 185–189, 214, 246
  –transference, 63, 73, 177, 189
Couvreur, C., 77
creativity, 189, 190–192, 248
  of analytic field, 236
  work of, 222–236, 248

Danckwardt, J. F., xii, 10, 165–178, 244, 245, 246, 249
Dare, C., 53, 56
Darstellbarkeit [visual or pictorial representation], 147
darstellen [represent], 150
Darwin, C., 37
David, C., 127
daydream:
  -life, 166
  -thinking, 166
  -work, 166
day-residues, 168
"dead mother", 201
de Ajuriaguerra, J., 109
death drive, 64, 107, 124, 145, 153, 243
death instinct, 55, 56, 60, 62–64, 70, 73, 74, 170–175, 242, 243, 249
  negation as manifestation of, 173
  pathogenic, 174
  pathoplastic, 174
death wish, 199, 209, 221
decussation, 136
defence(s):
  ego function, 243
  manic, 184, 191
  mechanism(s), 5, 39, 50, 51, 119, 222, 239, 240, 243
  negation as, 176, 245
  vs. offensive mechanisms, 191
neurosis, hallucination as, 77–80
pre-oedipal, 243
primitive, 60
schizoid, 187, 194, 246

Index

Degas, E., 227
déjà raconté, 95, 96, 111, 143
déjà vu, 111
Delorme, B., 151
delusion, 77, 79, 80, 91
delusional fantasies, 199
de M'Uzan, M., 127
denial(s) (*passim*):
   as defence, 22, 241
   operation of ego, 3
   defensive stucture of repression, 22
   and dialogue, 30, 31
   vs. disavowal, 25, 27
   as erasure of piece of perception, 4
   of existence of object, 76
   graduated series of, 135
   vs. inadmissible recognition, 113
   and language, 28, 30
   logical, 27, 29
   as manic defence, 4
   vs. negation, 4
   negation as, 24, 25
   "no" as, 35
   of object's existence, 76
   as obliteration of awareness of painful external reality, 4
   of perception, 93
   splitting as, 89–91
   propositional, 29
   vs. repression, 27
   of separateness, 239
   of trauma, 247
   truth-functional, 35
   types of, 26
   verbal, 25, 27, 32
depersonalization, 129
depressed maternal object, preoedipal, 60
depression, catastrophic, 58
depressive position, 58, 59
Descartes, R., 140
destruction, instinct of, 7, 17, 170, 174, 197, 238
destructive drive(s) [*Destruktionstrieb*], 43, 45, 70, 101, 102, 106, 220, 243
destructive narcissism, 63
destructiveness, primitive, 60
Destruktionstrieb, *see* destructive drive
developmental phases, 24
developmental psycholinguistics, 21, 27–30, 239, 240

disappearance, 28, 243
disavowal, 2–27, 37, 46, 51, 72, 90, 94, 114, 116, 119, 125, 143, 176, 180, 220, 241, 243, 245
   vs. negation, 4
   and splitting of ego, 4
disavowed reality, 114
disinvestment, 71, 88, 106, 143
   psychic, 115
disjunction, 26, 37, 97, 119
"dismell", 29
displacement, 76, 118, 119, 127, 133, 150, 160
Donnet, J. L., 122
"Dora", 17, 82
Dorey, R., 174
Dorpat, T., 26
Dostoevsky, F., 75
double reversal, concept of, 136, 139
dream(s):
   alpha, 227
   anxiety, 106
   censorship in, 84
   in clinical example, 31–32, 48, 157–161, 178–179, 192–193, 209, 232–233
   Wolf Man, 94–95
   corroborative, 181, 246
   and hallucination, 81–86
   matrix, 236
   negation in, 167, 174, 176, 179, 244
   between analytic sessions, 166
   relevance of, to analysis, 176–178
   negative in, 165–179
   negative of, 245
   of "open-air closet" (Freud), 167–170, 244
   -psychosis, 113, 114
   repetitive, 95
   between sessions, 245
   -thought, 236
   waking, 227, 228, 234 [secondary narrative of, communication as, 233]
   transformations into, 229, 235
   -work, 156, 167, 168, 169, 174, 175
Dreyfus, R., 163
drive, 112, 170
   functioning, unconscious fantasy as, 125
   as instinctual impulse, 146
   investments, 136, 137

Index

model, 43, 241
motion, 118, 121, 132, 137
  psychic representatives of, 136
  theory, 100, 175
dual instinct theory, 70
Duparc, F., 77
Du Prel, C., 166
Durcharbeiten [working through], 163
Duyvendak, J. J. L., 44
dynamic unconscious, 22

ego:
  alienated in its specular
    identifications, 126
  childish, 26
  decision-making function of, 7
  first mode of defence of, expulsion
    as, 30
  ideal, 61
  instincts, 7
  masochistic, 61, 242
  pleasure-, 6, 15, 100, 104, 152, 169,
    173, 238
    archaic, 170
  reality-, 6, 15, 169, 239
  second ego for, 116
  sense of self-disappearance of, 72, 220
  splitting of, 4, 27, 116, 183
  subjective disengagement by, 220
  unconscious, 119
Eickhoff, F.-W., 176
empty circle, 197, 198, 247
  origin of, 202–204
enactment(s), 33, 198, 199, 204–208,
    211, 212, 216–219
  fragmentary, defensive, 219, 247
  self-destructive, 207
envy, 193
  of analyst, 73
  object-destructive, 243
  primitive, 59
  in transference, 57
  unconscious, of therapist, 64
Erlich, S., 210
erogenous zone(s), 104, 105, 124, 154
Eros, xiii, 7, 17, 43, 149, 153, 154, 156,
    163, 170, 172, 238
erotic cathexis, 54, 61, 64
eroticism, anal, 96
erotic object cathexes, 242
erotogenic zone, 105
Eshel, O., 200, 201

Etchegoyen, R. H., 188, 191, 205
excorporation, 100, 137
existence, judgement of, 41, 42, 132,
    180, 181, 183, 185, 188, 191, 194,
    241, 246
expulsion, 7, 17, 31, 43, 45, 170, 171,
    173, 238
external perception, and unconscious
  representation, interpenetration
  between, 112
Ey, H., 91, 126, 143

Faimberg, H., 225
fantasy, unconscious, as drive
  functioning, 125
father:
  murder of, 146–147, 149–151, 161
  primal [*Urvater*], 151, 163
  fausse reconnaissance, 111
Fenichel, O., 5
Ferenczi, S., 39, 154, 225, 240, 243
Ferguson, C., 37
Ferro, A., xii, 10, 222–236, 248
fetish/fetishism, 4, 26, 90, 118, 124
field, analytic, 226
  between analyst and patient, 223
  creativity of, 236
  functions of, 236
  theory, 224
  figurabilité [representability], 94, 144,
    151
  figurability, 149, 157, 161, 244
  work of, 157
  clinical example, 157–162
  figurer [represent, *darstellen*], 150
Fine, B., 37
first topography, 86, 103, 145, 146, 147,
    149, 155, 161
fixation, 133
Fliess, W., 146
floating attention, 78
Fonagy, P., 203
foreclosed homosexuality, 131
foreclosure, 3, 46, 51, 72, 80, 96, 97, 180,
    241
  of symbolic formation, 131
Fort-Da game, 174
free association(s), 57, 78, 155, 156, 187,
    188, 189, 228
  and narrative derivatives, 228
  vs. reveries, 228
  ruptures in flow of, 156–161

Fresco, N. O., 199
Freud, A., 4, 5, 26
Freud, S. (*passim*):
"Analysis Terminable and Interminable", 25, 36, 56, 62, 163
"The Antithetical Meaning of Primal Words", 166, 167
Beyond the Pleasure Principle, xv, 16, 70, 107, 145, 153, 171, 173, 174, 175, 221
"Cäcilie M, Frau", 14
Civilization and Its Discontents, 15, 151
"Constructions in Analysis", 17, 55, 181, 246
"The Dissolution of the Oedipus Complex", 4
Dora, 17, 82
"Dostoevsky and Parricide", 146
"Draft G: Melancholia", 201
dream of "open-air closet", 167–169, 174, 244
dual instinct theory, 70
"The Economic Problem of Masochism", 54, 70
The Ego and the Id, 7, 16, 52, 53, 54, 58, 61, 64, 65, 70, 91, 145, 146, 153, 162, 171, 173, 174, 175, 220, 241
"Fetishism", 4, 26, 90, 125
first topography, 86, 103, 145, 146, 147, 149, 155, 161
"Five Lectures on Psycho-Analysis", 154, 163
"Formulations on the Two Principles of Mental Functioning", 14, 87, 100
Fort-Da game, 174
"Fragment of an Analysis of a Case of Hysteria", 17, 25, 82, 205, 206
on function of judgement, 6–8
"Further Remarks on the Neuro-Psychoses of Defence", 77, 78, 92, 93
"From the History of an Infantile Neurosis", 48, 54, 94–99, 119, 121, 130, 143, 145, 163
"The Infantile Genital Organization", 13
Inhibitions, Symptoms and Anxiety, 4, 5, 10, 61, 146
"Instincts and Their Vicissitudes", 15, 86, 152, 163, 170, 171, 172, 173, 175

intellectual acceptance of the repressed, 5, 14, 71
The Interpretation of Dreams, 16, 82, 147, 153, 154, 166, 167, 168, 169, 172, 173, 174
Introductory Lectures on Psycho-Analysis, 173, 187
on isolation, 10
Jokes and Their Relation to the Unconscious, 14, 17
Leonardo da Vinci and a Memory of His Childhood, 163
"Lines of Advance in Psycho-Analytic Therapy", 154
"The Loss of Reality in Neurosis and Psychosis", 44, 90
"A Metapsychological Supplement to the Theory of Dreams", 86, 87, 143
model of mind, 228, 238, 241, 244
tripartite, 242
Moses and Monotheism, 101
"Mourning and Melancholia", 199
"Negation" (*passim*)
facsimile, 13–17
on negation, 23–27
on negative therapeutic reaction, 53–56
"The Neuro-Psychoses of Defence", 3, 45
New Introductory Lectures on Psycho-Analysis, 16, 89, 114, 154, 156, 171
"A Note upon the 'Mystic Writing-Pad'", 16
"Notes upon a Case of Obsessional Neurosis", 5, 13, 96, 223
The Origins of Psycho-Analysis, 16, 77
An Outline of Psycho-Analysis, 26, 125, 153, 205, 206
"Papers on Metapsychology", 91, 143
"Project for a Scientific Psychology", 16, 78, 81, 82, 143, 163
"Psychical (or Mental) Treatment", 76
"*Psycho-Analysis and the War Neuroses*, Introduction to", 145
"Psycho-Analytic Notes on an Autobiographical Account of a Case of Paranoia", 44, 79, 80
The Question of Lay Analysis, 163
Rat Man, 13, 96, 223

Index

"Remarks on the Theory and Practice of Dream-Interpretations", 181
"Remembering, Repeating and Working Through", 54, 205, 206
"Repression", 86
"Schreber", 79, 93, 96
second topography, 102, 105, 145, 146
"Splitting of the Ego in the Process of Defence", 26, 125
structural theory of mind, 52, 71
Studies on Hysteria, 14, 76
symbol of negation, 14, 17, 41, 50, 71, 169, 170, 174, 175, 240
theory of perception, 127–130
Three Essays on the Theory of Sexuality, 16, 163
Totem and Taboo, 146, 154
"Two Encyclopaedia Articles", 155
"The Unconscious", 14, 86, 171, 206, 212, 218
on unconscious repressed material, 13
"Wolf Man", 48, 54, 94–99, 119, 121, 130, 145
Freyberg, S., 199

Gampel, Y., 216
Gandhi, M., 237, 238, 239, 240, 249
Gardner, E. S., 232
Garland, C., 221
"gaslighting", 9
Gast, L., 174
Gedo, J., 30
Gewachsener Fels [biological bedrock], 150
Gilbert, M., 2
global identification, 199
Goethe, J. W. von, 153
Gogol, N., 75
Goldberg, A., 27, 30
Green, A., xiii, 10, 50, 70, 71, 75–144, 162, 179, 180, 187, 199, 201, 244, 246
  negative hallucination, 72, 86, 157, 161, 202, 242, 249
  of thought, 8, 120, 220, 243
Gregory, R. L., 109, 110
Gribbin, J., 200
Grid, the (Bion), 223, 226
Grinberg, L., 199
Grinstein, A., 168
Grotstein, J. S., 2, 172, 200, 224, 228, 229

Grubrich-Simitis, I., 199, 204
guilt, 56, 62, 69, 146, 149, 161, 213, 219, 220
  borrowed, 54, 61, 64, 242
  unconscious, 52, 54, 55, 58, 61, 64, 73, 150, 242

hallucination(s), 45, 46, 49, 228
  auditory, 93, 94
  defence neurosis or psychosis, 77–80
  and dreams, 81–86
  negative, 8, 72, 75–144, 157, 159, 161, 202, 220, 242, 243, 244, 249
  phenomenal field of, 111–117
  and repression, 117–121
  and speech, 130–136
  oneiric, 122
  and perception, 90–92
  positive, 76, 78, 87, 90, 93, 98, 114, 129
  regression to, 87
hallucinatory confusion, 77, 86, 138
hallucinatory fulfilment, 84, 85, 100, 101, 107
hallucinatory negativization, 135
  and unconscious representation, 121–123
hallucinatory psychosis, 45
  wishful, 86
hallucinatory satisfaction, 104, 151
hallucinatory state, quasi-endopsychic, 156
hallucinatory wish-fulfilment, 81, 84, 85, 94, 99–109, 117, 118, 119
Hartmann, H., xiv, 30, 126
Hécaen, H., 109
Hercules, 168
Hoffmann, E. T. A., 75
Hoffmeister, R., 37
Holder, A., 53, 56
holding interpretations, 218
hole(s):
  "-object", 202, 220
  psychic, 7, 196, 204, 220
Holocaust survivors, children of, 196–221, 247
  clinical examples, 207–217
Homer, 49
homosexuality, 131, 158, 159, 244
  foreclosed, 131
homosexual transference, 159
horizontal split in psyche, 25, 27
Horney, K., 57, 58, 59, 60

Hume, D., 235
Husserl, E., 140
hypnotism/hypnosis, 75, 76, 78, 94
hypochondria, 92, 98
Hyppolite, J., 34, 50
hysteria, 77, 78, 168, 184
hysterical conversion, 76
hysterical identification, 131
hysterical symptom(s), 82

id, 7, 25, 27, 53, 89, 102, 104–106, 116, 142, 244
  as ego's second external world, 137
Oedipus of, 145–164
ideational representative [*Vorstellungs-Repräsentanz*], 132, 145
identification, 54, 60, 61, 63, 65, 162, 209, 210
  with aggressor, 37
  with analyst, 57
  with damaged parent, 199
  global, 199
  hysterical, 131
  with maternal object, 73
  in pathological mourning, 199
  primary [*primäre Identifizierung*], 147
  primitive, 199, 204
  projective, 125, 131, 175, 214, 227
  role of, 73
  unconscious, with sadistic object, 64
identity:
  perceptual, 134, 135
  thought, 134
implication:
  biconditional, 37
  material, 37
impulse [*Regung*], 148
incest, 148, 161, 162, 180
incorporation, 30, 100, 137, 193
infantile neurosis, 98, 99
infantile trauma(s), 150, 156
infigurable [unrepresentable], 132
inside/outside, 241
instinct(s), ego-, 7
instinctual impulse(s) [*Triebregung*], 15, 17, 145–154
  drive as, 146
intentionality, bias of, 130
internal perceptions, 91–94
interpretation(s):
  evasion of, though negation, 223
  holding, 218
  line of, 229
  narrative, 224
  negation of, 194, 246
  unsaturated, 224, 225
  weak, 224
interpretative paranoia, 114
introject(ion), 15, 60, 100, 108, 144, 170, 221, 238
inverse action, undoing as, 6
inverse thought, negation as, 6
inverted truth, 3
investment, withdrawal of, 88, 115
Isaacs, S., 125
isolation, Freud on, 10

Jackson, D., 37
Jacob, A., 163
Jacobs, T. J., 205, 206
Jacobson, E., 27, 36
Janin, C., 108
Jewish Museum, Berlin, 196, 198
Joseph, E., 37, 171, 188, 191
jouissance, 95, 161
judgement:
  of attribution, 180, 194
  concept of, 180
  of existence, 41, 132, 180, 181, 194, 246
  vs. attributive judgement, 42, 241
  in clinical practice (case study), 183–193
  function of, 14, 15, 17, 42, 169–171, 182, 238, 246
  Freud on, 6–8
  intellectual, function of, 182–183
  negative, 35, 194, 246
  repression as intellectual substitute for, 14, 171, 237
Jung, C. G., 98

Kadishman, M., 197
Kapit, R., 38
Keats, G., 222
Keats, J., 222
Keats, T., 222
Keller-Cohen, D., 37
Kernberg, O. F., 64, 243
Kestenberg, J. S., 199, 210
King, P., 126, 162
Kinston, W., 198, 202
Kirshner, L., 203
Klein, H., 210, 220

Index

Klein, M., 4, 30, 40, 43, 50, 58–60, 107, 124–126, 190, 191, 193, 210, 240
Koch, B., 30
Kogan, I., xiii, 10, 196–221, 247, 248, 249
Krell, R., 199
Kris, E., 220
Kristeva, J., 10

Lacan, J., 34, 50, 80, 97, 123, 126, 129, 140, 143, 187
Laforgue, S., 39, 40, 240
Lagache, D., 143
language:
  acquisition, 36
  and denial, 28, 30
  and speech, Saussurian distinction between, 133
Laplanche, J., 25, 26, 56, 61, 62, 83, 90, 97, 144, 162, 165, 171, 172, 205, 221
Laub, D., 197, 198, 199, 202, 203
Laufer, M., 199
Lavallee, G., 144
Leclaire, S., 144
Leibniz, G., 140
Leonardo da Vinci, 111
Lerner, H. E., 7
leugnen [to deny], 26
Levinson, S., 33
Levi-Strauss, C., 42
Levy, J., 65, 242
Libeskind, D., 196, 197
libido, 79
Lichtenstein, H., 37
life drives, 153
life instinct, 62, 171–175
l'imaginariser [to imaginarize it], 133
linguistic "no", 246
linguistic phenomenon, no as, 180
linguistics, 21, 27, 129
linking:
  attacks on, 8, 173
  function of, 173
Lipkowitz, M. H., 199
Litowitz, B. E., xiii, 10, 21–38, 239, 240
Löchel, E., 174
Loewald, H. W., 60–63
logic, 21, 22, 94, 97, 149, 249
  negative operator in, 24
  symbolic, 23, 28
  logical denial, 27

279

logical negation, 29
Lust-Ich [pleasure-ego], 42
lying, 3, 177, 214
  vs. negation, 3
Lyons, J., 24, 33, 34

Mahler, M., 126
Maldonado, J. L., xiv, 10, 180–195, 245, 246, 247, 249
manic defence(s), 58, 59, 184, 191
  denial as, 4
Manson, C., 232
Marty, P., 92, 127, 162
masochism, 56, 62, 70, 101, 106
  moral, 54, 55, 101
  secondary, 62
masochistic ego, 61, 242
material implication, 37
maternal object, 60, 63, 65, 73
  identification with, 73
  preoedipal, 63
  depressed, 60
maternal reverie, 154
Matte-Blanco, I., 37
Maupassant, G. de, 75
McDougall, J., 92
McLaughlin, J., 206
McNeill, D., 37
McNeill, N., 37
megalomania, 91
Meir, G., 1, 2
melancholia, 124
  psychic hole in, 201
melancholic object, 220
Meltzer, D., 169
Melville, H., 223
memory(ies):
  erasure of, 197
  fragments from persecutory world, 219, 247
  hole, 198
  mnemonic, 81
  trace, 161
mental functioning, 22, 37, 80, 127, 139, 169, 174, 179, 221, 234
Merleau-Ponty, M., 126
Meynert's amentia, 45, 77
Micheels, L. J., 199
mirror role of mother's face, 129
mise en figurabilité [visual representability], 151
mnemonic memories, 81

model of mind, Freud's, 228, 238, 241, 242, 244
  tripartite, 242
Mom, J., 201
Monet, C., 227
Money-Kyrle, R. E., 185
moral masochism, 54, 55, 101
mother:
  –child interaction, 62
  "dead", 201, 243
  face of, mirror role of, 129
  traumatic abandonment by, 243
motor action, choice of, 7, 16, 238, 245
mourning:
  blank, 202
  pathological, 199
  work of [*Trauerarbeit*], 163, 198, 219
mutism, 235
Mutterbild Urzeitlich [primal mother image], 163

narcissism, 58, 131, 139, 245
  bodily, 115
  destructive, 63
  disordered, 57
  negative, 72, 220, 243
  paradoxes of, 180–195, 245
narcissistic inaccessibility, 53
narcissistic injury, 35
narcissistic neuroses, 124
narcissistic pathologies/personalities/patients, 58, 64, 181, 182, 187, 188, 192, 194, 223, 246
narcissistic rivalry, 182, 184, 185, 187
narcissistic withdrawal, 188, 189, 194
narrative derivatives, 236
  and free associations, 228
narrative interpretations, 224
negation (*passim*):
  between analytic sessions, 166
  in analytic situation, 165–166
  antidotes to, 224–229
  benign, 7
  capacity for, 21, 34, 240
  clinical vignettes, 229–233
  concept of, 1–3, 6, 7, 10, 32, 39–41, 50, 70, 71, 174, 176, 179
  dealing with, 10
  as defence mechanism, 39–50, 176, 239, 240, 243, 245
    against repressed, 70
  developing capacities for, 21–37
  developmental sequence of, 28

vs. disavowal, 4
  in dreams, 167, 174, 179, 244
  between analytic sessions, 166
  relevance of, to analysis, 176–178
  effects of, 180–195, 245
  forms of, 25, 30–36, 240
    developmental sequence of, 22, 28, 36, 239
  Freud's concept of, 13–17, 23–27, 40–44
  function of, psychological origin of, 42, 50
  and function of judgement, 6–8
  and drive theory, 170–171
  importance of, in logic, 21
  and instinct of destruction, 7, 17, 170, 238
  of interpretations, 194, 246
  as inverse thought, 6
  vs. isolation of affect, 5
  logical, 29
  vs. lying, 3
  malignant, 7
  as manifestation of death instinct, 173
  through morphology as prefixes to words, 24
  "neustic", 33
  performative, 24, 32–35
  as premature mechanism, 40
  propositional, 24, 32, 34, 38
  through prosody, 24
  vs. psychotic negativism, 41
  relational dimension of, 223–224
  vs. repudiation, 3–4
  semantic, 165, 166
  subsequent to repression, 41, 50, 240
  symbol of, 14, 17, 41, 50, 71, 169, 170, 174, 175, 240
  technical handling of, 8–9
  truth-functional, 28
  vs. undoing, 5–6
  use of, 8, 9, 31, 185
    by patient, 8
    by political leaders (Churchill, Meir, Nixon), 1–3
  in waking life, 168
negative (*passim*):
  concept of, 62, 70, 241
  as defence against repressed, 52
  of dream, 245
  in dreams, 165–179
  of trauma, 160
  unrepresentable, 145–164, 244

Index

work of, 70–72, 75–144, 180, 202, 220, 246, 249
   and perception, clinical example, 109–111
negative capability, 222–236, 248
negative hallucination(s), 8, 72, 75–144, 157, 159, 161, 202, 220, 242–244, 249
   phenomenal field of, 111–117
   and speech, 130–136
   of thought, 8, 220, 243
negative judgement, 35, 194, 246
   as intellectual substitute for repression, 14, 171, 237
negative narcissism, 72, 220, 243
negative operator, 23–25, 33
   in logic, 24
negative therapeutic reaction (NTR), 52–74, 101, 150, 166, 181, 220, 241, 242, 243, 246
   Abraham on, 57
   Asch on, 60–61
   case vignette, 65–70
   Freud's concept, 53–56
   Horney on, 57–58
   Klein on, 59–60
   Laplanche and Pontalis on, 61
   Loewald on, 62–63
   Olinick on, 60
   Riviere on, 58–59
   Rosenfeld on, 63–64
negative transference, 70, 102, 184, 192
negativism, character-based, 70
negativization, 95, 97, 112, 118, 121, 122, 123, 135, 143
   hallucinatory, 135
   and unconscious representation, 121–123
   of representation, 122
neurosis(es), 41, 43, 50, 51, 54, 55, 83, 94, 101, 130, 148, 168, 201, 207, 220, 241, 243
   defence, hallucination as, 77–80
   infantile, 98, 99
   narcissistic, 124
   obsessional, 13, 77, 92, 97
   traumatic, 145
"neustic" negation, 33
neutrality, benevolent, 78
Niederschlag [precipitate], 150
nightmares, 106, 108
Nissim Momigliano, L., 225
Nixon, R., 2

nonexistence, 23, 28, 46, 220
non-neurotic pathologies, 50, 51, 241
non-perception, 76, 118, 120, 134
non-representation, 102
Novick, K. K., 31
NTR, *see* negative therapeutic reaction

"O" (absolute truth and ultimate reality), 224, 226, 229
object:
   cathexis, 65, 242
   -destructive envy, 243
   loss, 201
   and negation, 44–46
   relation, 63, 107, 139, 162
   -representations, 116, 152, 160
obsessional neurosis(es), 13, 77, 92, 97
obsessive representation, 76
Ödipus Komplex [Oedipus complex], 146
oedipal rivalry, 184
Oedipus:
   complex, 27, 62, 145, 146, 147, 148, 149, 150, 155, 158, 159, 161, 162, 163, 180, 244
   dissolution of, 180
   inverted, 158
   traumatic sources of, 155
   two sides of, 147–150
   early, 147
   of the id, 145–164, 244
   negative, 147
   positive, 147
   of the *Ucs.*, 147–151, 161
   negative, 244
Oedipus Rex, 146, 162, 163
offensive mechanisms vs. defensive mechanisms, 191
Ogden, T., 226, 228
Olinick, S. L., 57, 60, 61, 242
omnipotence, 64, 106, 129
omnipotent fantasy(ies), 192, 194
O'Neil, M. K., xiv, 237–248
oneiric hallucination, 122
oneirism, 77, 113
"open-air closet", Freud's dream of, 167, 244
oral incorporation, 30
Orgel, S., 60
originaire [primal, *Ur*], 150

Palombo, J., 30
Pankejeff, S., 94, 95, 97

paranoia, 79, 86, 92, 113, 131
  chronic delusion in, 77
    interpretative, 114
  paranoid-schizoid position, 200, 223
parapraxis, 130
parents, trauma of, 199, 200, 203, 204
  see also Holocaust survivors, children of
parricide, 146, 180
  primal, 147, 148
  see also father, murder of
Parsons, M., 71
pathological mourning, 199
pathological and normal, distinction between, 83
patients with narcissistic disturbances, 182
Pea, R., 28, 29
Penrose, 200
perception(s):
  denial of, splitting as, 89–91
  distortion of, and function of intellectual judgement, 182–193
  external, and unconscious representation, interpenetration between, 112
  Freudian theory of, 127–130
  and hallucination, 90–92
  internal, 91–94
  and preconscious thought, 117, 119
  and representation, 138, 141
  unconscious, 118, 119
  theory of, 111, 127, 128, 129, 137
  visual, 128
  and work of negative, clinical example, 109–111
perceptual identity, 134, 135
performative negation, 24, 32–35
persecutory anxieties, 199
perversion(s), 43, 90, 124, 125, 168, 243
phallic rivalry, 186
phenomenal field of negative hallucination, 111–117
Phillips, R., 199
philosophy, analytic, 28
phimosis, 233, 235
Picasso, P., 227
pictogram(s), 227, 228, 234
pleasure:
  double link of, 104
  -ego, 6, 15, 100, 104, 152, 169, 173, 238
  archaic, 170

function of, 103
principle, 15, 17, 24, 56, 107, 108, 109, 153, 154, 156, 169, 170, 172
pleasure–unpleasure principle, 81
Podell, D., 202
Polanski, R., 231, 232
Pontalis, J. B., 25, 26, 56, 61, 62, 63, 162, 165, 171, 205, 221
positive hallucination(s), 76, 78, 87, 90, 93, 98, 114, 129
possession, 63
post-Bionian field, 226
precipitate [*Niederschlag*], 150, 151, 163
preconscious representation, 86
preconscious thought, 117, 119, 120
  and perception, 117, 119
  and unconscious representation, 117
prediction (attribution), 23
pregenital fixations, 131
Prelinger, E., 199, 203, 210
preoedipal maternal object, 63
  depressed, 60
primal crime [*Urverbrechen*], 146, 163
primal fantasy(ies) [*Urphantasien*], 112, 119, 123, 163
primal father [*Urvater*], 151, 163
primal fixation [*Urfixierung*], 163
primal horde [*Urhorde*], 163
primal instincts [*Urtriebe*], 163
primal man [*Urmensch*], 163
primal mother image [*Mutterbild Urzeitlich*], 163
primal murder, 146, 148
  negation of, 150–152
primal parricide, 147, 148
primal process [*Urvorgang*], 151, 152
primal repression [*Urverdrängung*], 146, 163
primal scene [*Urszene*], 98, 99, 163, 226
primal state, 146
primal trauma [*Urtrauma*], 163
primal word [*Urwort*], 163
primäre Identifizierung [primary identification], 147
primary identification [*primäre Identifizierung*], 147
primary process(es), 81, 85, 86, 138, 143, 150, 160, 161, 166
primary representation, 45
primitive defences, 60
primitive destructiveness, 60

Index

primitive identification, 199, 204
primordial symbolization, 41
Principle of Convergence-Coherence, 154
projection(s), 26, 88, 105, 116, 129, 144, 173, 204, 220
  onto analyst, 60
  as archaic judgement, 170
  destructive, 102
  Freud on, 13, 80
  destroyed article on, 128, 143
  language as, 93
  of narcissism, 131
  and symbolic thinking, 175
  of threatening introject, 60
projective identification(s), 125, 131, 175, 214, 225, 227
propositional negation, 24, 32, 34, 38
protective shield, 89, 146, 148, 221
  and repression, 136
proton pseudos, 82
psyche, horizontal split in, 25, 27
psychic disinvestment, 115
psychic hole(s), 7, 196–221, 247
  as absence of psychic structure, 198, 202
  and black hole, 200
  in melancholia, 201
  negation of traumatic experiences, 201
  origin of, 202–204
  in psychoanalysis, 201
psychic representations, 196–221, 247
psychic structure, absence of, psychic holes as, 198, 202
psychic trauma, 156, 198
psychic truth, 3, 59
psychic working out [*Verarbeitung*], 163
psychoanalysis, *see* analysis
psychoanalyst, *see* analyst
psycholinguistics, developmental, 21, 27, 28, 239, 240
psychoneurology, 121, 144
psychoneurosis(es), representational, 155
psychopathology, 61, 79
psychosis(es), 7, 17, 38, 43, 88, 90, 92, 98, 116, 124, 125, 126, 127, 131, 183
  blank, 122, 202
  dream, 113
  and dreams, 114
  hallucination as, 77–80

hallucinatory, 45
  wishful, 86
hallucinatory investment in, 113
psychosomatosis, 92
psychotic negativism vs. negation, 41
psychotic states in childhood, 124
pure trauma, 201
purposive ideas [*Zielvorstellungen*], 155, 156

Quinodoz, D., xiv, 202, 220

Rabelais, F., 168
Rakoff, V., 199
Rangell, L., 7
Rat Man, 13, 96, 223
Rau, J. H., 199
Real, Imaginary, Symbolic (RIS), 126
reality:
  disavowed, 114
  -ego, 6, 15, 169, 239
  principle, 24, 87, 109, 154
  repression of, 114, 124
  -testing, 6, 15, 16, 42–44, 50, 82, 87, 89, 117, 143, 149, 152, 170, 238, 241
recorporation, regressive, 115
reference (existence), 23
refusal, 4, 21–37, 72, 239, 240
regression, 31, 58, 61, 98, 119, 127, 160
  animistic, 163
  to hallucination, 87
regressive recorporation, 115
Regung [impulse], 148
Reich, W., 186, 187
re-introjection, 175
Reiter, B., 172
rejection, 13, 21–37, 45, 52, 58, 72, 97, 99, 159, 176, 189–241
Remler, J., 37
Renik, O., 206
reparation, 191, 213
repetition:
  binding of, 109
  compulsion, 116, 134
  restitutive, 131
representability, 94, 121, 133, 134, 135, 144, 151, 192
  visual [*mise en figurabilité*], 151
representation(s) (*passim*):
  of absence of representation, 119, 121
  absence of, 197

representation(s) (*continued*):
  negativization of, 122
  object-, 116, 152, 160
  obsessive, 76
  and perception, 138, 141
  psychic, 105, 196–198, 205, 206, 217–219, 247
  of absence, 197
  and psychic holes, 196–221
  as reference point of psychoanalysis, 128
  repression of, 121
  theory of, 126
  thing-, 97, 114, 115, 128, 132, 133, 142
  transference, 135
  visual or pictorial [*Darstellbarkeit*], 147
  word-, 91, 92, 114, 128, 132, 133
representational psychoneurosis, 155
représentations [repressed ideas], 145, 150, 158
repressed (the):
  intellectual acceptance of, 5, 14, 71
  return of, 78, 84, 122, 131, 138
repressed ideas [*représentations*], 145, 150, 158
repressed material, unconscious, 13
repression (*passim*):
  classical, 125
  defensive structure of, 22
  dissolution of, 3
  end-point of, repudiation as, 3
  of instinctual wish, 169
  lifting of, negation as, 3, 14, 41
  mechanism of, 243
  negation subsequent to, 41, 50, 240
  and negative hallucination, 117–121
  negative judgement as intellectual substitute for, 14, 171, 237
  and protective shield, 136
  of reality, 114, 124
  of representation, 121
  use of, by childish ego to get rid of undesirable instinctual demands, 26
repudiation, 13, 46, 51, 241
  as end-point of repression, 3
  vs. negation, 3–4
resistance(s), 9, 32, 34, 36, 53–64, 70, 74, 93, 135, 150, 181, 187, 205, 242, 246, 248
  chronic, 57
  to cure, 53, 62
  against free association, 57
  to recovery, 56
  to signification, 203
  transference, 60–62
  restitutive repetition, 131
  return of repressed, 122
  reverie(s), 93, 225, 227, 232, 236, 248
  vs. free associations, 228
  maternal, 154
Ricoeur, P., 24
Riviere, J., 57, 58, 59, 242
Rizzuto, A.-M., 30
Robertson, B. M., xv, 10, 52–74, 241, 242, 249
Robutti, A., 225
Rocha Barros, E. M., 227
Rodari, G., 40
Rosenfeld, H., 57, 63, 64, 182, 183, 191, 242
rupture of self, 197

sadistic object:
  cathexes, 242
  unconscious identification with, 64
sadomasochistic patients, 60
Sandler, A.-M., 206, 216
Sandler, J., 50, 53, 56, 171, 206, 216
Schafer, R., 205, 206
schizoid defences, 187, 194, 246
schizophrenia, 86, 200
Schnipper, O. L., 199
Schreber, D. P., 79, 93, 96
scotomization, 39, 40, 90
Searle, J., 33
secondary masochism, 62
second topography, 102, 105, 145, 146
Segal, H., xiv, 184
self, vertical split within, 27
self-destructive enactments, 207
self-prohibition, 37
self psychology, 27
semantic no/negation, 29, 30, 165, 166, 169, 174, 175, 179, 245
semiology, 78, 83
separateness:
  denial of, 239
  reality of, denial of, 238
separation, intolerance of, 131
setting, analytic, 31, 77, 94, 131, 140
  preservation of by analyst, 130
  as space–time allotted for speech, 130
Shalekhet [Fallen Leaves], Jewish Museum, Berlin, 197
Shapiro, T., 31, 32, 38

Index

Sifneos, P., 92
signification, resistance to, 203
signifiers, key, abolition of, 115
Slobin, D., 30, 33, 37, 38
soma, 127, 142
Sonnenberg, S. M., 199
Sophocles, 163
Sowa, J., 37
speech:
   and language, Saussurian distinction between, 133
   and negative hallucination, 130–136
Spillius, E., 57, 242
Spitz, R., 29, 30, 37
split-off knowledge, 219
splitting, 72, 93, 94, 116, 124, 131, 134, 173, 220, 222, 224, 243
   as defence, 77
   and denial of perception, 89–91
   of ego, as result of disavowal, 4
state of session, 156, 161
Stein, R., 31
Steiner, R., 126
Stern, D. B., 22, 27
Stewart, W., 27
Strachey, J., 41, 45
structural theory of mind (Freud), 52, 70
sublation [*Aufhebung*], 37
sublimation, 106
superego, 37, 52–62, 142, 163
symbiosis, 137, 200
symbolic formation, foreclosure of, 131
symbolic function, 175
symbolic logic, 23, 28
symbolic notation, 23
symbolic thinking, 175, 179
symbolization, 80, 175
   primordial, 41
symbol of negation, 14, 17, 41, 50, 71, 169, 170, 174, 175, 240

Taine, H., 46
talking cure, psychoanalysis as, 205
Tao Te Ching, 44, 51
Target, M., 203
Tate, S., 232
Thanatos, 172
therapeutic failure, 56
therapeutic success, 65, 242
therapist, *see* analyst
thing-representation(s), 97, 114, 115, 132, 133, 142

   unconscious, 128
thinking, power of, 16
thought:
   disorder, 122
   identity, 134
Tomasello, M., 28, 37
Tomkins, S., 29
transference, 31, 59–63, 69, 99, 130, 131, 133, 154, 162, 187–191, 205, 209, 212, 215
   –countertransference, 63, 73, 177, 189
   envy in, 57
   homosexual, 159
   negative, 70, 102, 184, 192
   onto object, 123
   representations, 135
   resistance, 60–62
   onto speech, 123
transformational processes, 145, 157, 159, 161
   general theory of, 153–154
   primal, 150–152, 154
      binding capacity of, 155
transitional space, analysis as, 225
Trauerarbeit [work of mourning], 163
trauma:
   infantile, 150, 156
   negative of, 160
   parents', 199, 200, 203
   psychic, 156, 198
   pure, 201
traumatic neuroses, 145
traumatic screen, 220
Triebentmischung [defusion of drives], 43
Triebregung [instinctual impulses], 145, 148
truth:
   -functional negation/denial, 28, 35
   inverted, 3
   psychic, 3, 59
Tuckett, D., 225
Turner, F. J., 217
Tustin, F., 200

unconscious ego, 119
unconscious envy of therapist, 64
unconscious fantasy(ies), 69, 85, 122, 155, 185, 191, 192, 195, 198, 202, 204, 208, 210, 213, 215–219
   as drive functioning, 125
unconscious guilt, 52, 54, 55, 58, 61, 64, 73, 150, 242

unconscious identification with sadistic object, 64
unconscious representation(s), 72, 77, 85, 86, 88, 94, 108, 112–123, 128, 129, 132, 133
  and hallucinatory negativization, 121–123
  and perception, 118, 119
    external, interpenetration between, 112
  and preconscious thought, 117
unconscious repressed material, 13
undoing, 3
  as inverse action, 6
  vs. negation, 5–6
unfulfilled expectations, 28
unrepresentable [*infigurable*], 132, 145, 147, 157, 158, 161
unrepresentable negative, 145, 157, 244
unsaturated interpretations, 224, 225
Ur [primal, originaire], 150
  Urfixierung [primal fixation], 163
  Urhorde [primal horde], 163
  Urmensch [primal man], 163
  Urphantasie [primal fantasy], 163
  Urszene [primal scene], 163
  Urtrauma [primal trauma], 163
  Urtrieb [primal instinctual drive], 163
  Urvater [primal father], 151, 163
  Urverbrechen [primal crime], 163
  Urverdrängung [primal repression], 146, 163
  Urvorgang [primal process], 151
  Urwort [primal word], 163

Verarbeitung [psychic working out], 163
verbal denials, 25
Verdrängung [repression], 26, 41
Ver Eecke, W., 34, 35, 37, 38
verleugnen [to disavow/disown], 13, 25, 26
Verleugnung [denial/disavowal], 26, 46, 51, 90
verneinen [to negate], 13, 25, 26, 41
Verneinung [negation], 24–26, 40, 41, 46, 48
  as denial, 24

vertical split within the self, 27
Verwerfung [repudiation/foreclosure], 46, 51, 99
Viderman, S., 162
visual drive, 128
visual perception, 128
visual representability [*mise en figurabilité*], 151
"Voids" (Jewish Museum, Berlin), 196, 197, 247
  "Memory Void", 197, 198, 202
  "Voided Void", 197, 198
Volterra, V., 28, 29, 37
Vorstellung [primary representation], 45
Vorstellungs-Repräsentanz [ideational representative], 132

waking dream thought, 227, 228, 234
  secondary narrative of, communication as, 233
Waldhorn, H., 37
Wallace, J. G., 109, 110
Watzlawick, P., 37
Weber, G., 79
Wegner, P., 177
Whitehead, J., 9
Widlöcher, D., 224
Wilbur, R., 37
Wilden, A., 32
Wilson, A., 221
Wilson, President T. W., 46, 221
Winnicott, D. W., 101, 125, 129, 139, 142, 151, 152, 160, 162, 225
wish-fulfilment, 86, 99, 121, 123, 168
  hallucinatory, 81, 84, 85, 94, 99–109, 117–119
wishful hallucinatory psychosis, 86
"Wolf Man", 48, 54, 94–99, 119, 121, 130, 145
word-representations, 91, 92, 114, 128, 132, 133
words as tools for thinking, 120
working through [*Durcharbeiten*], 163, 184, 187, 194, 195, 209, 213, 216, 218, 220

Zielvorstellungen [purposive ideas], 155

On Freud's "Negation"

FEB 1 5 2012